MARITIME ANTIQUES

AN ILLUSTRATED DICTIONARY

BY THE SAME AUTHOR:

Coast, Estuary and Seashore Life (John Gifford Ltd.)

Collecting World Sea Shells (John Bartholomew & Son Ltd.)

Collecting Fossils (John Bartholomew & Son Ltd.)

Collecting and Studying Mushrooms, Toadstools and Fungi (John Bartholomew & Son Ltd.)

Grass and Cereals - A First-Look Book for Children (Franklin Watts Ltd.)

The Book of Seaweed (Gordon & Cremonesi)

Maritime Antiques

An Illustrated Dictionary

ALAN MAJOR

with illustrations by Barbara Prescott

A. S. Barnes & Co., Inc.,
New York & San Diego
The Tantivy Press Ltd.,
London

Maritime Antiques
An Illustrated Dictionary
©1981 by The Tantivy Press Ltd.

The Tantivy Press Ltd.
138-148 Tooley Street
London SE1 2TT.

A.S. Barnes & Co., Inc.,
11175 Flintkote Avenue
San Diego
CA 92121.

Library of Congress Cataloging in Publication Data

Major, Alan P
Maritime antiques

I. Title.

1. Nautical paraphernalia—Collectors and collecting

V745.M34   623.8'6'075   80-29624

ISBN 0-498-02496-2

Photoset in Great Britain by the Five Arches Press, Tenby,
and printed in the United States of America.

1 2 3 4 5 6 7 8 9   84 83 82 81

Dedicated to one of the finest maritime nations and peoples of the world, Britain and the British, and to the memory of all those through the centuries who have ventured upon the seas and seen the wonders thereof.

Contents

Author's Foreword

THE subject of nautical antiques is vast, covering not only objects used on ships but also articles devised by mariners for their own amusement or profit. In a work of this popular length it would be impossible to include everything, but I have tried to cover as wide a field as possible over the centuries. Thus if a collector of nautical antiques has no interest in navigational instruments, he or she will find compensation in accounts of such things as scrimshaw work, seaside souvenirs, figureheads, or sand glasses. Some subjects must naturally have more attention than others, especially where there is now a mounting interest - or where very little literature has already been published. I have for example catered not only for the wreck enthusiast, but also for collectors of maritime art. The Americans, so keen in the nautical antiques market, have special attention. Indeed the real intention of the book is to act as an introductory reference work for the beginner but at the same time as a tool for the seasoned collector.

Some sources of information have been difficult to trace and cannot be precisely acknowledged. Copyrights have not been infringed, but if I have failed to make any precise acknowledgments then I would be glad if the relevant authors would inform me so that the matter can be corrected in future editions.

Words set in SMALL CAPITALS give cross-references to items elsewhere in this dictionary.

Canterbury, Kent

ALAN MAJOR

Acknowledgments

To compile a dictionary on such a wide subject as this would be impossible without the advice and assistance of numerous private experts as well as those employed in museums, commercial companies, etc. The author has been fortunate in receiving such help, and wishes to place on record that assistance has been given to him by those listed below. He extends to them his sincere thanks. He also thanks Miss Barbara Prescott for her excellent co-operation as illustrator.

J. Kenneth Major, Esq., industrial archaeologist, Reading, Berkshire.

R. J. Hutchings, Esq., curator, The Waterways Museum, British Waterways Board, Stoke Bruerne, Northamptonshire.

William H. Lapthorne, Esq., local and naval historian, Broadstairs, Kent.

Gordon T. Clarkson, Esq., curator, The Scottish Fisheries Museum, St. Ayles, Anstruther, Fife, Scotland.

Mr. Kenneth Davis, OBE, general manager and registrar, Dover Harbour Board, Dover, Kent.

A. M. Cubbon, Esq., director, The Manx Museum, Douglas, Isle of Man.

K. J. Beken, Esq., FRPS, Beken of Cowes Ltd., Cowes, Isle of Wight.

The Colchester Oyster Fishery Ltd., Fingringhoe, Colchester, Essex.

Mrs. Margaret Baal, First Tower, Jersey, Channel Islands.

Société Jersiaise, The Jersey Museum, St. Helier, Jersey, Channel Islands.

A.M. Knebel, Esq., Director, E. Felton & Partners, Ltd., Sandwich, Kent.

P. Butler Henderson, Esq., Buscot Manor, Faringdon, Oxfordshire.

F. M. Underhill, Esq., FSA, Upton, Didcot.

Richard Hunter, Esq., Aughton, near Sheffield, Yorkshire.

Andrew Ward, Esq., Mosborough, Sheffield, Yorkshire.

A. Zealand, Esq., Keeper of antiquities and bygones, Dundee Museum, Dundee, Scotland.

Last, but by no means least, the author wishes to thank Donald Cowie, Esq., Founder and former Editor of *International Antiques Yearbook*, for his splendid work in checking and preparing the manuscript ready for publication.

12

Photograph Acknowledgments

THE author wishes to acknowledge with sincere thanks the generosity of the following in supplying photographs to illustrate this book:

William H. Lapthorne, Esq., local and naval historian, Broadstairs, Kent, for the half-block model photograph on page 100.

K. J. Beken, Esq., FRPS, Beken of Cowes Ltd., Cowes, Isle of Wight, for the schooner *Westward* photograph on page 36.

J. Kenneth Major, Esq., industrial archaeologist, for the whaling try pot photograph on page 41.

Richard Hunter, Esq., Aughton, Sheffield, Yorkshire, for allowing his Nelson items on page 140 to be photographed.

Andrew Ward, Esq., Mosborough, Sheffield, Yorkshire, for photographing these items.

U.S. Naval Academy Museum, Annapolis, Maryland, U.S.A., for photographs of Admiralty models on pages 75 and 203.

Mystic Seaport Museum, Mystic, Connecticut, U.S.A., for scrimshaw photographs on pages 110, 120, 150, 183 and 246.

City of Dundee District Council Museums and Art Galleries Department, Albert Square, Dundee, Scotland, for astrolabe photograph on page 24.

Science Museum, London SW7, for French prisoner-of-war ship models on pages 157 and 159.

Société Jersiaise Museum, St. Helier, Jersey, Channel Islands, for ship portrait painting photograph on page 204.

The British Waterways Board, Melbury House, Melbury Terrace, London, NW1 for narrowboat item photographs on pages 133, 134, 135 and 136.

The Commanding Officer, H.M.A.S. *Cerberus*, Royal Australian Navy, Westernport, Victoria, Australia, for permission to use the figurehead photographs on pages 85 and 87.

S. A. Lilliman, Esq., Kempston, Bedfordshire, for postcard photograph of *Osborne* on page 154.

Maritime Antiques

An Illustrated Dictionary

A

Admiral Jug. A kind of toby jug; specifically an earthenware ale jug made in the shape of a seated admiral. The originals were manufactured in commemoration of Lord Howe's naval victory on June 1, 1794, but other admiral subjects were subsequently chosen. Sometimes the subject is a sailor from the lower deck.

Admiralty Draughts. Specifications, establishments, plans, outlines drawn up, given by the Admiralty to naval and civil dockyards for the construction of a vessel and/or its appurtenances. These even included the figureheads and "gingerbread" work in the days of sail, especially during the seventeen years 1773 to 1790 when, to reduce costs, an Admiralty order required that drawings should be officially approved for all carved works on new ships. Fortunately some of these old "draughts" still survive, so it is possible for us to form a clear idea of how the ships were built and exactly what they looked like. During the American War of Independence the British Admiralty also had draughts made of the lines and specifications of captured American-built ships, including drawings of the figureheads and "gingerbread" or gilded, carved work.

It should be noted that the old draughts as such often gave rise to problems and were substantially modified in execution. The master shipwrights would suggest changes; sometimes the draught was merely an outline and the master shipwright himself filled out the details. So it became expedient to have not only these blueprints but also actual models of the ships. This helped naval officers who were not always able to visualise a ship from plans. Phineas Pett probably introduced the custom of accompanying the draughts with models, in 1607.

How complicated and detailed some of the draughts were can be judged from the still-extant Admiralty specification to the carver

17

William Savage of Chatham for the original huge group figurehead for the *Victory* in 1765. (Nelson's *Victory* later had a different figure-head.) L. G. Carr Laughton quotes in his *Old Ship Figureheads and Sterns*, 1925:

A new large figure for the head cut in front at the upper part with a bust of His Majesty, the head adorned with laurels, and the body and shoulders worked in rich armour and his George hanging before; under the breast is a rich shield partly supporting the bust and surrounded with four cherubs' heads and wings representing the four winds smiling, gently blowing our success over the four quarters of the globe. On the starboard side of the headpiece the principal figure is a large drapery figure representing Britannia, properly crowned sitting on a rich triumphal arch, and in one hand holding a spear enriched and the Union flag hanging down from it, and with the other hand supporting the bust of His Majesty, with one foot trampling down Envy, Discord and Faction represented by a fiend or hag: at the same side above and behind Britannia is a large flying figure representing Peace crowning the figure Britannia with laurels and holding a branch of palms…"

And so it goes on for a page or two more. How William Savage, wood carver, contrived to follow all this and translate it into a group figurehead of extreme beauty can be seen at the National Maritime Museum, Greenwich. Here still is the actual model he carved prior to creating the full-scale figurehead.

Alarm Gun. A gun fitted on merchant ships, fishing vessels and others in the 18th and 19th centuries, fired as a fog signal or warning.

Albatross Items. The albatross is a bird of the petrel family, having a goose-sized body; very long, narrow wings with a span of as much as twelve feet; and characteristic tube-like nostrils on top of the beak. Thirteen species mostly dwell in the southern hemisphere, where they live far out in the oceans, continually gliding over the water. They have never been popular with mariners, who have feared them superstitiously (see Coleridge's "Ancient Mariner"), and often they have been positively hated (mostly for their alleged attacks on

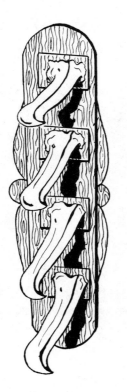

Coat rack made from albatross beaks.

men who have fallen overboard). Thus sailors frequently kill them when they have the chance, afterwards making particular use of the beak. This would be used as the handle for a walking-stick or, stuck in wood, as a wall hatrack or clothes-hanger. The complete head would sometimes be used for these purposes. Then, after the bones and flesh had been removed, the webbed feet would be converted into tobacco pouches. The strong, thin, wing bones would be used as rigging on ship models, or as pipe cleaners (see SHARK WALKING STICKS).

Alidade. The moving indicator or rotating arm with sights of an ASTROLABE. It was used for deduction of altitude; it also meant the vernier or indicator of optical or surveying instruments. Another definition could be: "A sighting device as part of an astrolabe, quadrant or other graduated instrument, which is moved about a graduated arc's centre to indicate the number of degrees cut off on the instrument's limb."

Alt-Azimuth. An instrument for deducing altitudes and azimuths (or arc of the heavens extending from the zenith to the horizon).

Alum Bay Sand. Colourful fine sand, including white, from the shores of Alum Bay, Isle of Wight, as supplied by action of the elements on the cliff strata. Used in souvenir SAND BOTTLES and SAND PICTURES.

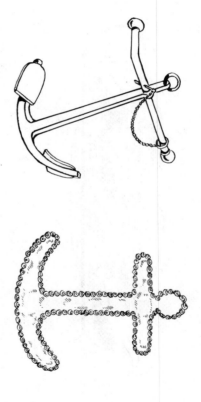

Folding stock anchor.   *Anchor wall plaque.*

Anchor. An implement for mooring ships and boats floating in water, which becomes embedded by its hooks or flukes in the sea or river bottom. Often these are dredged up from old silted harbours or anchorages, or found at the sites of wrecks. An anchor has several parts: first a strong shank, at one extremity of which is the crown. Two arms branch from the crown, terminating in broad palms or flukes, the sharp extremity of which is the peak or bill. Second, there is the stock, fixed at the other end of the shank in right angles to the plane of the arms. Then the ring or shackle, to which the cable or rope is attached, is above the stock. The shank or central bar of the anchor is tapered to the stock, which is a bar at right-angles to the shank. There is a shoulder on the shank just below the stock to keep the stock in position. On some of the early iron anchors still preserved the stock is missing because it was of wood and rotted with age in the sea.

There have long been several types of anchors, such as the best and small bower, the sheet, stream and kedge (the last-named being used for anchoring in a stream or sheltered water and for warping the vessel from one place to another). Bower anchors often weigh about 37½ cwt., stream anchors about 12 cwt., and kedges about 6 cwt. Sheet anchor is a corruption of the Old English "shot" anchor, maybe because it was shot or let go from the ship. The folding stock anchor can be stowed on deck easily. An oval hole on the shank where the

20

stock passes through enables the right-angled elbow at one end of the stock to pass through easily, each end of the stock having an acorn shape. A flange on the opposite side to the elbow, and a slot cut through it, keeps the stock in position when in use. A wedge-shaped pin in the slot is chained to the stock. To stow the anchor the wedge is knocked out and the stock is pulled through the hole in the shank so that it can be laid parallel to it. Nelson's *Victory* has two bower anchors. These were used to moor the ship. They were hauled up to the catheads, projecting from each side of the bows, by a hand-operated capstan. The *Victory* also had two sheet anchors.

A hollow-shanked anchor was devised in the 1850s by a Lieutenant Rodgers. This increased the strength of the anchor without adding to the weight. Another Rodgers invention, the patent pickaxe anchor, had a movable iron stock. Then there was the development of pivoting the arms and flukes to the stock, making them movable; this enabled the anchor to take an easier, firmer hold, and helped to prevent the cable from becoming fouled. Next they tried a self-canting anchor, of which the arms revolved through an angle of 30 degrees each way; the sharp points of the flukes of this were theoretically always ready to enter the sea floor. (See Pering's *Treatise on the Anchor*, Plymouth, 1819, and George Cotsell's *A Treatise on Ships' Anchors*, London, 1856.)

Anchor Light.   A lamp with all-round illumination.

Anchor Wall Plaque.   Usually a plaque with a wood base, cut in the shape of an anchor, adorned with various shells, particularly those with mother-of-pearl lustre, sometimes also having a raised padded area, perhaps heart-shaped, near the stock of the anchor, for use as a pin cushion or wall ornament. The mariner would purchase this ashore to give to a sweetheart, wife or parents as a love token or keepsake. Anchor wall plaques were widely sold during the Victorian and Edwardian periods, adorned with suitable lettering, as SEASIDE SOUVENIRS.

Anemometer.   A gauge for measuring the speed and direction of the wind, with rotating vanes and recording dial graduating from 1 to 12 Beaufort scale, or in metres per second. Invented in 1727, early rotary examples were hand-held and used with a 15 or 30-second SAND GLASS. Later examples were fixed to the mast.

Aneroid Barograph or Barometer. An instrument to measure and record on paper the variations of atmospheric pressure during a period of time. First of the two main types is Vidi's barograph or barometer that consists of several metal vacuum chambers, with an interior spring to prevent their being damaged by crushing. They were compressed by atmospheric pressure changes, these being noted by a stylus on a drum. The sensitivity of the instrument depended on the number of vacuum chambers in it. The second type is the Bourdon aneroid barometer, which contains a vacuum tube, elliptical in section and bent to form a circle. Changes in pressure alter the tube's section and increase or reduce the circle's diameter, this being mechanically noted on a drum by a stylus or a dial by a needle.

Aneroid Barometer. The true aneroid barometer, as opposed to Bourdon's, was invented in 1849. A metal box without liquid is used instead of the mercury in the conventional barometer. It works by the effect of atmospheric pressure on the sides of the metal box.

Angels. Another name for CHAIN SHOT.

Armillary Sphere. An item of navigational equipment, made of wood and brass. The name is derived from the Latin *armilla*, meaning a hoop or bracelet. Such spheres were first made by the ancient Greeks, having sights and being used for astronomical observations. They were widely used on ships in the 16th and 17th centuries to discover the solar system's important coordinates. The earth is shown as a small globe in the centre of the sphere, which is itself formed by two rings at right angles to the line of the poles. Another broad ring, representing the equator, joins them at their midpoint. The globe representing the earth is, in some large examples, made of wood or glass, and shows the oceans and continents. The tropics of Cancer and Capricorn, and the arctic and antarctic circles, are represented by four narrower rings. A broad ring crossing the narrow tropic rings at an angle represents the ecliptic or path of the sun. The sphere is mounted in a meridian ring that is set itself in an equatorial ring.

The polar axis angle of the armillary sphere could be adjusted to set the latitude. The sphere would be rotated on this axis to take the time factor into account. Portable armillary spheres for use at sea were generally contained in a two-halved, rounded case that supported the horizontal ring, and they were small and compact. Much larger armillary spheres were made for use on land, particularly to instruct students in the workings of the solar system. Valuable examples have the whole sphere supported on the back of an Atlas figure. The armillary sphere was superseded in the early 18th century by the ORRERY.

Arnold, John, (1736-1799, **and** *fl.* 1760-1795). Cornish-born watch- and clock-maker who became famous for his work on the development of reliable marine chronometers, a name which he himself invented. One of his instruments was taken on the *Resolution* by Captain Cook in 1772. Associated with THOMAS EARNSHAW until they accused each other of plagiarism. Awarded £3000 by the Commissioners of the Board of Longitude for his work on the marine chronometer.

Artificial Horizon. An instrument to take hydrographic sightings at a mooring during calm weather, or on land. It was also used during conditions of poor visibility, fog and heavy rain, when the true horizon was obscured. A pioneer attempt at such an instrument was John Elton's attachment of two spirit levels to a HADLEY'S OCTANT. This was not very successful, but two types of artificial horizon were developed later. One was the enclosed level mercury horizon of 1812. It had a separate trough and spare bottle of mercury to refill the horizon. The second was the mirror horizon, which had adjustable legs and was provided with a separate spirit level to check that the instrument was standing correctly. Both types were housed in a wooden box with hinged lid when not in use. The instrument was also employed with a BOX SEXTANT for terrestrial observations. (See SEXTANT.)

Astrolabe. An instrument dating back to ancient Greek, Persian and Arab times for ascertaining the positions of the heavenly bodies. It was primitively a kind of sextant, made obsolete by the eventual introduction of the quadrant and sextant.

23

The Dundee astrolabe, dated 1555, one of the oldest surviving nautical navigation instruments in the world.

An astronomical astrolabe, sometimes much ornamented, was used by land surveyors in the 12th century. The mariner's astrolabe, or astrolage, was developed from this as an aid to navigation in the early

15th century. This was superseded in the later 17th century by the CROSS-STAFF.

Columbus used an astrolabe, and Elizabeth I of England had her own personal model made for her about 1560 by the astronomer-magician Dr. John Dee. This contained the first known circular slide rule, and may still be seen in Flamsteed House, at the National Maritime Museum, Greenwich.

The astrolabe used for astronomy contains a ½-¾in. thick bronze disc or ring with the top and bottom partly cut out to lower wind resistance. The upper half is the more perforated, whereas the lower half is less cut out and thus heavier to provide the weight required, so that the instrument can be suspended correctly and vertically by one hand from the metal ring at the summit. The astrolabe's gravity, when suspended by the ring, provides the axis zenith-nadir, with the graduated ring representing the meridian. Then the astrolabe has an ALIDADE or rule with two pinnules, through which sightings can be made. The two sights or pinnules are lined up with the heavenly body being observed, to obtain a reading which is the altitude or zenith distance of the heavenly body, from which the observer can obtain his latitude.

The mariner's astrolabe, the astrolage, as developed from the first, has a heavy pierced disc and a ring for suspension, the rim being engraved with scales of degrees on its edge. Its diameter can be between 6 and 12in., it is about ¼in. thick, and weighs about 4½ lb; it is often made in copper. Although used well into the 18th century, the mariner's astrolabe is sufficiently rare now to be valuable as an antiquity, whereas astronomers' astrolabes are plentiful and not so widely sought.

The oldest mariner's astrolabe known could well be the example in the Dundee Museum. It is in excellent condition, not having been involved in a shipwreck or otherwise damaged. Probably it is Portuguese and might have been made by Lopo Homem, a leading instrument-maker of Lisbon in the mid-16th century. This instrument is 8¾ in. in diameter, and weighs 6 lb. 6 oz. The points on its alidade are distinguished from each other by a cross-cut into one of them. By using only one point as an indicator all the time it was probably possible to reduce errors in reading due to the unevenness of the instrument. There are five small circles arranged in the form of a cross that may be the maker's or an inspector's mark. The name Andrew Smyton and the date 1688 have been crudely stamped on the back of the instrument, but elsewhere the date 1555 is engraved, which makes it one of the oldest of all surviving navigational instruments. An even older astrolabe, attributed to the same maker, Homem, and dated 1540, disappeared from a Palermo collection during the Second World War. Others have been found in Armada wrecks, and one very old one was dredged up from Manilla harbour in the Philippines.

The Dundee astrolabe was found by J.D. Boyd, director of the Dundee Museum, among some material at the old Dudhope Museum, closed in 1939. The instrument had no known history, but might once have been among a collection of scientific instruments made by Thomas Dick of Dundee, an astronomer and writer of the 19th century. Andrew Smyton, whose name is stamped on the back, was a Dundee shipowner who traded in salt to the Bay of Biscay ports, where the instrument was made. On the other hand it may have been looted from an Armada ship and so came into Smyton's possession. Keen collectors should visit St. Columba's Church, Burntisland, Fife, where a late-17th century painting shows a mariner with an astrolabe.

Atlantic Neptune Prints. These prints were commissioned about 1780 by the British Admiralty for use during the American War of Independence, and showed American ports, harbours, landscapes and charts. A complete collection of about 275 prints is now a valuable rarity.

Atlas. A collection of MAPS, CHARTS and plates bound into a volume or volumes for convenience. Probably the term was first used by GERARDUS MERCATOR for his collection called *Atlas sive cosmographicae meditationes*. The first part, with 51 maps, was published in 1585, but Mercator died before the work was completed. The title page had an engraving of Atlas, the Greek giant of mythology, bearing a GLOBE and a pair of DIVIDERS. Mercator's son Rumold published the complete atlas of 107 maps in 1595.

Prior to Mercator, however, Claudius Ptolemy had published a book, *Geographia*, in 1477 which contained the earliest printed maps, covering the known world (Europe, Asia and the Mediterranean coast of Africa). Perhaps the first true atlas was a volume of maps published by ABRAHAM ORTELIUS (1527-1598) in 1570. This had seventy maps on 53 sheets and was called *Theatrum orbis terrarum.*

Ptolemy's *Geographia* went through several editions in the 16th century of universal exploration, and was still being published and used a hundred years later, when the maps were described as "anti-ent". A very useful and influential curiosity of this trade was Ortelius's miniature or pocket atlas published in 1575. It measured only 4 × 7 in., and contained over a hundred small maps.

Other early atlases were those of Gerard de Jode (his *Speculum orbis terrarum* appeared in two volumes, 1578), JAN JANSSON, whose *Atlas novus* constituted a monumental eleven volumes in 1661; Jodocus Hondius with his *Atlas minor* in 1607; and the outstanding Johann Blaeu, whose eleven-volume *Atlas major* covered in 1662 all the known world, one volume being devoted to America and yet another to China.

It will have been noted that the pioneers in this craft were nearly all Netherlanders, but the British swiftly took the helm from their rivals. Christopher Saxton, born at Tingley near Leeds in 1542 (date of his death unknown) produced a fine, hand-coloured atlas of his own country in 1579. Two engravers, William Hole and William Kip, issued between 1610 and 1637 a series of maps copied from Saxton's. Then John Speed (born 1552, but date of death unknown) devised perhaps the finest of all atlases, his *The Theatre of the Empire of Great Britaine.* It was published 1610/1611, and continued to be published until at least 1770. Speed owed much to Saxton, but Blaeu and Jansson of Amsterdam owed as much themselves to Speed.

Probably the first sea atlas was Lucas Jansen Waghenaer's *Spieghel der Zeevaerdt* of 1584. It had 23 maps in the first part and 22 in the second, either sold separately or bound together. An English edition called *The Mariners Mirrour* was published by Anthony Ashley in 1588. Meanwhile the first atlas devoted to America was *A Supplement to Ptolemy's Geography* as published by Cornelius Wytfliet in 1597, although Herman Moll issued a late 16th-century atlas, *The World Described,* that contained American maps (with California shown as an island). Later we have Thomas Jefferys' *American Atlas,* of thirty maps in 1776, and his *West Indian Atlas* of 1775.

The beginning of the atlas was wholly a plagiarist's scramble. The

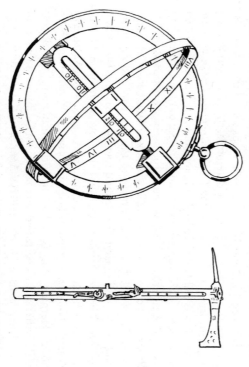

Augsburg Dial.

Combined axe and wheel-lock pistol:
late-sixteenth-century.

makers stole from each other without compunction. There was no copyright law. Plates were hawked about after the original publisher's death. It is very difficult to ascribe originality to any of these cartographers - or to Shakespeare for that matter. It was not until 1795 that the Hydrographic Department of the Admiralty was founded and official maps and atlases began to be produced.

Among the last privately-produced atlases of interest to mariners were Jefferys' *The French Coast*, 1761 (although some of the engravings have obviously been copied from Jan van Loon's French atlas *Le Neptune François*) and *The Channel Pilot* of 1799, which was based on the surveys made by the Royal Navy master mariners John Stephenson and George Burn. It showed the harbours, bays and "roads" of the English Channel. Aaron Arrowsmith published his *New General Atlas* in 1817. René Bougard's *Little Sea Torch* in 1801 had twenty-four charts and twenty sheets of coastlines.

Mention might also be made of Matthew Carey's *American Atlas*, 1795; J.F.W. des Barres' *Atlantic Neptune*, published for the Royal Navy 1776-1781; and of the largest atlas of all, Claes Visscher's, which was issued in the mid-17th century, measured 6 ft high, and contained thirty-five to forty large wall maps by various Dutch experts.

Augsburg Dial. A type of SUNDIAL specifically one of the DIPTYCH dial types, made of gilt and silvered brass and of IVORY, comprising an hour-graduated ring, the plane of this being angled to coincide with the observer's latitude. A perpendicular axial gnomon at the ring's centre is aligned to represent the polar axis. There is a hexagonal baseplate. During use the ring of the instrument shows the shadow of the sun moving at a regular speed around it. Emanating from Augsburg in Germany at first. The ring dial or GEMMA'S RING and the NUREMBERG DIPTYCH OR SUNDIAL are based on the same principles. The Augsburg dial could be used at all latitudes, so was superior to the Nuremberg diptych, but was never so accurate as the ring dial.

Axe Pistol. A pistol, either flint-lock or wheel-lock, with an axe blade attached as a combination weapon, as used on board ship in the late 16th century.

Azimuth Compass and Vertical Compass. A form of compass divided into degrees, with vertical sights used for taking the azimuth of a star. The azimuth of a star is the distance of that body in angular degrees from north or south point of the meridian: the angular distance measured along the horizon between the meridian of a place and the vertical circle passing through the centre of a celestial object and the zenith. Designed with an azimuth circle, and made in England by Ralph Walker, 1793, the instrument was part of the standard equipment, as a bearing compass, of Royal Navy ships between 1795 and 1819. With it, magnetic variation could be measured to about a tenth of a degree, and it supposedly solved problems of longitude, but the achievements of this very sensitive compass were never fully appreciated or utilised because of the lack of knowledge of the laws of magnetic deviation at that time.

B

Backstaff. This was an instrument used for deducing altitude when at sea, so named because it was employed with the observer's back to the sun. It was also known as DAVIS'S QUADRANT, the English quadrant, or, in France, Quartier l'anglois or Quartier de Davis. It was an ingenious improvement on the CROSS-STAFF, and on the QUADRANT and MARINER'S ASTROLABE. The light of the sun in his eyes tended to dazzle an observer who used the more primitive cross-staff facing the sun. He had to turn his back, so Captain JOHN DAVIS devised the backstaff in 1590. He described it in his book *The Seaman's Secret*, 1594. Constructed of lignum vitae or mahogany wood section 5/8 × 3/4 in., with an overall length of 22-24 in., it had a main limb about 24 in. long, on the end of which was a right-angled accessory called the horizon slit. Two arcs, usually of boxwood, divided the quadrant. The smallest arc was calibrated to 60 degrees, and was positioned above the main limb together with a shadow vane. The larger arc, calibrated to 30 degrees, was at the main limb's further end, and had a sighting vane, also an auxiliary limb, about 18 in. long, for strengthening support. Extra rigidity was given to this auxiliary limb by a cross-member between the two limbs. The cross-member would be used as a hand grip.

When using the instrument, the observer stood with back towards the sun; and the shadow vane was altered to between 10 and 15 degrees less than the sun's estimated altitude. With his left hand holding the cross-member, the observer looked through the horizon slit and raised or lowered the backstaff until he saw the horizon through the sight vane. Then he adjusted the shadow vane until the shadow of its upper edge was on the upper edge of the horizon slit. The total of the readings on the two arcs cut by the edges of the vanes would then give the altitude of the sun. In *The Mariner's New Kalendar, also the Description and Use of the Sea Quadrant, Fore-staff and*

Nocturnal, by Nathaniel Colson, published London, 1722, will be found an engraving that depicts the use of a backstaff.

This instrument was universally successful, and remained in use for almost 200 years, save in the Dutch fleet, which preferred the cross-staff even in the 19th century. Backstaffs were made in Ireland and America, but most came from England. Some fine examples were produced with IVORY insets at the joints, and with Tudor roses, fleur de lys, diamond shapes, and sun and star decorations.

Bale, Bayle.   An old name for a ship's bucket. From this arose the term "baling out", the removing of water from a boat with bucket or similar receptacle.

Baleen.   An elastic, horny, blackish-brown substance, in thin, parallel plates, from the sides of the upper jaw of a baleen whale. These plates would vary in size from a few inches to as much as 12 ft long. Because of its strength, flexibility, elasticity and lightness, the material was formerly employed for many purposes, which included the making of umbrellas, corsets, and brushes. The baleen plates were known in commerce as whale-fins. Mariners would carve them into SCRIMSHAW ORNAMENTS and similar articles, which are now rarer and more valuable than scrimshaw made of WHALEBONE and walrus tusk.

Bar Shot.   A type of shot, similar to a pair of dumb-bells, fired by CANNON to destroy sails, rigging and masts, and thus slow down the enemy vessel.

Bargee-ware.   Pottery made of a red base decorated with white clay and Wenger's colours. It was manufactured in the late 19th and early 20th centuries, and became particularly popular with the narrowboat and barge people who worked on the canals; hence its name.

Barometer.   An instrument for measuring atmospheric pressure or weight to determine likely weather changes. There are two forms: the liquid, and the later ANEROID. The liquid type usually (but not always) employed mercury, and was itself divided into two kinds. The earliest, or cistern barometer, was basically a long glass tube closed at

Eighteenth-century ship's barometer-thermometer.

one end, filled with mercury, and with its open end inverted into a cup containing mercury. The column of mercury in the tube moved until balanced by the weight of the atmosphere. The second type, known as the siphon, had no cistern, and consisted of a U-shaped glass tube with one side larger than the other. The reading was made from the difference in the mercury level of the two sides. However, construction was faulty: the glass tube would be uneven along its length, and the mercury inaccurate thanks to the presence of air and water in it.

An Italian named Torricelli accidentally discovered the principle of the first mercury tube about 1643. The Englishman Robert Hooke invented the first wheel or dial barometer in 1665. The mercury's movement in this was measured by a sphere that floated in the shorter side of the U-tube, and by a counterpoise attached by a thread over a wheel pulley to a needle pointer which rotated around the calibrated brass wheel or dial. The credit for the first good barometer is usually given to another Englishman, Henry Jones, and to the later improvements of the great clockmakers Tompion and Quare.

Marine or ship's barometers were developed as a separate instrument, and differed from the domestic type, often column-shaped, and constructed with a THERMOMETER and a HAIR HYGROMETER incorporated. Edward Nairne (1726-1806), an English instrument-maker, constructed the first maritime barometer about 1773. He realised it had to be strong, able to withstand the rough usage and violent movements of shipboard, so mounted his on gimbals, with a weight at the base to keep the instrument upright. A long, narrow tube became a characteristic of the marine barometer. Even so, these first mercury examples were often inaccurate in rough weather. The ship's movement caused the mercury to rise unnaturally, and sometimes even broke the glass tube.

A typical example of a fine old ship's barometer-thermometer is a long, narrow instrument consisting of a wooden case, often mahogany, walnut or ebony, either with the thermometer and barometer opposite each other at the summit of the case, or with the case in two hinged parts. Then the barometer will be on the left-hand side and the thermometer on the lower right-hand side. A protecting, sliding wood panel in a vent above the thermometer enables the barometer scale to be read alone without opening the entire case. The scales will be, perhaps, in lemon-wood, with hand-written grada-tions. Such instruments were beautifully made, and have been polished to a high patina. During the 17th century appropriate words were added to the primitive graduations. Possibly George Sinclair, the English instrument-maker, was the first to adopt this nice prac-tice in 1688, when he used the words: "Long Fair; Fair; Changeable; Rain; Much Rain; Stormy; Tempest." The true father of weather forecasting, Admiral Robert Fitzroy (1805–1865), devised the Fit-zroy marine barometer, on which were the words: "Rise for Cold; Dry or Less Wind - Except Wet from Cooler Side; Fall for Warm, Wet or More Wind - Except Wet from Cooler Side." From the 1860s onwards the wording stabilised to "Very Dry, Settled Fair, Fair, Changeable, Rain, Much Rain, Stormy," and have remained more or less the same since.

Bathometer. An instrument, invented in 1875, to measure the sea's depth.

Battle Glass. Another name for a large SAND GLASS that "ran" for 4 hours. Used on board ship during battles or in rough weather, when the violent movement of the vessel might adversely affect the mechan-ism of chronometers and other time-keeping and navigational equipment.

Battle Lanterns. These were used during naval engagements to light the gun decks.

Beadwork. Product of the ancient craft of stitching small, plain or coloured beads, perforated oval or round balls of glass or clay, sometimes opaque to resemble pearls, to cloth, canvas or other material, to form patterns or scenes. Used by mariners to adorn purses and the like for gifts or sale. Beads were exported to North America for trading with the Indians, and to India and other eastern countries. Beads were used as barter for African slaves.

In the mid-19th century mariners, particularly deep-sea whalers, produced many items of beadwork, such as PIN-CUSHIONS, slippers, purses, handbags, and numerous domestic articles. They used beads

34

to cover boxes, cushions, vase covers, table mats, and particularly, if sometimes optimistically, love-tokens. Their hands might be hard and horny, but the seamen often transformed such articles into objects of exquisite beauty. Although late examples of the art could be based on a stencilled canvas obtained from a shop in port, yet the majority were designed by the mariner himself, using a nautical scene, patriotic emblems such as national flags, or hearts with an inscription, motifs beloved of the 19th century sea-farer. Some items of beadwork would be the result of cooperation between men. One seaman would attach the beads, and another would fix the chain or clasp to a purse. Some beadwork was not made by the sailors but merely purchased in a foreign port.

Bearing Compass. This is a compass for the taking of bearings from sea-marks, which are sights on shore whose position is known in relation to the magnetic north. Consequently the ship's position could be plotted on a chart. The bearing compass is also used at sea to measure the angle between a known star and the magnetic north, which enables a calculation to be made of the deviation of the steering compass. The first of these bearing compasses was no more than a square box containing an ordinary compass, with slits on opposite sides that had cross-hairs for sighting. In the 18th century two-armed sighting vanes with cross-hairs and a central pivot were added. The sun's azimuth was measured from the shadow that fell on the compass card, thanks to lowering or raising the arm with the cross-hairs.

Beken of Cowes. This is the name of a firm of marine photographers of Cowes in the Isle of Wight, whose early photographs, and postcards made from them, have become collectors' items. An entire series records the modern history of yachting and shipping generally. Alfred Beken and his son Frank moved in 1888 from Canterbury to Cowes, where the father bought a chemist's shop, and eventually received a Royal Warrant for supplying medicines and scents to Queen Victoria. Alfred was a keen photographer, and indulged his hobby by taking pictures of local scenes and happenings. Frank, also a keen photographer from an early age, developed the craft as a business. In due course he was commissioned by wealthy yacht-owners and even by royalty to take pictures of themselves and their vessels.

Photograph by Frank Beken, FRPS, of the racing schooner Westward in the Solent in 1911.

The business flourished as Edward VII gave his encouragement to yachting. George V, who raced *Britannia* from Cowes, bestowed on the Bekens a Royal Warrant for marine photography. A similar warrant was bestowed much later by the Duke of Edinburgh. Frank Beken was followed by Keith Beken in the business, and Keith's son Kenneth is the proprietor at the time these words are written. The present premises are close to the old chemist's shop.

The Bekens have a collection of some 60,000 black and white negatives, many on old 8 × 6 in. glass plates, as well as some 20,000 colour transparencies. These photographs not only deal with royalty on the island, yachts and sailing vessels, but also the arrival and departure of famous steamships in Southampton Water, as well as naval occasions.

Belaying Pin. A fixed spike or pin of wood or iron on a ship for belaying or hitching a rope round and making it fast. Several of these would be positioned on the rails of sailing ships.

Bellamy Eagles. These wooden eagles were carved in the flat by the famous American figurehead artist John Haley Bellamy (1836-1914), for mounting on the paddlewheel boxes of river steamers. The eagle was chosen as a favourite motif because it was the national emblem, and a particularly favoured bird at that time. Probably the finest was Bellamy's magnificent eagle on the FIGUREHEAD of the U.S.S. *Lancaster* of 1875. This was a ram-bowed steam frigate, and the eagle was a bird of particularly aggressive appearance, with outstretched wings, tail feathers that splayed out, and strongly-clawed feet. It may still be seen at the Mariner's Museum, Newport News.

Belt Buckles. As worn by sailors and naval officers, these were affixed to regulation issue belts, and had appropriate national and nautical motifs, from flags to anchors.

Bernoulli, Daniel (1700-1782). Swiss mathematician who won an academy prize in Paris for a marine chronometer in 1747. He had an idea for a screw propeller in 1752, long before such came into use, and he wrote notable papers on the tides.

Berthoud, Ferdinand (1727-1807). Skilled craftsman who became clockmaker to the King of France and the French Navy. In the 1760s he produced several CHRONOMETERS. His first products were large and clumsy, thanks to the use of heavy weights, but he eventually produced more convenient instruments with mainsprings. One of his fine later chronometers was used by JEAN BORDA on his circumnavigation of the world in 1776. It had the seconds, minutes and hours on separate dials. Berthoud wrote several books on his subject.

Bill of Lading. Ship-master's detailed receipt of goods to consignor.

Binnacle. The housing or box for a compass on a ship. It was

37

introduced about 1662 to avoid compass deviation, although local iron objects continued to cause this for a long time after. Even as late as the *Victory*, iron objects kept in a drawer on top of the binnacle produced grievous errors in compass readings. The subject was not properly understood until modern times.

The old binnacle had a lantern and window, which enabled the compass to be read in darkness. A double-wick candle was used in the earliest days, with a funnel on top of the binnacle to take away the heat and smoke. The name binnacle was originally applied to a small shelter for the steersman, although in the early 17th century it was actually "bittackle," from the Portuguese "bitacola" and the French "habitacle," meaning a little dwelling. Primitive binnacles consisted of a small wooden cupboard near the tiller, secured by wooden pins, and so designed as to carry compass and candle without showing a light outboard. Elegant examples, made of wood or bronze, would have a stand carved with nautical motifs, such as fish and dolphins. When iron came to be used for shipbuilding it was important to protect the compass from its influence, so binnacles were increasingly designed to eliminate compass deviation. They ceased to be just wooden cupboards, and were developed as wooden stands for the compass bowl, often two compasses alongside each other, separated by the illuminating lamp. They were constructed with wooden pins to reduce deviation. Finally in the 19th century of all-iron ships, the binnacle was to become an all-brass fixture surrounding the compass, with a protective, non-ferrous coat.

Major developments in the 19th century were the Kelvin-Bottomley and Thomson binnacles. Lord Kelvin (then William Thomson) devised in the late 1870s a patent compass and binnacle that completely revolutionised the device. It was the first successfully to incorporate all the requirements for an accurate instrument in one model, and was the basis for subsequent binnacle-compasses. It was simple in design, having a mahogany or teak box, a brass cover, brackets for oil lamps, and - most important - cells containing magnets to counter the deviation of the compass caused by the iron hull of the ship. Sometimes the binnacle pedestal of brass would have adjustable iron bars, known as Flinders tubes, to deal with this deviation in different latitudes. A characteristic binnacle of 1895 is made of wood, brass, and steel, with a printed paper compass card. It is essentially a hollow cylinder on a square base attached to the deck, incorporating a plumb level, and having racks inside the cylinder for corrector magnets. An observation window in the brass cap allows the gimballed, heavy card compass to be seen. The exterior of the case has two brackets carrying soft iron spheres, inscribed "Lord Kelvin's Patents", and numbered.

Binnacle Clock. A clock made for use aboard ship, to show the nautical watches, and to strike from one to eight.

Binocular. An optical instrument through which both eyes look, at the same time, to see enlarged objects at a distance. The true inventor was J. Lippershey of Holland (1608); then Père Rheita constructed, in 1643, a binocular device which consisted of two cardboard telescopes side by side. But interest lapsed until 1823, when the original Dutch device was improved by a Viennese optician, J. Voigtlaender. J. Lemaire developed his central focussing device in 1825; and the true prismatic binocular was introduced by A.A. Boulanger in 1859. The instrument could now be smaller. Ernst Abbe's prism binocular of 1893 at Jena foreshadowed the modern instrument, which not only magnifies the view perfectly but gives a stereoscopic effect.

Blaeu, Willem Janszoon (1571-1638). Dutch cartographer of eminence who not only made celestial and terrestrial globes, but also published maps and books. There are several versions of his name. He studied with the Danish astronomer Tycho Brahe, and used the knowledge thus acquired for positioning the stars on his celestial GLOBES. He used as many as five pictorial constellation images. He published a book called *A Tutor to Astronomy and Geography or an Easie and Speedy Way to Know the Use of both the Globes, Celestial and Terrestial,* and another of his works was *The Sea Mirror containing a Brief Instruction in the Art of Navigation and a Description of the Seas and Coasts of the Eastern, Northern and Western Navigation,* published in Amsterdam, 1625. This contained at the time the most modern summary of navigational information relating to north-west Europe, and it was translated into several languages, including English. Mariners used it extensively. His sons John Blaeu (1596-1673) and Cornelius Blaeu continued the business in partnership after his death, and published several important atlases, succeeding the main great volumes of their father's maps (that, in their turn, had owed much to the English cartographers, Saxton and SPEED).

Blower. Common name for a speaking tube, of which there were several in the wheelhouse, communicating with various essential parts of the ship. Each speaking tube had its own nameplate, indicating to whom it communicated. The ends were formed into mouth-pieces, in which whistles were fitted. Actually "voice pipes", as they called them originally, were used in the Royal Navy long before engines and engine-rooms. The ninety-gun *Formidable*, Rodney's flagship in 1781, had "voice pipes" made of lead; and Rodney's flag captain Symonds was concerned whether his admiral would approve of seeing the tubes as they had to pass through his cabin. He wrote to Rodney in 1781:

The mizen-mast and tiller ropes with the leaden pipes for conveying the voice down the gunroom are now exposed to view. Would you wish them covered in and cased round or left as they are?

We do not know Rodney's answer to this letter, but the *Formidable* had formerly been a private ship, a possible reason why the tubes had been left exposed.

Blubber Pot. Also called a try pot. It was a large, cast-iron cauldron with massive lugs, set up in the try works or brick ovens for rendering blubber, on board whaling ships, and first used on American whalers in the 1760s to refine the blubber. It would sometimes have lettering to indicate the maker's name and address, such as "Johnson and Son, Ironfounders, Old Crane Wharf, Wapping", and "Coalbrookdale". Such pots have been found abandoned across the world from the islands of the South Seas to Greenland and Antarctica, wherever whaling took place, and remain either unwanted debris or convenient receptacles for water, growing plants and trees. Such will be found at the east and west ends of the garden front of Faringdon

Cast iron blubber pot, or try pot, at Faringdon House.

House, Oxfordshire, and in a garden behind Faringdon church. This mansion, built between 1780 and 1785, was bought shortly after completion by a whaling master with a whaling fleet. Like WHALEBONE arches they are frequently found in and around seaports connected with the whaling trade.

Blunderbuss. A form of hand gun used by the naval and military services from the 1650s onwards (also a civilian weapon). Ten blunderbusses were included among the small arms of first-rate vessels. The barrel was wide at the muzzle to scatter the shot. These barrels were sometimes brass or bronze, although normally steel. Early examples carried aboard British naval ships did not have a bayonet, but later flintlock examples had a long, triangular cross-section spring bayonet on top of the barrel just behind the "bell" or widening. The bayonet was almost the length of the barrel when folded back against it. A lock secured it to the stock when it was not in use. The blunderbuss became a veritable pike after the gun had been fired and the bayonet was released and brought forward.

Blunt Instruments. These have nothing to do with causing

41

"grievous bodily harm" but were the compasses, measuring devices, barometers and other nautical items made by EDMUND and GEORGE BLUNT in America.

Blunt, Edmund March (1770-1862). American hydrographer and publisher who issued the *American Coast Pilot* in 1796, the *New Practical Navigator*, 1799, and Bowditch's *New American Practical Navigator* in 1801. In addition he prepared charts and made nautical instruments. His company and bookshop was the centre of American nautical publishing and instrument making at the beginning of the 19th century.

Blunt, George William (1802-1878). Son of the above who was associated with his father and brother Edmund in the preparation of charts and making of instruments. Edited *The Young Sea Officer's Sheet Anchor*, 1843.

Boarding Axe. A hand weapon, part of the ship's side-arms. It was T-shaped, with an expanded crescent blade and a straight or curved spike with bevelling. The axe-head was screwed or riveted to a wooden handle. This handle had a hook for fastening to the seaman's belt. It would be used offensively against the enemy during boarding, or to clear away rigging. There was a late 16th century development in the form of a combined axe and wheel-lock pistol.

Boarding Dirk. A dagger-like hand weapon with blade, hilt and scabbard. The hilt's guard was a simple straight or inverted cross-bar or quillon. There could be an escutcheon in the centre of that cross-bar, showing armorial bearings or an anchor. Early examples are the most elaborate in design, with eagle-head or trefoil-ended cross-bars, while the boarding dirks of the 19th century were much simpler, with hardwood hilt grip, plain cross-bar, and triangular-section blade. The boarding dirk was used to fend off blows, being held in the left hand while the right hand used a sword. It was essentially a thrusting, stabbing weapon for close in-fighting. It should not be confused with DIRKS made for wearing as part of the uniform on ceremonial occasions.

Boarding Pike. A thrusting, spear-type weapon, with a long handle, up to 8 ft long, but shorter than the pikes used by the military. It was part of the ship's side-arms used by the crew together with PARTIZANS, HALBERDS and SPONTOONS when boarding an enemy or repelling would-be boarders. The pointed, lanceolate, leaf-shaped head had a cross-piece. On fighting ships, such as the *Victory*, the boarding pikes would be housed around the foot of each mast, out of the way but ready for instant use.

Boatswain's Whistle or Bosun's Pipe. A whistle used in the Royal Navy to pipe high-ranking officers and other important persons on board a ship and when leaving it. Also for other purposes such as "piping down the hammocks" when the crew off-duty took down their hammocks stowed by day in the nettings round the ship's side and poop end. Boatswain is one of the oldest seafaring titles, and comes from the Old English "batsegen", meaning boat's swain or husband, at that time the actual commander of the ship. The term was applied later in the Royal Navy to the warrant officer who had charge of the sails, rigging, colours, anchors, cables, and cordage. He came to have similar duties in merchant ships, where he would also be general overseer or foreman of the crew, summoning them to their duties.

The boatswain's whistle first came into use as part of his equipment in the 15th century. It also became an actual badge of rank. Such a

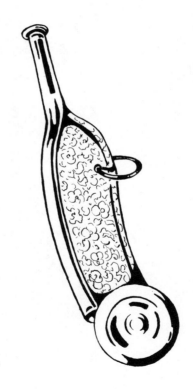

Nineteenth-century boatswain's whistle.

gold whistle was worn by Sir Edward Howard, Admiral of England under Henry VIII. He was about to board a French galley when his own ship fell off. Sir Edward was killed, but, just before that fatality, contrived to fling his gold whistle over the side so that it did not fall into enemy hands.

We read that captains could carry such whistles, but did not always do so. They were principally the prerogative of the "Boatswaine and Cockson", the last being the man in charge of the cock or cog boat. Boteler writes in his *Dialogues* of 1643 how the "cockson", on duty "with his silver whistle cheered up and directed his gang of rowers and kept them together". From about 1671 the whistle was known as a "call". The actual sound of it was, and is, high-pitched, with several notes; the idea being for it to be heard above the noise of the sea at times when it would be useless to shout.

Boatswain's whistles have been made of many metals, but mostly of tin, copper, and brass, sometimes silvered to protect them from corrosion or discoloration in use. Pure silver examples go back to about 1750, but were rare until about 1800. Then they became more general, although they were used only on important occasions. The flat plate on them, usually bright, plain, but sometimes engraved with initials or the ship's name, is called the "keel", while the barrel, usually decorated at each end with an anchor or other nautical motif, is called the "buoy". The pipe of the whistle, normally bent a little in an S-shape, is the "gun" or "cannon".

A considerable number of common silver whistles were made in the late 19th century by Hilliard and Thomason of Birmingham. Modern examples can be identified because they are usually made of chrome or nickel-plated brass. The value of old whistles depends on the rarity of the type plus the fineness of the decoration on the "keel", not to mention general condition and size (the length varying from 3 to 6 in.). Interesting types are those formerly made at British-controlled ports and naval stations overseas, such as Malta and the Cape of Good Hope.

Bollard. This is a strong post of wood or iron on the deck of a ship, used for hitching ropes. Sailing vessels had several of them, mounted on the main deck, forecastle head, poop and main rail. They varied in

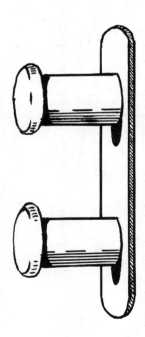

Main deck bollards.

size according to the kind of rope they had to carry, small bollards being used when the rope was too big and heavy for a BELAYING PIN.

Bone Carvings and Work. Bone was often used, sometimes as a humble substitute for IVORY, for cheap items, or because it was easily available, for the making of prisoner-of-war SHIP MODELS, also working models, games and games boxes, pen-holders, toys, fans, buttons, tobacco stoppers, doll cradles, lace bobbins, and some SCRIMSHAW work.

Bootlegger's Pistol. A percussion cap, box-lock pistol with underhammer action and without a trigger guard, the butt sometimes being of the type called "saw handle". At the top of the butt there was an extension to give a better grip. The name came from its use by smugglers, particularly those of New England.

Borda, Jean Charles de (1733-1799). French astronomer geodesist, nautical engineer, navigator, who rose to captain in the French Navy. Between 1771 and 1774 he sailed to the Azores, Cape Verde Islands, along the African coast, and to America, determining latitudes and longitudes, and testing astronomical instruments. He was responsible for several new methods and instruments, including the "cercle de reflexion" or reflecting circle, made in one piece with a telescope and a mirror. His most important invention was this device, the purpose of which was to reproduce angles in nautical observations.

As a member of a commission set up to determine the length of a degree along the meridian between Dunkirk and Barcelona, he formulated his "rule of Borda". Author of *Description and Use of Circle of Reflection*, 1778.

Branding Iron. An iron tool that was used when hot to put a mark or marks on an object to indicate ownership, contents or weight. Fishermen employed it particularly to brand barrels of fish.

Bridge Jugs. Also known as Wearmouth Bridge jugs, a ware produced in SUNDERLAND PINK LUSTRE WARE in the 19th century. Wearmouth Bridge, the favourite subject, was opened in 1796, altered in 1859, and finally replaced in 1929. There are thirty-three recorded views of the bridge on transfer-printed jugs.

Bristle. A long-handled brush, used with the SPONGE and WORM to clean the bore of a cannon by a ramming process.

Bristol Glass. Glass was made at Bristol in the late 17th century, and one manufacturer, Jacob Little (died 1752), is associated with opaque white glass. The famous "enamel glass", made at other centres but never so superbly as at Bristol, is dense white, like porcelain, painted with enamels in imitation of china painting. "Bristol Blue", now a generic term for any dark blue translucent glass, should strictly be applied to glass of the kind between 1761 and 1790 that was not necessarily made at Bristol but contained the necessary Saxon smalt. Items such as ROLLING PINS and SAILORS' LOVE TOKENS as well as walking sticks, decanters and other ware often had a nautical flavour and were purchased as gifts by sailors.

Brockbanks and Atkins (producing from 1815 to 1835). These were London makers of marine chronometers.

Buccaneer Musket or Boucanier. A musket, 5 ft 6 in. long, weight 14 lb, with a walnut stock, copper furniture, and a 0.708 in.-calibre barrel itself measuring 4 ft 4in., which was favoured by pirates of the Caribbean area from the mid-17th century to mid-18th. There were other sizes and weights, one being the "demi-boucanier",

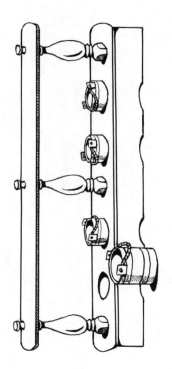

Bucket rail.

12 lb, with a barrel 4 ft long. But these weapons were so cumbersome that they rarely saw real action at sea. They have too often attracted the attention of forgers.

Bucket. A vessel for holding and carrying of water; made of wood, leather or metal. Buckets in the days of sail would mostly be of teak bound with several hoops of brass or iron, with two wood ears for the rope handles, and stands of teak in which they were housed. Thus several buckets would be housed alongside each other in a bucket rail, as at the break of the poop. Others would be in the cook's stores and galley and in the cabins. Fire buckets on naval vessels, at the end of the 18th and beginning of the 19th centuries, were made of leather with copper rivets.

Bufford Prints. These were produced by the 19th-century American lithographer John H. Bufford. His favourite subject was the railroad, but he also excelled in nautical themes.

Buncombe Silhouettes. An unusual manifestation of this craft, by John Buncombe, Newport, Isle of Wight, in which the face is normally black like a silhouette but the body has the relevant and colourful naval uniform, hand-painted in detail. These uniforms, in which Buncombe specialised, were very well done. His prints have been copied since.

Bunting. A thin, coarse woollen material used for small PENNANTS and for FLAGS.

Burgee. A small flag or PENNANT, shaped to a single point or swallow-tailed, plain-coloured or with the ship's name, or company's name, or club badge or similar motif. These have been particularly flown by yacht and sailing club members. Examples of defunct shipping and yacht club burgees are now valuable collectors' items.

Bussa. A metal contraption, rather like a coiled spring, used in the West Country of England during the 19th century for cooking pilchards.

Bussa Pot. Also called a pilchard pot (and not to be confused with a GREATCROCK). It is a deep, round pan, with vertical sides and internal glaze, used in Devon and Cornwall for salting pilchards. In the 18th and 19th centuries these pilchards formed a large part of the normal diet of West Country people. Often a single family would salt down more than a thousand pilchards for winter consumption. First a layer of salt was spread on the bottom of the bussa pot, then a layer of pilchards was placed on this, the process being repeated till the pot was full, after which a piece of flannel would be placed on the top to stop the fish from becoming "rusty", then a heavy stone to press down the contents. The crude coastal potteries of Devon and Cornwall, particularly at Truro and Barnstaple, provided the bussa pots.

Buttersworth, James E. (fl. 1850s-1870s). English ship portrait painter who emigrated to New York in the late 1840s, and did much to cultivate the European method of marine painting in America.

Buttons. Discs or knobs sewn on clothing for fastening and decorative purposes. A vast number of nautical buttons have been made throughout history; not only for naval and merchant sailors, but also for men working in ancillary services such as lifeboats, coastguard stations, lightships and lighthouses. It is probably best to concentrate on collecting naval buttons. We know that the foul anchor as a device on them was first used (as an official seal) by Howard, Earl of

Nottingham, in 1601 when he was Lord High Admiral, but it probably goes back much earlier.

Naval uniforms in 1748 had buttons of a bright white metal with a central rose device. In 1774 the buttons were made flat, with the rose replaced by an anchor and cable. Rank could then be distinguished by the spacing of lapel buttons. In 1787 they were gilded for commissioned officers, and the cable round the anchor was abolished. Those of admirals had an anchor surrounded by a laurel, whereas it was surrounded by an oval ring for other ranks. The anchor was surmounted by a crown in 1812, and at the same time an anchor and cable button was adopted by the merchant marine. In 1825 branch badges were added to the buttons, masters having three anchors, physicians having a snake round an anchor, pursers having two anchors with cross-cables. In 1828 it was ordered that all coats should be worn buttoned up. Then in 1837 engineer officers were given buttons with a steam engine and crown device, but this was denied to them in 1856. Meanwhile the crown and anchor button, for all branches was standardised in 1843. In 1879 buttons were ordered to be worn between the stripes on the sleeves of all officers, but the wearing of three buttons between the stripes was abolished for commissioned officers in 1891, and in 1918 warrant officers were forbidden the same privilege.

Bussa for cooking pilchards.

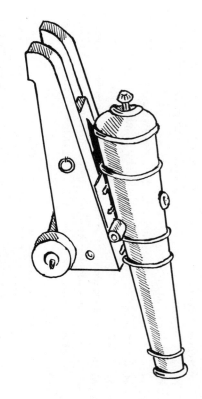

32-lb cannon, as used in English ships against the Spanish Armada.

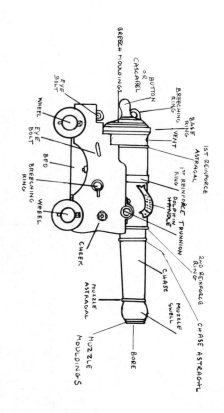

Parts of a naval cannon.

C

Canal Horn. A horn, usually of brass and similar to those used on stage coaches, which was blown by men on NARROWBOATS to warn lock-keepers and others of their approach, before the steam whistle was invented.

Cannon. Item of naval artillery, bronze or iron, carried in broadsides mounted on one or more gun decks, usually comprising heavy, smooth-bore muzzle-loaders on wheeled carriages run inboard for loading and for recoil. It had trunnions, two horizontal pivots or projections from each side, cast with the barrel. It rested on the trunnions and pivoted up and down on them to alter the muzzle's angle and so shorten or lengthen the distance of the shot. Such angling was, however, limited by the size of the gun ports through which the weapon was aimed. Other parts of the cannon were: the cascabel or knob or button, sometimes pierced so that the gun could be fired with a red-hot poker instead of the usual CANNON IGNITER or LINTSTOCK; the breeching ring, one end of which was attached to the breeching rope and the other to a ring bolt in order to absorb part of the recoil; the base ring; the vent; the astragal; the reinforce rings; the chase; the muzzle swell; the dolphin.

The old weapons had a low trajectory, so they would be used primarily to batter the enemy's wooden hull, or destroy his rigging with special shot. Naval construction was vitally altered about 1460 when cannon were introduced on ships. Previously naval and merchant vessels were built to sustain platforms or "castles", from which archers and spearmen launched the only frail weapons that were then available. The ship had to be built in quite a different way when long rows of heavy cannon were installed on each side. The first iron cannon were cast in England in the 16th century, superseding bronze, but the more primitive metal continued to be used elsewhere until the mid-17th century.

Early cannon were cast solid, and the barrel was drilled out afterwards. Originally they were encircled with rings to strengthen the barrel, but these became purely ornamental afterwards. The shot fired were cast-iron balls or roundshot, the calibre or diameter of the bore or interior of the barrel being based on the weight in pounds of the roundshot (6, 12, 18, 24, 32, and 36). The long cannon of the *Victory* weighed 3 tons and was 9 ft 6 in. long. It fired a 32-lb roundshot that, at close range, was able to penetrate 3 ft of oak. The extreme range of this gun was 1½ miles.

The wheeled carriages of the cannon were made of elm, and sometimes weighed as much as half a ton themselves. Both the Army and the Navy used the same type of carriage, the only difference being that the naval carriage had wheels of wood (called trucks) to avoid damage to the deck. These naval carriages were painted red, there being a legend that the colour was chosen to make the blood of the wounded rather less conspicuous and off-putting. Coastal defence gun carriages had iron wheels painted grey, and black barrels. The ships' cannon of the Royal Navy were imprinted with a crown and the crest of the reigning monarch at the time the weapon was cast. In other navies the cannon had similar royal crests, imperial motifs, arms of ports or cities, crests of governors, names of makers

Cannon Igniter. A long-handled instrument, with a stock, butt, trigger, and guard, also a flint or percussion lock, used in the 18th and early 19th centuries, for igniting the flash powder on a cannon and so firing the missile.

Capstan. A device made of iron and wood for hauling up anchors and cables, taking down the foresail tack, aboard ship, or for drawing light boats above high watermark. The cable is wound round an upright cylinder revolving upon a pivot. At intervals in the upper part of the cylinder there are one or two rows of square holes, in which poles or bars are inserted to act as levers for the turning. The cable coils beneath these bars. The centre-line capstan on the *Victory* had fourteen sockets around its upper part for the capstan bars. If ten men stood to a bar then 140 would be required to hoist a heavy item. The

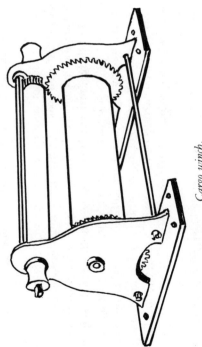

Cargo winch.

main capstan, used for weighing the anchors, would require 280 men. The decorated top of the centre-line capstan was detachable, so that the ship's fiddler or other musician could stand in its place and perform while the men heaved the bars.

Cargo Winch. A hand-operated winch with two wooden rollers. It resembled the old domestic mangle. At each end of the rollers, one of which was large and thick and the other thinner, were gear wheels with a pawl that engaged the top wheel. The thinner upper roller had a squared end on its spindle to which the crank handle fitted. These winches were used on sailing ships to haul cargo into and out of the hold. For light loads just the upper roller was used but for heavy cargo the lower roller, with its superior gearing power, was brought in. The *Cutty Sark* had a cargo winch between the main mast and the main hatch.

Carronade. A short-barrelled (about 5 ft) naval gun of $1\frac{1}{2}$ tons, with a very big bore, for throwing heavy shot of 68 lb at close range. Nicknamed "smashers", because of their destructive power, the heavy shots would penetrate 3 ft of oak at a range of 2 miles. A smaller example, 3 ft long, of 12 cwt, used a 3 lb powder charge to throw a 24 lb shot.

Carronades were named after the Carron Iron Company of Stirling in Scotland, who first made them in 1779. They were originally called gasconades because a Henry Gascoine designed the guns (together with General Robert Melville) in 1778. The Carron Iron Company made not only these fearsome weapons but much later produced cast-iron cooking ranges for sailing ships and barges. The carronade was not mounted on trunnions but on a kind of sliding carriage or sledge, so devised (with a king-pin affixed to the ship) that it could have a wider trajectory than ordinary cannon. It had about twice the fire-power and was about half the size and weight of any equivalent-calibred cannon of its period. It played an important part in the British naval victories of the Saintes, 1782; the Glorious First of June, 1794; Camperdown, 1797; and Trafalgar, 1805.

Cartridge Box. An upright wooden cylinder, made of bound slats, with a rope handle at first, which was used to contain the cartridges used in the firing of cannon and to convey them from the ship's powder magazine to the gun decks. On naval vessels in the 18th century the powder charge was contained in a paper cartridge that was loaded bodily into the cannon, whereas with land guns this powder was placed in the barrel with a ladle. The cartridge was used on ships to prevent the powder from getting wet; besides that, it was much more convenient on a rolling ship during battle. Sir Jonas Moore, the armaments engineer (1691-1741), first described their use. This paper cartridge had the disadvantage that remnants of it tended to accumulate in the cannon, so it was replaced just before the Seven Years' War in 1756 by a flannel cartridge that burned up entirely.

The name cartridge box was also applied to a real box, made either of copper or brass, with an airtight screw lid, used for the safe housing of cartridges.

Some years ago there was discovered in warehouses at the Portsmouth dockyard a great stock of fine leather cartridge cases, with leather handles and the royal coat of arms in colour, that had been left over from the Nelson period. Dealers acquired these, sold them profitably, and they became collectors' pieces, but were soon reproduced in large numbers and often strange shapes, most of them ending as umbrella stands in ambitious households.

Cary, John (died 1835). English map-engraver and publisher, as well as maker of celestial and terrestrial globes. His family continued his business after his death, and their globes in particular achieved a considerable reputation, being made until about 1850.

Case Shot. Used like GRAPESHOT this comprised a bag of lead musket balls upon a circular wooden disc, which was made to fit the calibre of the weapon that fired it. Such shot acted nastily like shrapnel on men and rigging alike.

Casks. This cylindrical wooden vessel, made of staves bound by metal hoops and having flat ends, has from time immemorial been used to transport and store flour, meat, water, butter, apples, beer, fish, and other commodities. Casks for fresh water, sometimes holding 100 gallons each, were kept on the poop, and were made of wood with several copper or brass hoops. They were closed by a wooden lid, half of which was secured to the top of the cask, while the other half was hinged and could be turned back when water was required. These lids often had locks to prevent men from stealing more than their ration. The side of the cask had several rings which were used to lash it to the deck for security in rough weather. Some casks have the shipping company's and the vessel's names on them. Smaller emergency casks of drinking water were stowed in lifeboats, with the name of the vessel in capital letters. The casks used to stow commodities aboard ship in various sizes had their own names - the hogshead which held 54 gallons, the tun 216, the butt 108, the barrel 36, the kilderkin 18, the firkin 9, and the pin $4\frac{1}{2}$. All were constructed to be watertight, save those used for packing pilchards, that purposely had badly-fitting staves so that the oil and brine used in packing the fish could drain away into pits beneath where the casks were stowed (see BUSSA). Most ports had cooperages to make and supply the casks (see HARNESS CASK and SMUGGLER'S KEG).

Caulking Tools. These were used for stopping the seams between the boards of a ship with mixture of tow, oakum, and pitch, to promote a watertight condition. There were rave hooks, caulking irons, caulking mallets, adzes and draw knives. The long-headed, short-handled round mallet with iron bands was used with the iron for driving the caulking material into the seams, and the rave hook was used together with the ripping iron for removing the old caulking

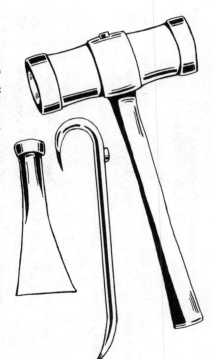

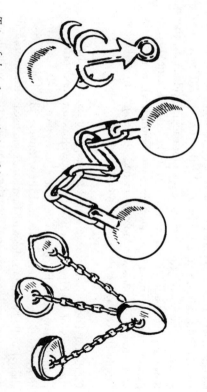

Caulking tools: mallet, rave hook, and caulking iron.

from the seams. The caulking gear aboard ship was usually stowed in the sail loft with the ship's spare sails and sailmaker's equipment.

Chain Shot. A type of shot, two iron balls linked by a chain, which was used to destroy masts and rigging, tear sails, and thus slow down an enemy ship. Also called ANGELS.

Types of shot: 1: a variation of bar shot, to destroy rigging and sails; 2 & 3: chainshot, to kill and maim enemy crew.

Charts. A chart is a mariner's sea map, showing outlines of coasts, depth of water, rocks and other hazards, currents, and tidal streams. The earliest surviving date from about 1300, but certainly had predecessors long before that. Early examples were called a periplus or coast pilot, mainly a description of a sailing route with instructions. There are references to an example from 450 BC, which concerns a voyage to Gibraltar and along the west coast of Africa. Many early charts are undated, and can be judged for age only by their style. A chart actually dated 1311 was produced by a Petrus Vesconte at Genoa. It was called a charta or tabula. Another very early example is The "Carte Pisane", $41\frac{1}{4}$ in. by $19\frac{3}{4}$, on vellum. It covers Europe, including the British coastline, from the Atlantic to Bruges in the north, and then through the Mediterranean to old Trebizond. It probably dates from the second half of the 13th century. The old examples, known variously as Portolan, compass or rhumb charts, are all crossed by rhumb lines, which radiate from the centre in the directions of the winds or compass points. Later these charts were enclosed in a frame and devised on vellum or sheepskin, having a scale, one or more compass roses to help the mariner on his course, as well as flags and coats of arms, with coastal places named on their left. Some of the charts produced by Italian and Catalan cartographers at this time had other useful information, such as the pole star for the north and a cross for the east; they would show inland seas. The Catalans relinquished the circular map shape, and introduced the type of chart that endures to this day.

Until the 16th century charts were based on the assumption that the world was flat, being termed "plane sailing" charts. Pedro Nunez realised about 1537 that such charts were inaccurate; he was responsible also for developing the use of the rhumb line more accurately. It was, however, GERARD MERCATOR who solved the problem of representing the globe on a flat surface. In his world map of 1569, known as Mercator's Projection, he kept the converging meridians equidistant, but stretched the latitude scales between the meridian as they receded from the equator. This Mercator's Projection was responsible for charts that enabled seamen to lay down a compass course on a straight line. (It was not altogether a new idea; a Nuremberg compass-maker named Etzlaub had tentatively employed it prior to Mercator.)

All the same, many conservative mariners preferred to continue the use of "plane sailing" charts, which were employed by many East Indiamen until as late as 1750. The earliest surviving sea chart of northern Europe, is the *Caerteven de Oostersche zee* of Jan van Hoirne, Antwerp 1526. But the oldest surviving sea chart intended for actual use aboard ship was a map of the eastern Mediterranean from the Straits of Messina to Palestine, published in Venice, 1539, by G. Vavassore. This was a true sea chart for navigation. Cornelius Anthonisz then came forward with his nine-sheet woodcut chart in 1544. From about this time charts were always included in what the Germans called seabooks. The French called these documents routiers, a name that was debased by the English to RUTTERS. Such seabooks contained sailing directions and other useful information, as well as charts.

One of the best-known examples of early sea charts was Lucas Jansen Waghenaer's *De Spieghel der Zeevaerdt* of 1584, published as an ATLAS, together with charts. It is a beautiful production, having still the conventional symbols for anchorages, reefs, navigation marks, fathom depths, tide details, buoys, churches, postmills, gallows, areas netted for fishing, wrecks, and other hazards. Such old charts were decorated with sea monsters, ships firing guns, mermaids and mermen, and cherubs puffing winds from all corners of a hand-coloured cartouche that contained dedications or sailing instructions. They would also have elevations of the coastline as seen from the sea. The Dutch produced some of the finest charts during the 17th and 18th centuries. BLAEU was a foremost maker, but less artistic than Waghenaer. Other famous Dutch makers were J. van Keulen, Anthonie Jacobsz and Henrik Donckers. Most were published commercially, but often with the encouragement of a royal, princely, or ducal warrant, using information gathered by mercantile or naval navigators. Foremost among these was Captain Greenville Collins (fl. 1679-1696). As "Hydrographer to the King", Charles II, he surveyed the British coastline from 1681 to 1688, producing a set of forty-eight charts that paid particular attention to the ports and harbours of Britain, including the islands of Scotland and Scilly. They were published as *Great Britain's Coasting Pilot* in 1693, being the first set of charts devoted to the British Isles entirely. The work was re-issued fifteen times in the 18th century, some editions being dedicated to such as Samuel Pepys and King William III.

In an effort at standardisation, the Admiralty established the first Hydrographical Department in 1795, and an initial series of 736 Admiralty charts was issued in 1825. An important set of charts came from Thomas Jefferys in 1775. It was called the *North American Pilot*, and consisted of twenty-two charts. Jefferys had already published in 1761 his *The French Coast*. (The French themselves had Nicolas Bellin's *Hydrographie Française*, from Paris with a hundred charts in 1765.) The new century was ushered in with William Heather's five-sheet *Charts of the Harbours of the British Channel*, 1801, and William Faden's *French Coasting Pilot*, forty charts, 1805. America then had Nathaniel Bowditch's *New American Practical Navigator*, published in New York in 1832. The copyright of this, and of Bowditch's NAUTICAL ALMANACS and navigational manuals, were purchased by the U.S. Hydropgraphic Office in 1866, which continued to revise and issue them for many years. Most of the great sea powers undertook similar work in the 19th century. The 20th century saw the sea chart as a true scientific instrument, but also as a means of making money with prolific forgeries of the old ones.

Charter Parties. An item of the merchant ship's papers, specifically contracts for cargo, important to the captain in his SHIP'S PAPERS BOX.

Chronometer. An instrument for measuring time with particular exactitude, differing from ordinary time-pieces in having a device incorporated for compensation according to changes of temperature and the like. The chronometer on ships of the Royal Navy was kept by the master, who checked the ship's time at noon each day.

A foremost problem of navigation for centuries had been how to find longitude. There were complicated tables to ascertain latitude, but not longitude; and although these tables enabled a navigator to find the local time, he was unable to place his exact position at sea because he did not know the time at zero meridian. Various devices were suggested for overcoming this, from double-balance wheels to pendulum suspension.

It was JOHN HARRISON, the English clock-maker, who first invented a successful chronometer. This was in 1735; and it incorporated a gridiron pendulum which compensated for changes in temperature through the unequal contraction of two metals. This instrument was followed by Harrison's longitude watches of 1760 and 1764. As early as 1714 the "Commissioners for the discovery of Longitude at sea" had been established and authorised to reward inventors who arrived at a solution. Harrison did not at first satisfy the Commissioners. Other clock-makers had been at work, such as JOHN ARNOLD (1736-1799), THOMAS EARNSHAW (1749-1829), and THOMAS MUDGE (1717-1794). Eventually the Commissioners awarded £3000 each to Arnold and Earnshaw.

At the same time the Frenchman PIERRE LE ROY (1717-1785) had been producing an escapement which left the balance wheel free in the larger part of its movement. Marine chronometers in the future were to owe much to this, but Le Roy eventually abandoned his work after a quarrel with his friend and rival FERDINAND BERTHOUD. Berthoud, of Swiss origin, worked on the chronometer's development in the 1760s. His particular achievements was the invention which incorporated two circular balance wheels that oscillated in opposite directions. Harrison's gridiron pendulum was used by Berthoud, but eventually abandoned in favour of a mainspring. Berthoud was thus able to produce the true precursor of the modern chronometer, a smaller instrument than any predecessor. The British Commissioners, thanks to their not giving Harrison his proper encouragement, had indirectly enabled the French to take the lead. Pierre Louis Berthoud (1754-1813) continued the work of his uncle Ferdinand; and other French improvers of the device included Gannery, Jacob, Motel, Dumas, and Breguet.

The first more or less completely accurate chronometer was produced in the 1820s; thereafter it was just a matter of simplifying the design and construction. From about 1830 the standard marine chronometer was contained in a brass-bound mahogany box, with a lid on it that swung open so that the time could be read through a glass pane. A key would be used to open a second lid that gave access to the mechanism, which swung on two sets of gimbals to maintain its level accurately in spite of the movement of the ship. (Walnut, rosewood or satinwood would sometimes be used for the box instead of mahogany.)

By the 1850s most good ships had proper chronometers, although there remained mariners who preferred taking bearings from the heavens. They continued to use the last, together with tables of lunar distances, until the late 19th century, just as arithmeticians sometimes insist on doing their own figuring even when possessed of an electronic calculator. Modern chronometers, from about 1800 onwards, do not possess the attractive decorations of early devices, nor mean so much to the collector. There are, however, some who seek Victorian examples, the controls of which are outside the clock's rim.

Circumferentor. An instrument, probably invented by Gemma Frisius (1508-1555), an instrument-designer of Louvain, which was used on survey ships and by surveyors to measure vertical and horizontal angles, and to chart coastlines in the 17th and 18th centuries. It is essentially a surveyor's compass, and was introduced into England by John Norden (1548-1625), an English surveyor. Eventually it was superseded by the theodolite. It should not be confused with the earlier HOLLAND CIRCLE. It comprises a compass with magnetic needle, around which is a graduated, non-magnetic brass ring or circle,

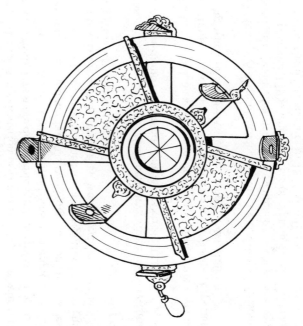

Circumferentor by Macarius, 1676.

61

divided into 360 degrees, mounted on a horizontal brass bar, on which two sight rules or alidades are positioned vertically to the outer ring. There are two slots parallel and longitudinal to the strip's edge. Some had a fine wire through the centre of the sights. The needle would be positioned at north, using the compass, and the sight rules would be fixed on two predetermined points, so that their azimuths could be noted and the survey related properly to cadastral maps, which are maps of territorial property. When mounted horizontally on a stand, the circumferentor was used to measure horizontal angles, and when shackle-suspended it could measure vertical angles.

An example of an English brass circumferentor of the early 18th century has a 9 in. diameter, and comprises a silvered compass with inset spirit level, engraved at the circumference with 2-degree scales, the inner in four quadrants, and the outer, 0 to 360 degrees, all mounted in a glazed box on a cross-frame, with two detachable sights. The frame rotates over a circular cut-away plate engraved on the circumference with a nought to 360-degree scale, against which is the fiducial edge-line or point from which measurements are made. This is taken as the basis of calculation or comparison against which the cross-piece is read. Two more detachable sights are fixed to the plate, which is mounted on a universal staff-head fitted to a single adjustable metal column. The compass box has two wing-nuts on either side to enable a separate bridge to be attached for other sighting instruments. The circumferentor and GRAPHOMETER were overtaken in the 19th century by the REFLECTING CIRCLE.

Clemens, Andrew (fl. late 19th century). American craftsman (deaf and semi-dumb) who made bottled SAND PICTURES.

Coat Rack. A rack on a wall or secure site for suspending coats and other clothing, sometimes using boat cleats for hooks. Especially interesting when of SCRIMSHAW carved wood or WHALEBONE.

Cocked Hats. A form of headgear worn by naval officers, sometimes with gilt, braids, feathers, and escutcheons. They were worn athwart until about 1795, when officers of captain's rank and below starred to wear them fore and aft. In 1825 all officers were ordered to wear them fore and aft. The value of surviving hats depends largely on whether the wearer's name is marked on the inside leather, and on the importance of that name and rank, especially when connected with some notable deed or event. It is particularly interesting to possess such a hat in its original dome-shaped metal box.

Cod-Fishing Knives. On cod-fishing vessels, entrails were removed with a gutting knife (see Kipling's *Captains Courageous*). The cod's head was severed with a guillotine, the fish next being opened with a slicing knife that had a blade with a pointed end, cleaned with a scraping knife, the backbone being removed with another knife that had a rounded blade, then washed and thrown into hold, box or cask. A small shovel was used to throw salt on to the catch to preserve it. Sometimes instead of a guillotine a knife with a rough-edged blade was used to strike off the heads of the fish by hitting the back of the knife with a hammer.

Colt, Samuel (1814-1862). American small-arms manufacturer. His .36, six-shot naval percussion revolver of 1851 was purchased in thousands by the Royal Navy for use in the Crimean War. It had an octagonal barrel, which was replaced by a round barrel in the version of 1861.

Commemorative Ware. Useful or ornamental small articles of pottery, porcelain, glass, wood, or metal produced to commemorate some notable deed. The production of such articles for wide commercial use was begun about 1780. A notable example is the SUNDERLAND PINK LUSTRE JUG. The battle of Trafalgar was celebrated by a huge emission of commemoratives for sale. Nelson would be depicted on them, encircled by a laurel wreath, and with some such patriotic verse appended as "Show me my country's foes, the Hero cry'd, He saw - He fought - He conquer'd And He died". Towards the end of the 18th century a speciality was naval commemorative glassware. PRIVATEER GLASSES were particularly popular. A typical commemorative glass bowl, decorated with enamel subject. A typical commemorative glass bowl, decorated with enamel by William Beilby of Newcastle, was made for the launching of a ship, the *Margaret and Winnieford*, at that place in 1765. It depicts a ship in full sail, with decorations of a coat of arms and lacings. It represents one of the finest achievements of the otherwise tragic

Beilby. Towards the end of the 19th century, with the growth of the "wakes" and general holiday habit, seaside souvenirs of a miniature kind were increasingly produced by such as Goss, whose particular articles in fine bone-china are likely to impart considerable value to collections of them in the future.

Compasses. A mariner's compass is an instrument with magnetic needle on a pivot which always points north, and thus allows the relative position of the other points of the compass to be ascertained. The device comprises the needle, the card or fly, the bowl, a jewelled cap, and a pivot. The card is above the needles in nautical compasses. There are at least two needles, and in some cases four, such as the Admiralty compass had after the Board of Admiralty had investigated the compasses in use in 1837.

At first the card of a compass was made of cardboard, but thick paper or mica with a paper facing was later used. The actual design of the compass card is curiously much older than the compass itself. The symbols on it probably originated in ancient Arab instruments, which were orientated to Mecca and not to the north. Maybe Flemish navigators named the intermediate sub-divisions of thirty-two points or rhumbs about 1390. On early European compasses used by Mediterranean navigators the eight principal points of the card or "wind rose" were signified by eight winds, the sirocco, ostro, africo or libeccio, ponente, maestro, tramontano, greco, and levanter. The point of north was a broad arrowhead, with the letter T for tramontano. This developed during the late 15th century into a spear or fleur de lys. The point of east was marked with L for levanter and later a cross. This cross survived in British compasses until the early 19th century. Compass cards varied according to nationality, and the cardinal points were indicated by and decorated with many various motifs, figures of Faith, Hope, and Charity, sailing ships, birds, fish, reptiles, bulls, white triangles on a black background, leaves, stars, and crowns over anchors. These compass roses began to be developed into designs that gave more accurate readings in the 17th century; but it was not until the 19th century that the division into 360 degrees from north clockwise was more or less standardised.

It is considered that the compass first evolved from a magnetised iron needle that had been rubbed with a LODESTONE to magnetise it.

Those first needles would be encased in straw upon some water in a dish, so that when undisturbed the needle would turn freely and point north. By considering the stars and wind direction, a course with any luck could be set. The first use of the lodestone for this purpose on a length of iron has been variously credited to the Arabs, Chinese, Greeks, and Etruscans. The Chinese knew about the lodestone and its properties in the second century of our area, and probably the Arabs devised the first magnetic compass after contact with those Chinese. It is not known who invented the needle on pivot. Meanwhile the first recorded reference to a nautical compass is that of Francesco da Buti, who wrote in 1380 that "sailors use a compass at the middle of which is pivoted a wheel of light paper, on which wheel the needle is fixed and the star [wind rose] is painted".

Then there was the development of the placing of the pin-mounted needle at the centre of a disc of wood, the last being divided into thirty-two sections of 11 degrees 15 min each, to accord with the main wind currents that prevailed in the Mediterranean. It is believed that an Italian next developed the sea compass by mounting a magnetised needle on a thin card. That needle was of metal wire, lozenge-shaped, the larger diagonal indicating the north-south axis. Some early sea compasses, particularly those of the Chinese, had an astronomic dial centred around the compass. An English scientist and librarian of the British Museum, Gowin Knight (1713–1772) devised an "improved steering compass", also a method of increasing the magnetic flux of the needles, but this instrument did not succeed in overcoming the moments of inertia. This was a period when nautical instrument-makers everywhere were trying to solve the many problems of an effective compass. One major problem was that the north of the card was not true north, an important fact realised about 1490 by either Cabot or Columbus or both. Then it was realised that this deviation was variable. Another major difficulty was that rough weather and unstable ships upset accuracy anyway. Attempts to solve this problem were the DRY COMPASS, and the LIQUID COMPASS as developed in Denmark about 1830. The card in this last floated in a bowl of distilled water. The water contained 35 per cent of alchohol to prevent freezing, and there was an expansion chamber to cope with the expansion and contraction of the liquid. Gimbal rings kept the bowl and compass card level under all conditions. Compasses of this type were introduced into the Royal Navy in 1845, but their use did not become general until a long time after.

Another problem was that metal aboard ship caused deviation. This problem had to be solved finally when iron-hulled ships became the norm, but Commander Matthew Flinders had conducted experiments between 1800 and 1803 which proved that if magnets and iron bars were placed in strategic positions in relation to the compass, then the deviation of the needle could be corrected. His Flinders bars or tubes did in effect solve the problem, which was finally settled by the magnificent work of WILLIAM THOMSON, first Baron Kelvin (1824-1907). His compass of 1876 used eight lightweight needles attached to threads of silk. The threads radiated from a pivot, an inverted aluminium cup with a crown of sapphire, to the rim of the compass. The use of several needles solved the problem of moments of inertia. Thomson's compass was much more sensitive than the regulation naval version of the 19th century, thanks to the fact that the cards, the flies, the needles and the cups were much lighter in weight. The card in the Admiralty compass weighed 1525 grains, while Thomson's was only 180 grains. His needles were shorter; and Thomson's compass on its rigid platform, with its sprung-gimbal suspension, was so successful that it remained in use until the coming of the GYRO-COMPASS well into the 20th century.

Compass Lantern. A lantern used to illuminate the compass in the BINNACLE during darkness. Heat from the lantern was taken away by a funnel on top of the binnacle.

Conchometer. An instrument, invented in 1828, for measuring conch shells, an early aid to listening.

Cosmolabe. This resembled an ASTROLABE and was employed for astronomical observations.

Crab Measure. Fishermen and fishery inspectors used this to check the width of the carapace or shell of a crab. If this shell fitted easily between the two lugs then the crab was smaller than the regulation size allowed to be caught, and so was returned to the sea.

Fisherman's crab measure, circa 1870.

Crank Pump. A pump that, hand-cranked with a cast-iron wheel, was used for expelling water from the ship. It would be sited near the main mast. Rotation of the wheel drove long crank-shafts that descended into the pump-well at the bottom of the hold.

Crossing the Line Certificate. A mock certificate issued aboard ship to a passenger who had crossed the equator for the first time and had undergone the somewhat harrowing but humorous "crossing the line" ceremony. A crew member arrayed as Father Neptune would perform the ceremony with the glad help of other veterans. Much ducking and mock shaving was involved. Some of the earlier certificates are well worth collecting. One has the typical wording:

I, Neptune, being the true and rightful Monarch of all the oceans and of all the creatures that dwell therein hereby bestow THE FREEDOM of the SEVEN SEAS upon that noble and gallant mariner. [space left for name of the recipient] who has crossed that line, called the Equator, which divides our hemispheres. Let all who owe me allegiance allow the above-named to pass without let or hindrance in pursuit of that which is truly pleasing.

This certificate would be signed by the master, and the name of the ship and date of the ceremony would be added. Travellers wisely carried this certificate on all voyages, or they would most certainly be made to undergo the somewhat gruelling ceremony again.

Cross-staff. This simple instrument was also known as the fore-staff, baculus, balestilla, and arballista, being thus called because of its resemblance to a cross-bow and its use for taking a sun-sight (hence the expression "shooting the sun"). Originally an astronomer's aid, it was adopted by mariners for measuring the angle of the altitude of the sun above the horizon at sea. One more name for it was Jacob's Staff, thanks to its physical resemblance to the constellation Orion, formerly Jacob on medieval star maps.

The cross-staff was first described by Levi ben Gerson, a Jewish scholar of the Languedoc, in 1342. After that Vasco da Gama (1460-1524), the Portuguese navigator, on his way to discover the sea route to India in 1498, took aboard an Arab pilot who used an early cross-staff for navigation.

It was originally a bone, ivory or wood staff, $2\frac{1}{2}$ to 4 ft in length, approximately $\frac{1}{2}$ in. square-sectioned, with a sight, and calibrated with different scales on each of the four sides, each scale applying to one of the vanes. There were three or four alternative and bevelled cross-pieces, vanes or transoms, right-angled. They would cover 10, 30, 60, and 90 degrees. They would either be plain or decorated with an engraved geometric or floral design. The sights could be moved up and down the staff, one at a time. The variation in the sizes of the cross-pieces, vanes, or transoms improved the accuracy of the readings, thanks to their manoeuvrability. Different-length vanes were used to measure different altitudes.

To obtain the altitude of the sun, the user fitted one of the transoms, vanes, or cross-pieces to the staff, and pointed the whole instrument at the sun (resting the opposite end of it on the skull-bone beside his eye). The lower or bottom edge of the cross-piece was then put in alignment with the horizon, and the upper or top edge of it was moved up or down the staff. Thus it could be aligned by a sight with the lower edge of the sun, so that the sun's altitude could be read from the appropriate staff scale.

The cross-staff was not only difficult to use, but often entailed damage to the eyes from the sun's keen rays in the tropics; eventually a piece of coloured or smoked glass, to muffle these rays, was used. The instrument had the disadvantage that the user had to angle his vision to see two objects simultaneously. On the other hand some dexterous users would employ the cross-staff like a BACKSTAFF. They would turn their backs to the sun and take a reading from the cross-staff with the help of two cross-pieces and the shadows falling from one on to the other. Most maritime nations had abandoned this primitive instrument by the end of the 18th century, but Holland continued frugally to use it well into the 19th.

Cutlass. A broad, single-edged, naval sword, usually but not always curved. The blade would be partially grooved for lightness, and an anchor would often be engraved on that blade, near the shoulder and close to the guard. The name has been misapplied to any sword used by a pirate or seaman, but should properly be employed only to a regulation-issue cutlass as adopted by the Royal Navy in the 18th century. This standard British naval sword had a long blade, sometimes as much as 28 in. - a flat blade, the black iron hilt of which had a broad, circular shell guard, together with a knuckle guard in the form of a disc. Sometimes the plain iron hilt was of the semi-basket type, or was in heavy brass. After 1889 Royal Navy cutlasses had straight blades, and in 1900 the iron grip was changed to one with leather sides riveted to the sides of the tang. The cutlass originally replaced the BOARDING AXE as a seaman's side-arm. Those in other navies varied considerably in type of hilt. Some 19th century Russian cutlasses had no knuckle-guard, but just a cross-bar, while the grip was studded. American cutlasses of that period were characteristically narrower in the curving blade, and, with their broad knuckle-guards and brass-ended grips, were among the finest ever made.

Cutting Shovel. This was used by the crew to sever or to help the severing of blubber in strips from the carcase of a whale which was chained alongside the whaling ship.

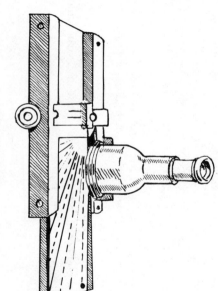

Distance finder.

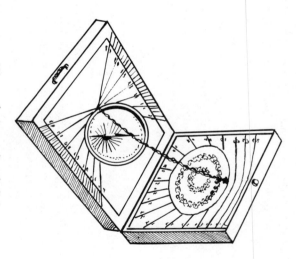

Nineteenth-century diptych dial.

D

Dabney, John, Jr. (fl. 1739). English instrument-maker, apprenticed to London instrument-maker Jonathan Sisson (1690-1749), who emigrated to Boston, U.S.A., in 1739, and became one of the first nautical instrument-makers in the Americas.

Davis, John (1550-1605). English captain and navigator, also amateur scientist and author, whose Canadian coastal explorations resulted in his name's being given to the Davis Straits. One of his books, *The Seamen's Secret*, of 1594, contains his celebrated description of a BACKSTAFF; another, *The World's Hydrographical Description*, 1595, proposed the use of the terrestrial globe as an instrument of practical navigation, and also described sailing on a rhumb line. He was killed in December 1605 during a skirmish with Japanese pirates, when he was piloting an English ship near Bintang.

Davis's Quadrant. The BACKSTAFF, also known as the English quadrant, and, by the French, as the Quartier de Davis.

Dead-Eyes. Circular blocks of hard wood, usually lignum vitae. Each contained three holes, and they were used to secure rigging to the ship's hull. Probably pre-Roman in origin, and used throughout the ages, they were required in very considerable numbers for modern sailing ships such as the clippers.

Deck Chair. An item of furniture still found on beaches and in parks, but originally designed for the use of passengers and for easy stowing on liners. Developed from the hammock, and consisting of canvas stretched on a collapsible wooden frame. Luxury liners eventually had cane-seated, mahogany chairs, which, however, could similarly be collapsed.

Depth Thermometer. A THERMOMETER housed in a strong brass cage with a sturdy base and uprights, used by deep-sea fishermen to discover the water temperature at various depths. It was believed that if the temperature of the water was right then the fish could more easily be caught. Also used on hydrographic ships in ocean surveys.

Dieppe Models. Miniature SHIP MODELS complete with sails and other fine details, made of IVORY in Dieppe during the 18th century, by the ivory carvers for which that French port was famous. Later many of these carvers were pressed into the French Navy during the Napoleonic Wars, captured by the British, and, while imprisoned as prisoners-of-war, became responsible for a vast amount of PRISONER-OF-WAR WORK and bone ship models (See BONE) and the like.

Diorama. The background and base details of a SHIP MODEL in the round or HALF-BLOCK, and of SHIPS IN BOTTLES, including variously a sky and clouds, sea birds, a choppy sea, a coastline with cliffs and/or rocks, a lighthouse, signal station, harbour buildings, and jetties. The sky and cloud diorama was usually painted blue and white; the sea was made from putty or plaster-of-paris painted appropriately. Such things as lighthouses would be made of wood. Another form of diorama, used on land, consists of illuminated pictures seen through an aperture.

Diptych Dial. A form of portable sundial, hinged in two parts connected by a cord. The part acting as a lid was at right-angles to the base so that the cord, tightened, acted as the upright gnomon or style to cast the shadow. Chiefly produced at Augsberg, Germany, in the form of the AUGSBURG DIAL and NUREMBERG DIPTYCH.

Dirk. Originally from Scotland, this is a slender, short sword or poniard. Naval dirks as used for boarding the enemy had a pointed and triangular blade, a hardwood grip, and a leather scabbard with metal chape for protection. The guard was a straight cross-bar, or two inverted or straight quillons with sometimes a central escutcheon. Various kinds of dirk were issued in the 18th and 19th centuries, particularly to midshipmen, but not to senior officers. These could have blued and engraved, curved or straight blades, with an ivory grip, a lion's-head pommel, and the langets engraved with a crown and anchor.

Other navies made more use of this weapon than the British. The Germans favoured it particularly; their chief naval dirk originated in the Prussian Imperial Navy weapon of 1849. In 1861 its issue was stopped, because so many men used it in shipboard and tavern fights, but it was re-issued in 1871, and superseded eventually by the Model 1892 German naval officers' dirk. Thus German dirks are the most plentiful for collecting.

Distance Finder. A navigational instrument used for finding the distance of an object, and particularly the distance of another ship to keep vessels in station. It consisted of a small sighting telescope, with movable prism plate and a diagram base plate. The last was graduated in cables, and engraved with dividing lines that radiated outwards from a central point like sun's rays.

Ditty Box. A sailor's receptacle for holding needles, cotton, and small personal possessions, also materials and tools for model-making and SCRIMSHAW WORK. Possibly from the Saxon "dite", meaning neat or tidy. Its forerunner, however, may have been a bag made of "dittis", which was a form of Manchester cotton fabric. Ditty bags are mentioned in naval records of at least two centuries ago.

Dividers. A two-pronged hinged instrument or "pair of compasses", for measuring on scales or marking off distances on a chart, introduced about 1703, made of brass usually in early versions, but later of other metals with steel points.

Dockyard and Shipyard Models, Civil and Naval. Models of planned ships originally developed to show the King, his ministers, and Admiralty officers what the ship would look like when completed. In 1649 the Admiralty issued an order to naval and civil shipbuilders that an accurately detailed model of every ship proposed for the Royal Navy was to be constructed beforehand, so that the Navy Board could better visualise the full-scale ship. Samuel Pepys, as Navy Secretary, partly used ship models to assist his instruction by naval shipwrights in the craft of naval architecture. Possibly the famous Phineas Pett, mentioned often by Pepys in his *Diary*, inaugurated the useful practice. He was a master shipwright at Chatham, and in 1607 produced what is the first model of its kind, that of the *Prince Royal*, which was launched at Chatham in 1610. It was constructed exactly to scale, even to the smallest details.

The best early ship models were skeletal in construction, but money was later saved by cutting them from blocks, hollowed out and finally planked. Rigging was not erected on official models unless a new type was being tried, and the early skeletal models were deliberately unplanked so that full construction methods could be revealed. Later on the planking was affixed but could be taken off. A method of half-planking was sometimes used, but not in Holland, France and Spain. There were some models that showed not a specific ship to be built but a suggested new class or type of vessel. Some still in existence show types of ship that were never subsequently built.

It was not customary to decorate the models with figureheads, "gingerbread" work and other embellishments, mainly because such would not be decided upon until a definite order was given for a ship's construction. But such models were extremely valuable as guides to naval officials and shipwrights, and could be similarly useful after a ship was constructed, when they would sometimes be sent to naval colleges for the instruction and edification of trainee officers. Models would even be constructed just for such educational purposes. The National Maritime Museum at Greenwich has an H.M.S. *Victory*, known to have been used in a Portsmouth dockyard academy opened in 1733 to train young men for the naval service. There were similar instructional models of various parts of the ship, such as sliding keels, rudders, and capstans.

It was, moreover, the practice in 17th- and 18th-century France to build ship models that were large enough in scale to enable men to sail them on calm lakes before naval experts and thus demonstrate their seafaring capability. Then British shipyards of the 19th century developed the modern tank test, while some hull models would be made to demonstrate how the full-scale vessel could best be cradled and launched.

The model collector can also look for engineers' miniatures of marine engines, armaments, anchors, even dry- and floating-dock

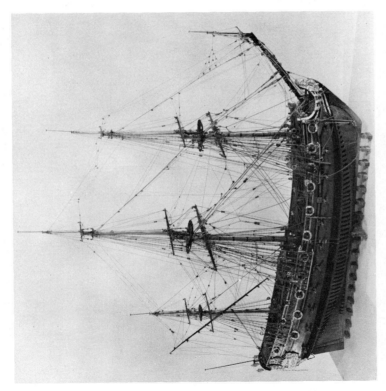

Admiralty model of an unidentified English fourth rate 52-gun ship of 1695.

models. Such will be found in the dockyard and maritime museums still.

Finally there is a whole class of ship models not made for naval and shipyard or instructional purposes, but just "for fun" by private craftsmen everywhere.

Document Case. Not unlike a hat box, this would be round in shape, with a hinged lid and metal band round the side, and a clasp fitting over two lugs so that it could be padlocked. It was used for secret and important documents and ship's papers. The document case dates from the 17th century, and can be beautified with a nautical, state, or heraldic emblem. The lid would be furnished with

75

a handle, and the case as such either complemented the SHIP'S PAPERS BOX or was an alternative to it.

Dry Compass. A compass without liquid in it, prior to the LIQUID COMPASS as developed in the 19th century.

Dry Compass Card. The card showing the compass positions, and used in the dry compass as above. Early examples were drawn by hand. By the late 17th century they were engraved and printed, the north often being indicated by a nautical or state symbol. These cards, from the 13th to the 16th century, were mounted in lidded wooden bowls, but from the 16th century they were placed in brass bowls on gimbals, the last-named to stop the ship's movement from affecting the instrument. The area of the needle or lozenge was enlarged to increase the sensitivity of the card, but this added weight caused wear of the pin; it could be blunted and thus affect the card's rotation. So pins with hardened, ruby tips and caps of agate were introduced. In the 18th century the card was fixed with glue to a disc of mica to avoid distortion, but Thomson's card was much better and lighter in the 19th century when it was printed on Japan paper. Strong silk threads formed a framework, from a stone cap and brass ring, to hold aluminium wires on which the silk paper card was glued, with the bar magnets below it.

Duck's-foot Pistol or Gun. This was also known as a mob pistol. It was a rare type of VOLLEY GUN and dates from the late 18th century. Essentially it was a box-lock, flint-lock pistol with four to seven barrels fitted to a single breech-block. These barrels spread out fanwise from the breech so that they covered approximately a 45 degree angle. There were a touch-hole and priming pan, with four to seven connecting passages fanning out from that touch-hole to the four to seven barrels. Such a fearsome weapon, loaded with grape-shot, would often be used by the command when faced by a mutinous assembly of seamen, and would obviously have had a profound psychological effect. Whether such a weapon was ever discharged effectively is another matter. But it can be seen as the primitive precursor of the modern machine gun.

Dudley, Sir Robert (1573-1649). This English navigator and hydrographer left England in 1605 after a naval career, and lived in Florence, where he worked on several nautical inventions. He collaborated with an Italian engraver to publish a HYDROGRAPHICAL ATLAS called *Dell' Arcano del Mare*, "Of the Secret of the Sea", 1645-1647. This was the first sea atlas of which every chart had Mercator's projections; also the first to give the magnetic declination of a large number of places, and the first to show the prevailing winds and currents at all important harbours and anchorages.

Dutchman's Log. A variation of the use of a LOG to ascertain the speed of a ship, being a piece of wood thrown overboard at the bow, whose time was measured between two marks on the gunwale or between two seamen similarly positioned.

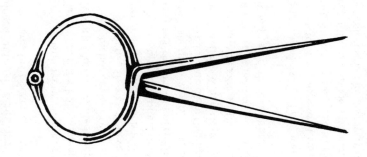

Nineteenth-century dividers.

E

Earnshaw, Thomas (1749-1829). English marine chronometer and clock-maker. He was employed by John Brockbank, then established his own business in London, 1795, to work on an improved CHRONOMETER. He received £3000 for this from the "Commissioners of the Board of Longitude". He was friend of JOHN ARNOLD until they quarrelled over alleged mutual plagiarism. Earnshaw's marine chronometers are very rare; his pocket chronometers less so.

Earring. Metal or wood or ivory ring worn as decoration by a seafarer long after landlubbers had abandoned them to the ladies. Associated especially with bloody-minded mariners of the piratical type. They often had the anchor device, symbol of the sailor's patron saint, St. Nicholas of Myra. It was believed that if a man fell overboard then his earrings with the anchor device would save him from drowning; St. Nicholas would put a hook through one of the rings and pluck him out of the sea to safety. It was also an identity device. Frisian Island fishermen would wear one earring with the name of the wearer engraved inside it, so that he could be identified if drowned and half-eaten by fish. When those fishermen retired from the sea they gave the engraved ring to their eldest son for wearing. Trawler fishermen of Lowestoft used to wear a single gold earring, as they believed that it improved the eyesight.

Egyptian Ritual Ship Models. These were models placed in ancient Egyptian tombs for the purpose of carrying the soul of the defunct, his *ka*, along a river to the next world. At first full-scale boats were left in the tombs, but models were in due course preferred for economy and space purposes. The discovery of these has taught us much about the early days of shipbuilding and navigation. There were two principal types of model: the first was of a vessel used for the ordinary purposes of life, the transport of passengers and cargo; the second type was ritualistically funerary, with a mummy model of the defunct and of mourners aboard, symbolising the transport of the soul to its new abode. Both types had masts, spars, and sails, and much other interesting equipment, including oars. Most of the surviving Egyptian ritual ship models date from the 23rd to the 20th centuries BC. Those found in the tombs of Tutankhamen and Meket-Re are particularly fine.

Embroidery. Ornamentation of fabrics by needlework, in coloured thread on a plain cloth ground. It was a regular spare-time employment of seamen in the 18th and 19th centuries, producing not only gifts but also articles for sale. Materials at hand would be used, a piece of stiff cloth or canvas, and even threads drawn from other cloths. A design would be drawn on the fabric, then followed with stitches of coloured thread or cotton. Cotton wool would sometimes be sewn on for clouds. More elaborate materials would be acquired in ports. When ships were depicted their rigging could be drawn in silk thread. The finished article was sometimes framed and glazed for protective purposes. A frequent theme was that 19th century favourite "The Sailor's Farewell", showing the sailor parting from his loved ones while a boat with other sailors waited to transport him to his ship. Another favourite was the perennial *Victory* to celebrate Trafalgar. Embroidery BEADWORK was also popular, especially on heart-shaped and padded PIN-CUSHIONS, and on such as bags and purses. Coloured wool-work was another method of making gifts for wives and sweethearts. Lazy mariners would purchase similar articles in ports. There developed out of this in the 19th century a trade in SEASIDE SOUVENIRS. Seaside shops eventually existed for this purpose, and for providing embroidery materials that young ladies purchased so that they could make nautical items themselves. Today, alas, the seaside antique shop often sells not so much the carefully hoarded results of this Victorian niceness as modern reproductions.

Endicott Prints. American lithographs of naval subjects, first published by Endicott and Swett of New York in the 19th century.

Engraved Eggs. Thick-skinned emu and ostrich eggs were engraved in bas relief by sailors, often with remarkably artistic results.

Engraved Shells. An occupation for spare hours on the lower deck was the engraving of large seashells. The periostracum or outer surface was cut away to reveal the interior layers forming a design in mother-of-pearl or coloured shell, with the outer layer forming a design or scene in relief. Thick, calcareous shells such as those of the helmet and conch were the most favoured, and survive as antique curios, ranging in colour from cream and milky-white to amber, orange, reddish-brown and deep golden-yellow. Romantic words were sometimes painstakingly engraved, such as "To dear Mother", "I love you always", "Be true to me", or just had the legend "A Souvenir from . . .". Such engraved shells were also purchased by mariners in foreign ports, where their fabrication became an industry, particularly in Italy (which still contrives them).

Ensign. A banner, flag, or standard. Thus the red ensign is the flag of the British merchant service, the white ensign that of the Royal Navy, and the blue ensign that of the Royal Naval Reserve. The Royal Navy was divided in 1625 into Red, Blue and White squadrons, with the Admiral's division carrying red pendants at the main, the Vice-Admiral's blue at the fore, and the Rear-Admiral's white at the mizzen. This was changed in 1653: then red, white, and blue ensigns or plain, coloured flags were the order, save that their upper cantons near the mast became white with a red St. George's cross. The appropriate coloured ensign had to be flown at the poop. In 1702 a much larger red St. George's cross was used on the white ensign to distinguish it from the French national flag of that time which, with its fleur de lys, often appeared plain white. It was not until 1794 that the French adopted the tricolour. In 1707 the UNION FLAG was added to the upper canton of all three ensigns, and just over a hundred years later this was modified with the Union of Ireland.

The red ensign for British merchant ships was officially ordained in 1674, and given the force of law in 1864, when the naval squadron system was abolished thanks to changes in battle tactics. The white ensign became the flag of the Navy as such, and the blue was given to the Reserve. From 1829 the Royal Yacht Squadron had the privilege of flying the white ensign, although other yacht squadrons were allowed to do the same until 1842, when the R.Y.S. was given the sole right. Those others then had to make do with the blue ensign.

Epaulette. Literally a shoulder ornament, first introduced into the Royal Navy in 1795 to help distinguish officers from men, and also to copy the practice in foreign navies. Admirals wore two epaulettes with silver stars; captains over 3 years' seniority had two of plain gold; captains under 3 years' seniority had one on the right shoulder; and commanders had one on the left shoulder.

Ephemerides, Ephemeris. A table giving the computed positions of a celestial body for a given period, such as successive days; also an astronomical calendar or almanac.

Equinoctial Ring. A simplified type of the astronomical ring; a bridge engraved with a declination scale that replaced the astronomical ring's sight-bearing third ring. A small curso, pierced to supply the index, would slide along the bridge. An observer would move the suspension mount along a scale of latitude engraved on the meridian or outer ring to the required position. He would set the index to an approximate declination on the bridge, then turn the free-hanging dial till light passed through the index and fell upon the hour scale engraved on the second ring to indicate the time. The device worked only if the index was correctly set and the dial was suspended with the outer ring in the plane of the meridian. Actually on the back of the meridian ring a 90 degree scale could be engraved, the divisions being radially drawn from a small hole at the centre on the opposite side of the ring. When a short pin was put in this hole, and the suspension mount moved to the zero position of the latitude scale, the diagram or nautical ring could be used for solar altitude measuring. Ring dials of this type could be engraved with scales of latitude both for the northern and southern hemispheres, or for the northern hemisphere alone. Possibly the invention of WILLIAM OUGHTRED.

Ex-voto Models (see below, and also VOTIVE SHIP MODEL).

Ex-voto Paintings. Sailors were the most superstitious of men in the old days, and liked to bestow gifts upon their patron saint, or the Virgin Mary, or other objects of fear and worship, especially when the ship and crew came home safely. Devotional pictures were prominent among these offerings, as well as religious figurines or models of ships. Among the earliest examples known are simple wash drawings of ships, bestowed upon small chapels in the Naples area. These paintings were executed on wood during the 18th century, and on canvas in the 19th. They tended to be small, as the chapels became crowded with such gifts. Either they were painted by a skilled member of the ship's company, or commissioned from a hack artist. Some celebrated painters started their careers with this kind of essentially sterile work. The hack would be given the story of the grave hazard from which the ship's company had been saved, and told to go away and make a picture of it. Of course all marine paintings are not "ex-voto". The true "ex-voto" can be clearly identified by the presence in it of an image of the patron saint or other deity, in some such position as hovering in the heavens above the ship in peril. Most clearly identified are those with a panel giving details of the perilous event, the ship's name, and the donor's name with his vow - traditionally the initials V.F.G.A., standing for *Votum fecit, gratiam accipit*, which could be translated as "He made a vow and received a favour from Heaven". The custom of arranging for the painting and giving of these pictures declined with the coming of the safer steamship.

F

Falconet. A breech-loading and essentially light gun, attached to a swivel mounted on a ship.

Ferrers, Vice-Admiral Washington, Fifth Earl of (1772-1778). A naval architect and astronomer, three of whose ship designs were exhibited at the Royal Academy in 1775.

Fiddlehead. Ornamental carved work on the bows of a sailing ship, culminating in an upward-turning scroll like the head of a violin.

Figurehead. A painted, carved-wood representation of a human or other figure, or of a head or bust only, projecting as an ornament from the bow of a sailing ship, usually symbolising the name of the vessel. It has a superstitious or religious origin, going back to ancient times in most seafaring countries. Maybe it was at first an "oculus" or eye painted on the bows to ward off evil and bring good luck. It is known that neolithic peoples, between 1000 and 500 BC, sacrificed an animal and tied the carcase to the bows of their ships. This custom was still being observed on the Coromandel coast of India in the 1870s. Human beings have similarly been killed and tied to the bows. One savage people would decapitate a virgin and stick her head on a spike in the bows of a ship, the idea being to placate a male sea god. Some of her blood was at the same time splashed on the bows, and this may be the origin of the custom of breaking a bottle of wine on a launching ship. The anthropologists suggest that the virgin became a carved wooden figure at a time of virgin shortage.

Carved sacred emblems, a solar disc, an ibex, a hawk, a ram, a lion's head, even the Pharaoh himself, were used on the stemhead of ancient Egyptian vessels, both of the Nile and the sea, as depicted on tomb and temple paintings, and on EGYPTIAN RITUAL SHIP MODELS. Animal heads were used on Minoan vessels. The Greeks of the 8th century BC favoured not only an "oculus" but also a stag's antlers, and they would have underwater rams in the form of charging boars and elephants. The Phoenicians were all for the horse. They thought of their vessels as swift sea horses, and so had a carved representation of that animal on the bows. The Romans carried on this custom, but varied the animal, and were particularly fond of riders on dolphins. Then they had figures and abstract patterns carved on the stem sides. The Vikings had figureheads consisting of dragons, horses, and serpents. These were very tall, carved and prominent, almost top-heavy. The stem and sternposts of a famous example, the Oseberg Viking Queen burial ship, found on the west side of Oslo Fiord, 1904, are carved upwards to form a serpent's head. By Viking law all fearsome figureheads had to be unshipped on return to port, lest they might offend the gods on land. Later on, the Danish and other north European ships had their prows ornamented with lions, bulls, or dolphins, often in copper gilt. We learn that one Sweyn had an entire ship in the form of a dragon, the stem bearing the head and the stern the tail. William the Conqueror's personal ship had a lion figure-head, and a stern-post consisting of a carved boy holding a trumpet with one hand and pointing seawards with the other. Thence ensued a period when figureheads were no longer practicable. This was during the 13th and 14th centuries, when fighting ships had "castles" at each end to accommodate bowmen. These were known as "fockse", from which evolved the term forecastle. But the carrack of the 14th century did have a horizontal beam projecting from the lower forecastle, and this would be carved at its extremity in the form of an open-jawed beast.

Then in about 1400 the figurehead was revived, and especially in the form of the figure of the seafarer's saint. At that time there was often an altar in the bows for a religious service, together with a figure of the saint for worshipping. But the sacerdotal theme did not last, especially when Henry VIII outlawed the Roman Catholic faith. In the 16th century figureheads became almost wholly laic. Galleon-head vessels had the forecastle reduced to form a flat bulkhead, and what was known as the beakhead had a figure appropriate to the ship's

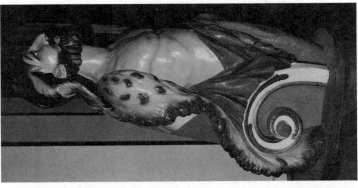

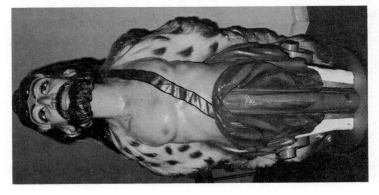

Figurehead of H.M.S. Encounter, 14-gun corvette, 1873-1889.

name, such as a unicorn attached to the beak of the warship *Unicorn.* Elizabeth I's ships had dragons, unicorns, tigers and lions, the royal beasts, not necessarily connected with the ship's name, as the *Mary Rose* had a unicorn, the *Swiftsure* a tiger, and the *Repulse* a lion. This lion became the favoured beast in the 17th century. It was usually gilt in the reign of James I. Dutch ships then had red lions, and the Spanish and Scandinavian navies used baroque versions of the beast, leaping or crouching, crowned or uncrowned, with an extended tail. The favoured lion in the 18th century was frequently combined with other figures, rampant and holding a shield or other device. The *Sovereign of the Seas,* a notable ship of the Carolingian period, had a great figurehead showing a king on horseback trampling on six nations.

Cromwell, for all his puritanism, did not himself disdain to have a ship, the *Naseby*, whose figurehead was a graven image of the Lord Protector no less, again trampling upon vanquished peoples, the Scots, the Irish, the Dutch, the French, the Spanish, and of course the English. That ship was re-named the *Royal Charles* with the restoration of the professional monarchy, and the figure of Cromwell was replaced by that of Neptune.

The 18th century was a period of very rococo figurehead design, the height of the art. The *Royal Anne* of 1704 had an ox, a female figure and cupids on each side, together with a large, crowned shield of the royal arms, supported by four cupids, beneath which were two female figures, nicely draped, and further cupids below them. The sloop *Cruizer* of 1732 had a very fat figure of a merboy, winged, who was blowing on a conch shell.

The cost of these figureheads could be considerable. In 1686 it had been found necessary to issue an Admiralty order to curtail such expenses. Similar orders were issued in 1727 and 1742, notably to reduce the size of the carvings. It was in 1771 that ships first had their names painted on them, initially as an incorporation of the figurehead design. Severe restrictions were finally imposed by Admiralty order in 1796. It was about time, as is shown by the ADMIRALTY DRAUGHT details for the *Victory's* group figurehead.

The American Navy, as formed on the outbreak of the War of Independence, followed European conventions rather slavishly, in that most early figureheads symbolised the name of the ship. Thus the *Hancock* of 1776, named after John Hancock, President of Congress, had a figure of that gentleman himself, with yellow breeches, white stockings, blue coat with yellow buttonholes, and a small cocked hat with yellow lace.

The figureheads of the Royal Navy soon began to decline in size and quality during the 19th century; from 1835 they consisted mainly of busts and half-figures. The first steamships had figureheads, but a projecting device became impossible with the introduction of straight-stemmed ironclads. The *Agincourt* of 1865 had just the royal arms across the stem. The *Prince Consort* of 1862 had a medallion portrait of Albert with Art and Music as supporters. The last figurehead on a major warship was that of the *Rodney* in 1884. It was an upright bust of the admiral, surrounded by scrollwork. An Admiralty

Figurehead of H.M.S. Pylades IV, 21-gun corvette, based in the Australia Squadron 1860-1870.

order of 1894 formally abolished figure-heads on large warships, but scrollwork continued until the early 20th century. The last Royal Naval ships to have figureheads were the *Odin* and *Espiegle* sloops of 1901, as they had suitable clipper bows. This *Espiegle's* figurehead showed a somewhat doubtful lady, who, during service on the India station, had a black mask painted over her eyes, which, for superstitious observers, was not the best of omens. The American Navy suffered the same gradual deprivation for the same reasons. Its naval figure-heads ended with a glorious burst in 1875, when U.S.S *Lancaster* was given that enormous eagle as carved by the great Bellamy (see BELLAMY EAGLES).

87

Very little is known about merchant ships prior to modern times (by modern is meant at least the last two centuries) as there are few surviving paintings, models, or plans of them. But East and West Indiamen of the 18th century had a variety of ornate figureheads undoubtedly, with the lion always predominant. The 19th-century expansion of population and world trade greatly increased the size of merchant fleets, and throughout that century figureheads were so popular of merchantmen that they were to form the basis of most modern collections. The fast clippers had very suitable bows for the purpose. These would be either curving, as a legless figure-extension of the cutwater, or a fuller-length figure standing on a knuckle cut into that cutwater. The early steamships had clipper bows, and could support figureheads, but when that clipper bow became obsolete, so did a rather lovely custom, which survived only in yachts and other small craft.

The subjects used for 19th-century mercantile figureheads were enormously varied. Traditionally they were intended to represent the name of the ship, or at least the trade in which that vessel was engaged, but it was considered very unlucky to change the name of a ship, and, even worse, to alter the figurehead. So often ships continued to carry figureheads that were quite irrelevant to their purpose. Needless to say the female figurehead was always very popular. In the otherwise inhibited Victorian age it could be surprisingly voluptuous, even seductive. No doubt it was intended by benevolent shipowners to provide food for reflection on long voyages. Those owners, however, would often allow their wives and daughters or even themselves to be depicted on a ship. Jenny Lind was a popular female figurehead of the period. Another was the famous feminine figure with a rose clenched in its hand. It was suitably derived from the French custom of giving a rose to the most chaste (or chased) girl of a village. There is such a girl figurehead on one of Dover's piers, taken from the barque *Roseau*, that was named from the port of Roseau in Dominica.

Figureheads with a projecting arm sometimes had it made so that the arm could be unscrewed and removed in rough weather or when entering a crowded port. There are, of course well-carved, and ugly, figureheads. Too many in museums or private collections have been either faked or badly restored, especially with crude re-painting.

Staring eyes are a fault - because artists thought they should be made thus to indicate how the figure was searching out a safe course for the ship. American figureheads may be identified by both their boldness and their clumsiness, also by local subjects such as American eagles, Wild West heroes and Red Indians. The last commercial sailing ships to be built with figureheads were the four-masted steel barques from the 1890s to the early 1900s, some of which survived until the beginning of the Second World War.

The wood used in a figurehead was oak, if the ship-owner did not mind the cost, and wanted a figure that would last, particularly withstanding the sea's violence, and knocks while in harbour. Pine was an alternative, also elm, but the last was a false economy, in that the wood deteriorated quickly and had constantly to be repaired and repainted. The figure would be carved from one block, or from two blocks laminated.

One can believe that the original painting of figureheads was good, sometimes excellent, but that paint would wear off and soon, alas, be replaced by the crude daubings of an inartistic seaman, layer after layer, until eventually the figure can be quite garish and unlike its young days. This applies particularly to figures from the more lowly vessels of the merchant marine. The Navy always did much better.

The collecting of figureheads has become a connoisseur's speciality and dealer's trade in recent times, with the result that genuine examples have become steadily rarer. Meanwhile carvers of great skill have entered the business with often splendid reproductions.

Fire Bucket. A wooden bucket, often of teak, with strong metal, sometimes copper hoops for strength, carried by rope handles knotted at each end, which held water for fire-fighting. Several would stand in countersunk holes between the balusters of the poop rail; BUCKETS used as fire buckets were also made of leather.

Fishing Floats. These were sealed glass balls used as net floats by fishermen. Later they were retrieved and painted or engraved with a local scene or nautical subject, then sold as SEASIDE SOUVENIRS.

Fishline Basketry. Baskets made by sailors, using fishline with fancy knotting. They are a 19th-century form of SCRIMSHAW. The basket had a grommet for base with fishline hitched to it. The lines worked to the rim, and finished off with coxcombing or buttonholing. After being stretched over the bottom of a basin and soaked, the basket was allowed to dry, and was painted or varnished.

Flag. This could be defined as a piece of thin woollen cloth called BUNTING, thickly hemmed along one edge called the hoist, into which is sewn a short length of line. The upper end of this line ends in a wooden toggle for making fast to the halliard shackle, and the lower end is an eyelet to be made fast to the other end of the halliard. Various types of flags have been flown on naval and merchant ships. The national ensign is self-explanatory; it is flown at the stern flagstaff, mizzen masthead or gaff peak, but at the bows of naval warships and over the bowsprit on some sailing ships. The differentiation between naval and merchant ships as regards flag-flying is largely a British custom; in many countries the same national ensign is flown on all ships, but Britain has preferred to distinguish merchant vessels by their flying of the red ensign, or "red duster", which has a miniature union flag in the corner nearest the hoist. The Royal Navy flies the white ensign, a flag with a white ground and red St. George's cross, but also with the union flag in miniature near the hoist. The Royal Naval Reserve has the same flag in blue instead of white.

For centuries flags have been used for transmitting messages: smaller kinds of various shapes, patterns and colours, called SIGNAL FLAGS. Up till the 19th century each national navy would have its own signalling system, but standardisation usefully came in the 19th century with the first international flag-signalling code, there being some natural confusion at first.

A subject in itself is house flags, the individual insignia of private shipping companies, which were flown on the mainmast of sailing ships from the windjammer to the river barge, and on the foremast of steamships. A collection of these would run into hundreds, some of them still familiar, but many meaning nothing now save to the shrewd expert who knows how to delve into old shipping magazines and marine records. The best place to buy genuine old flags is at seaport auctions of marine bric-à-brac. Useful old books of flagsignalling codes and instructions can be obtained.

Flint-lock Musket. A type of musket that was fired by using a flint in a hammer-head to strike a steel, causing a spark which ignited the powder charge. It is usually dated back to 1556, but a Florentine document of 1547 contains a reference to flint-firing. The marine type were carried aboard ship as part of the crew armament, together with pistols and CUTLASSES. On Royal naval vessels they were stored in a gun room when not required.

Flint-lock Pistol. The mechanism of the musket as described above was here used in a small hand-arm. (It should be mentioned that the same mechanism was attached to cannon aboard ships in Nelson's time, being first tried out rather primitively in 1755.)

Flower Shells. (SEE SHELL BOUQUETS.)

Fog Apparatus. Various items which, by making sound, have been used on board ships to warn of their approach during fog, also on lighthouses and lightships and warning buoys. Probably the original foghorn was an animal horn, through which a Viking crew member would prodigiously blow. The Chinese used a humming gong, which was a bronze disc in a frame on deck, struck by a mallet to make a vibrating sound, eventually used as an insignia by a famous film company, although not necessarily for warning purposes. Arbroath had a fog gong in 1898, and Irish lightships used it. A gong-boy struck the instrument at intervals. Another warning device was the ship's bell, also used on lighthouses. A cannon could be fired regularly on warships, and a gun on merchant ships, known as the ALARM GUN. Muzzle-loading guns were employed by some lighthouses, notably those at Lundy Island and Flamborough Head, although Flamborough later replaced the gun with pioneer rockets discharged by gun-cotton.

From about the middle of the 19th century the hand-operated foghorn superseded most other devices, being made of brass, and consisting of a large sealed cylinder about 18 in. long with a vent at one side in a smaller cylinder. The large cylinder contained a brass-knobbed rod with a leather washer at the other end. The principle was the same as that of a bicycle pump. The large cylinder would be held, or placed upright on a flat surface, and the knobbed rod would be pulled out and then pushed in quickly. The air thus compressed was pushed out through the smaller cylinder and its vent caused a mournful but sufficiently pervasive sound. These survived into the steamship era, and continued to be carried as a standby when otherwise replaced by steam devices; they will still be found on naval ships. But the engines of the steamship produced the steam whistle, then the compressed air whistle, and finally the siren foghorn that still booms across the narrow seas. Such sirens were installed on lightships and lighthouses, originally in 1877 at St. Annes and the Skerries and Shambles. There was also the manual pneumatic foghorn of T. Mathews, a Trinity House engineer, which was a foghorn connected with an air compressor activated by two pumps operated by a flywheel. The loudness of this device was increased by a cone above the mouth of the trumpet. Robert Foulis, a music teacher of St. Johns, New Brunswick, is often given the credit for the invention of the first practical steam foghorn in 1887.

Fore-staff.   (see CROSS-STAFF.)

Frisius, Gemma (1508-1555).   Instrument-maker of Louvain who developed an ASTROLABE that he called an *astrolabum catholicum*. It took as its point of reference not the celestial pole but the vernal equinox.

Froude, William (1810-1879).   This English engineer was probably the first to use SHIP MODELS in tests to discover the behaviour of new hull designs.

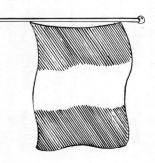

House flag of John Hardie & Co., Glasgow.

92

G

Galley Equipment. The galley, sometimes in the after end of the deck house, had much necessary equipment, including a cooking range with a sheet-iron surround, a chopping block with a groove for knives, a deal plank table with shelves underneath for storing pots and pans, a kneading trough for bread, and a cylindrical container with a tap, holding 11 gallons of water, the galley's ration. There would also be frying pans, stew pans, tongs, tormentors, meat forks, knives, sieves, baking pans, stew pans, ladles, colanders, axes, saws, coffee pots, not to mention an oil-burning storm lantern for lighting. The galley of the *Victory* is at the forward end, customary at that time, and contains an iron "brodie" stove, fuelled by coal and charcoal, the funnel of which passes through the deck above to the forecastle. There is a primitive water condenser in this galley, so that the ship's surgeon could have uncontaminated water for his operations.

Geminus Dial.   (see ROJAS DIAL).

Gemma's Ring.   Also known as the ring dial, this was a development of the AUGSBURG DIAL, a reasonably accurate sun clock. There was a ring to represent the meridian, a quarter of which was graduated with a scale of latitude from nought to ninety degrees; and another ring for the hours, which was graduated with Roman numerals. The third part was an axis with a sliding sight. This was set to the angle of the sun's declination in the month of observation. The device was suspended from a ring, and the sliding ring moved on the outer rim of the meridian ring. It would be set on the meridian ring scale to coincide with the latitude of the observer. The meridian ring was drawn into line with the meridian plane, when the axis represented the polar axis and the hour ring the equator. The sliding sight on the axis was set between 23.5 degrees south and the same north according to the month of the year. The hour on the hour ring was ascertained by the way the sun shone through a hole in the sight; thus the hour could be known for any given latitude. Until replaced by the CHRONOMETER the ring dial or Gemma's ring was a standard navigational instrument in the British and other navies.

Gingerbread Work.   A term applied to the large amount of gilded and ornate carved work on the hull, sides and stern of naval ships in the 17th and 18th centuries. Use of this decoration started to decline when the Admiralty, due to the increasingly high cost of the work, ordered in 1796 that unnecessary adornment should be eliminated, and gilt should be used only on the Royal arms and the ship's badge. Gilt on figureheads was progressively replaced by yellow or orange paint. Damage to a ship's decorations evoked the phrase: "The gilt has been taken off the gingerbread". Gingerbread was essentially a fair-ground confection in the old days, and thus had the connotation of tawdriness.

Glass Racks or Trays.   These, sometimes called swinging fiddles, were suspended over the tables in the saloons and captain's accommodation of sailing ships, to enable glasses to be available without breaking in rough weather. The racks swung by uprights from a cross-bar or beam, and the shelves had recesses to hold the feet of the upturned glasses.

Globe.   A model of the world, depicting the continents, islands, seas and oceans, sometimes with small spheres at the ends of wires to show the heavenly bodies and their paths. Globes showing the heavens (celestial globes) date from very ancient days; but the first terrestrial globe as such could not be produced until it was finally agreed that the earth must be round and not flat. The early globes were either hand-painted or covered with a gore, which was a printed paper pointed at the top, swelling towards the centre, and pointed again at the bottom. Several of these were used to cover the globe. They became common in the 16th century, on land in libraries, and on ships for use in navigation. Most of the early examples are quite inaccurate, although they did give a rough idea of land and sea

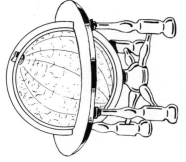

Seventeenth-century terrestrial globe.

surfaces. One famous maker was William Blaeu. The globes of this Dutchman were made of papier mâché covered with plaster of paris, on which gores printed from copperplate engravings were pasted and varnished. Blaeu's work dates from 1622. Another great craftsman was Padre Vicenzo Coronelli. He produced globes at the end of the 17th century, made to a standard diameter of 3 ft 6 in., provided with an equatorial ring and a meridian ring of copper marked in scales. This meridian ring slotted into the equatorial ring, and thus allowed the poles to be tilted at any required angle above the horizontal. On the larger globes of the late 17th and early 18th centuries, it was possible for the navigator to estimate with a fair accuracy local time, daylight length, and times of the rising and setting of the sun at his known position. The English navigator Martin Frobisher (1535-1594) ordered a marine globe and plain metal globe from an instrument-maker in 1576, for course-plotting. Terrestrial globes were chiefly important as a reasonably accurate means of indicating to a navigator his shortest course to plot. They were used on land both for educational purposes and to enable merchants to understand trade routes. There were also pocket terrestrial globes of the 18th century, housed in a leather or shagreen-covered spherical case, that had a celestial map pasted on the inside of the case cover. Three of the important 18th-century globe-makers were John Senex (fl. 1728-1749), Richard Cushee (fl. 1760), and Nathaniel Hill (fl. 1746-1764).

Godfrey, Thomas (1704-1749). American mathematician and instrument-maker, who claimed to be the inventor of the quadrant, although he was working on the same lines simultaneously as JOHN HADLEY, who is generally credited with the invention in Europe. James Logan, Irish-born American statesman and Chief Justice of the American Supreme Court (1731-1739), encouraged Godfrey's talent for optics, astronomy, and mathematics, so that in 1730 Godfrey successfully designed and made a quadrant which improved on Davis's quadrant or BACKSTAFF as then in general use. It was tested in Delaware Bay, after which a Captain Wright took it to Jamaica, where "he showed and explained it to several Englishmen, among whom was a nephew of HADLEY". The Royal Society had made, or was intending to make, an award to Hadley, who had designed and made a similar quadrant in 1734, but James Logan wrote and claimed at least equal recognition for Godfrey. The Royal Society, nicely recognising the American claim, awarded each inventor a prize of £200. Godfrey took his in household furniture, which would have proved a splendid investment if his descendants kept it.

Gorget. A crescent-shaped ornamental plate in gilt copper, worn round the neck by officers of the French Navy in full uniform.

Grape-shot. A cluster of small iron balls, held together in a frame, and fired from a smooth-bore cannon. They were superseded by shrapnel. They would be used against the enemy as an anti-personnel weapon to injure and kill many crew members at a single firing, also to cut rigging.

Graphometer. A surveying instrument for measuring angles, derived from the CIRCUMFERENTOR, invented about 1696, although a plan for the first of the type, a circumferentor with a graduated semi-circle, was published in France by Philippe Danfrie a hundred years before. Usually made of brass, it was used by land surveyors to survey coastlines, but also by naval cartographers, although the movement of ships made this rather difficult. It had not a full circle but a graduated semi-circle, plus a diametric bar with a sighting hole at each end. It was aligned to magnetic north with the help of a compass centrally situated between the scale and the bar. A bearing

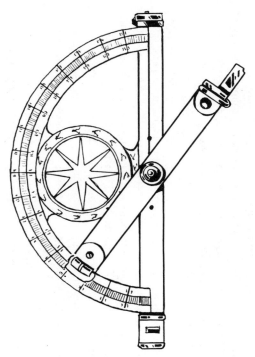

Eighteenth-century graphometer.

was taken by aligning a second alidade, with sighting holes at each end, which pivoted around the semi-circle. The graphometer was housed in a semi-circular box when not in use. It was among the navigational instruments used on survey ships, but was superseded in the 19th century by the REFLECTING CIRCLE, which was itself followed by the theodolite. It was known as a whole dial when the 360 degree circle was complete.

Grapnel, or Grappling Hook.   A small anchor with several flukes, attached to the end of a rope, for grappling an enemy ship. It would be slung over a rail or other projection of that ship, then the enemy could be pulled over for fighting at close quarters or boarding. It would also be used for mooring a small vessel - and for retrieving SMUGGLERS' KEGS.

Grappling-iron.   A grappling hook or GRAPNEL.

Great Crock.   A large pot used in North Devon for pickling pilchards. Not to be confused with a pilchard pot or BUSSA.

Gunter, Edmund (1581-1626). The English mathematician who invented in 1624 the GUNTER'S SCALE. Hence the old phrase "according to Gunter", which means precisely, or accurately.

Gunter's Scale. A wooden or brass ruler 1-2 ft long, engraved with scales of chords, logarithms, trigonometry functions and the like, used in navigation and for surveying. It was a predecessor of the slide-rule; and was employed for plotting on a chart, giving the logarithms and natural values of trigonometrical lines. When it was combined with a DIVIDER the same results could be obtained as with a SECTOR. It was first introduced in 1624, and remained useful until the late 19th century.

Gyro-Compass. A gyroscope with compass-card attached, developed especially for marine use, where the ordinary magnetic compass was unreliable for various reasons, especially the movement of the ship (see COMPASS). First used in Germany, 1906, it eventually replaced Thomson's compass.

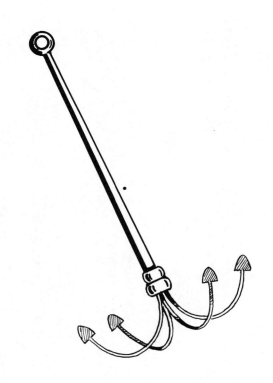

Grapnel.

H

Hadley, John (1682-1744). English mathematician who claimed to be the inventor of the quadrant, but whose claim was disputed by the American GODFREY. All the same he received £200 for his invention from the Royal Society (as did Godfrey).

Hadley' Quadrant, or Octant. Also known as the reflecting octant this was invented by John Hadley in 1731. It had a sector of 45 degrees, differing from the true sextant, which has a sector of 60 degrees. Hadley overcame a common fault in nautical angle-measuring instruments (the difficulty that an observer experienced in looking in several directions at once) by using mirrors. But good-quality mirrors were scarce at the time, and this in turn handicapped the instrument.

Hair Hygrometer. An instrument often incorporated with a BAROMETER, for discovering the degree of humidity of the air. It comprised a whisker or beard, actually the hair from a seed of wild oats, that formed a spiral when dry, and unwound when damp. It was, however, a somewhat inefficient instrument, as the oat beard tended to disintegrate with time and use, and had constantly to be replaced.

Halberd or Halbert. A form of spear or pike, from which it was distinguished by its axe-head with one or more spikes. It was mounted on a long wooden pole. There was a combined halberd and wheel-lock gun, 8 ft long, that must have required considerable strength to operate. The pure halberd was principally a military weapon, of the 16th century, but was adopted for naval use. The crew would use it to repel boarders. This naval version was stronger and longer than the military type, so that it could be used between ships. The difference between the naval and military halberd is the length of the pole, up to 8 ft in marine versions and only 5-6 ft in the land type. Halberds were used until the middle of the 18th century.

Half-block Models. This type of ship model had a flat hull on one side to be fixed against the background of a DIORAMA. Those made aboard ship were usually less than 3 ft long; often copied from the ship in which the maker was sailing. Simple models had the vessel stuck against a plain sea-green or blue background. Finer examples had a diorama consisting of a bright blue sky, white clouds and seagulls, a sea-green calm sea or a white-flecked choppy sea, with white at the base of the cutwater, along the hull sides and at the stern to indicate movement; plus either a buoy, a following smaller vessel, or variously a lighthouse, jetty, cliffs, and harbour houses. The hull, masts and bowsprit were usually nailed to the diorama backing, while the carved-wood sails and yards were glued to the masts, together with the rigging, ensigns, pennants and other details such as cannons and crew figures.

The half-block model was housed in a case about 6 in. to 1 ft deep, the background being smaller than the front, open part of the case, with the sides sloping inwards to improve the effect of perspective. Sometimes this case would be set in a picture frame, complete with glass, and there can be a label giving the name of the ship and its captain, or other details. Half-block models were also made in ship-yards, sometimes up to 6 ft long, fixed to a wooden panel as a background. The purpose of these was to show prospective buyers of a

Half-block ship model, circa 1870, made into a pipe-rack at a later date.

ship what they were buying. It was unnecessary to show the ship in the round because the sides of a ship do not differ from each other that much.

Then there was what might be called the working half-block model, made in dockyards or shipyards to assist the naval architects and the shipbuilders in their actual work. It saved money to have such a half-block instead of an all-round model. These shipyard versions were carved from the solid, with rudder, bowsprit and masts in the form of stumps, just to show their positions. As the model was three-dimensional, it could be cut into sections, each of which would be scaled up to give the builders the design of the hull over its length. Such models were particularly useful at the time of the clipper ship boom. It was all-important to design the fastest possible hull. Examples of whole shipyard models that survive are either fakes or duplicates made at the time of the originals, or of hull designs that were not used. A complete and genuine shipyard half-block model is of great interest, especially if it has a label or plate appended with details of the proposed ship.

Half-hour Glass or Clock.   This is a SAND GLASS that ran from one bulb to the other in half an hour. It was used at sea from the Middle Ages till the mid-19th century. The helmsman would turn the glass as the officer of the watch called the passages of the sun through the meridian. He turned it again at the end of the first half-hour, striking the SHIP'S BELL once. After the second half-hour he struck the bell twice, and so on. On Royal Naval ships a marine was positioned at the ship's belfry to strike the bell and to advance the hands of a clock face another half-hour each time the sand in the glass had completed its course. The common sand glass had bulbs protectively housed in a brass or wooden mount with top and bottom plates, with bars or columns between the plates to give some protection to the bulbs. The sand glass could be suspended by a ring.

Half-minute Glass.   A sand glass for just that time, used as log-timers, and surviving on sailing ships until the 20th century. Their bulbs were made in one piece, unlike the two-bulbed glasses made to measure longer periods.

Handbill. A small printed POSTER containing a notice or advertisement, distributed by hand. It would advise the departure of a vessel for foreign parts, announcing accommodation for emigrants, and space in the hold for cargo, also cargo rates. Such bills at ports were much more important in the old days than in the later days of newspaper and periodical advertising. A surprising number of early handbills remain in existence, or are brought into existence, for collecting.

Handkerchief. Maybe it was in the 18th century that the custom began of having handkerchiefs printed with nautical or seaside scenes. Certainly this became a mass-production industry in the 19th century. Artists would be commissioned to execute the original designs, but often the mills would use blocks or transfers that printers had produced and that were eventually used on a wide variety of articles besides handkerchiefs. The earliest of these handkerchiefs have very simple designs; the most recent, and the reproductions, tend to be more ornate. Seamen's INSTRUCTION HANDKERCHIEFS are quite different from the souvenir variety.

Handspike. An implement made of wood tipped with iron, used with the TURNSPIKE for manhauling a cannon's carriage wheels, and for raising its breech, also to train and elevate the weapon.

Hanger. A short, lightweight, single-edged sword, with a slightly curved blade, used by naval officers and seamen; a precursor of the CUTLASS.

Harness Cask. This conical, usually teak, cask with three brass hoops round it for strength, and a hinged lid, may have got its name from the way it is "harnessed" to ring bolts in the deck behind the mizzen mast, or on the monkey poop roof over the cabin accommodation. There were usually two aboard, one for salt pork; the other salt beef. The Royal Navy used to say that the name came from the fact that such casks contained salt meat and the meat was horse, and the only part on the animal missing was its harness. Some lower-deck humorists were regularly saddled with this joke.

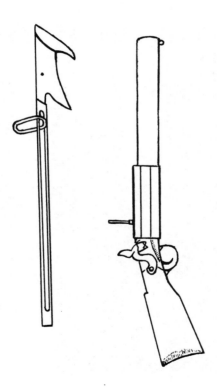

Shoulder harpoon gun and harpoon, circa 1850; percussion, with a brass stock for added strength.

Harpoon. A barbed spear with length of rope attached by a ring on the shaft, for whale-fishing. In the early days of whaling this well-balanced, long-handled weapon, with its sharpened and greased head, would be hurled at the leviathan by hand from a small, rocking boat. The whale would set off wildly, towing the boat. Eventually it would tire and be dispatched by further spears, carefully aimed into its vital parts, then towed to the whaling ship after a final harpoon with wider-fluked barbs had been inserted.

Harpoons were kept in leather scabbards. Attempts were often made in the old days to fire them from cross-bows (as arrows), and eventually they were to be launched from hand-held guns. The largest harpoons would be projected from a heavy-barrelled gun that was mounted on the whaler's deck. Probably the Dutch invented the first harpoon gun about 1731. American whalemen used a shoulder gun like a rifle, about 1860, to fire what amounted to a "bomb" into the unfortunate animal. In 1864 a Norwegian, Svend Foyn, nicely developed a gun to fire a harpoon with an explosive head. It was too heavy to be used in a rowed whaleboat, so was mounted in the bows of a specially built steamship. The whale line ran from the harpoon through spring tackle to absorb shock. This was controlled by a steam winch. The invention meant whales could often be dispatched by a single shot and hauled to the factory ship by the same harpoon and line, which led to the modern system of mass-production or mass-destruction whaling.

Harrison, John (1693-1776). Nicknamed "Longitude" Harrison because of his inventions, which included the marine chronometer, the remontoire, and the gridiron and grass-hopper escapements. The British Government offered in 1714 a prize of £20,000 for a timepiece that would accurately give a ship's longitude within 30 miles, compensating for movement and for temperature changes. Harrison, a carpenter at first, tried to meet these considerable requirements. He and his clockmaker brother James developed by 1726 two very accurate longcase clocks that were unaffected by atmospheric changes and involved a minimum of friction. This was followed in 1730 by a clock from which the pendulum had been eliminated, and in 1735 Harrison developed, with the financial help of the East India Company, a very large watch or "sea clock". This was taken on a naval ship to Lisbon in 1736. On the return journey it was found that the Harrison device was infinitely more accurate than the normal navigational methods of the time. Those methods were used on that return journey, and Harrison's device proved that they were 60 miles off course.

In 1737 Harrison and his brother sought financial help from the "Commissioners of the Board of Longitude", that had been set up to encourage inventors. The £500 they were awarded enabled them to move from Lincolnshire to London, and to enlist the help of skilled metal workers in the capital. James returned to Lincolnshire in 1739, leaving John to continue his work on the "sea clock". The Board of Commissioners were sufficiently impressed to award him another £500 in 1741, but with the proviso that he should complete the invention in 3 years. However, much longer than that was required; it was not until 1760 that Harrison had his fourth and best "sea clock" or "longitude watch" ready. It measured 5¼ in. across, had jewelled bearings, and was set in a silver case. (By then Harrison had received nine grants from the Admiralty, totalling £3000.) This first real chronometer was taken on Admiralty instructions by H.M.S. *Deptford* on a voyage to Jamaica. Harrison's son William sailed in charge of it. The chronometer enabled the ship accurately to make landfall at Madeira, but on the way to Jamaica it was alleged by the ship's navigator that whereas the ship was 13 degrees 50 minutes west of Plymouth, the Harrison chronometer gave a reading of 15 degrees 19 minutes. William maintained that the difference was due to inaccuracy of the ship's charts. He added that if his father's chronometer was correct then Portland Island would be sighted next day. It was; and on arrival at Port Royal, Jamaica, it was found that the chronometer, after 81 days' voyage, was only 2 seconds slow.

On the return voyage to Portsmouth, after 5 months' sailing, the variation of the chronometer was nearly 1 minute 5 seconds, which produced an error of 16 miles of longitude; so the Commissioners of the Board were not satisfied. There was a long and acrimonious argument between those Commissioners and Harrison and his son, who claimed their complete prize money. The Board eventually agreed there should be another test, for which Harrison should construct a better instrument. The old man (now 79) completed this, his fifth attempt, in 1764, fighting against bad health and eyesight. William took it on a test to Barbados, and this time the chronometer performed perfectly. Old Harrison was finally awarded his prize, but only half the money was paid over at first. The Commissioners required that Harrison should take his device to pieces and make a full explanation of its construction and working before the balance was paid over. He did this, but still did not get the money. There was a public outcry. Parliament was petitioned; pamphlets were published; and William became a perfervid campaigner for justice; his appeal even reaching the ear of the King. It was not, however, until 1773 that Harrison, by Act of Parliament, finally received the remaining £8750. Three years later the old inventor died, having spent those last years in constructing a chronometer that, after 10 weeks' trial in the King's private observatory at Richmond, was inaccurate by only $4\frac{1}{2}$ seconds.

The secret of Harrison's chronometer was a self-compensating piece of mechanism attached to the balance wheel, which he called a knib (now known as a compensation curb). Harrison also invented a recoil escapement that produced practically no friction, as well as the gridiron pendulum. Other clockmakers, JOHN ARNOLD, THOMAS EARNSHAW and THOMAS MUDGE, worked to improve and develop what became known as the marine CHRONOMETER.

Heard, Joseph (fl. 1839-1856). Little is known of the life of this very active ship portrait painter, celebrated for his pictures of the brigantine *Centaur*, 1839; the S.S. *Damascus*, 1856; the barque *Mary Ann Johnston*; and the *Annie Jane*.

Hester, Wilhelm (fl. early 20th century). German-born marine photographer, who skilfully photographed sailing ships in American ports and waters during the early years of this century.

Holland Circle. An altitude-measuring instrument from Holland, produced prior to the CIRCUMFERENTOR. A notable maker was the firm of C. & D. Metz of Amsterdam during the early 18th century. The Holland circle was similar to the circumferentor, but on its main circular plate it had four sights separated by 90 degrees.

Hollar, Wenceslaus (1607-1677). This Czech topographical etcher, engraver and draughtsman, was born in Prague, and died in London (completely destitute). At first he worked in Germany, then came to England and was admitted in 1636 to the suite of Thomas Howard, first Earl of Arundel, who recognised his considerable talents. Eventually he taught drawing to the Prince of Wales, and in 1666 was appointed "King's scenographer or designer of prospects". He was sent to make drawings of the town and fort of Tangier and the adjacent countryside. He was one of the first important etchers in England. His line can be spidery but was never inaccurate, and considerable historical as well as artistic value attaches in particular to his river and bird's-eye views of London and Amsterdam. Those of the old Whitehall Palace, are interesting and revelatory. This applies also to the ships in "The Fleets off Deal", the "Map of the Harbour of Newcastle", and "Dutch Shipping".

Hondius, Jodocus (1563-1612). Flemish cartographer, engraver, globe-maker, and map publisher, who issued his own ATLAS and also engraved MAPS for other cartographers, such as John Speed's "Theatre of the Empire of Great Britain", 1611-1612. He illustrated the voyages of Drake and Cavendish. He greatly admired GERARD MERCATOR, after whose death in 1594 he purchased plates from the family, and thus continued to publish revised editions of Mercator's atlas until his own death. Jan Jansson, whose sister had married Mercator's son, continued this good work afterwards.

Howitzer. A short CANNON for high-angle fire at short range. It came into naval service in the early 19th century. It was not mounted on trunnions; the barrel had a sledge or shoe mount. The weapon was attached to the deck by a kingpin. The shoe or sledge absorbed the recoil.

Hudson, J. (fl. 1860). English ship portrait painter, notable for pictures of the steam tug *Rescue*, the ship *Charles Henry*, the ship *Lota*, the barque *George Watson*, and the "Launch of the *Polka*".

Hurricane Dial. A curious meteorological instrument, usually made of brass, comprising a COMPASS ROSE, with several scales and pointers. When these were arranged correctly they were supposed to give the ship a safe route to steer around the path of an impending hurricane.

Hydrometer. Also called the English log, this was a mechanical LOG as invented by William Foxon, a carpenter-mariner at Deptford, and patented by him in December 1772. Prior to this, in 1688, the English physicist Robert Hooke had outlined a similar idea to the Royal Society, but nothing was done to develop this. (Hooke also established the laws governing the stretching of springs, which eventually enabled an accurate marine timekeeper to be developed.) Foxon's invention was a mechanical instrument, fixed on the taffrail, that relied for its action on a vane, fly, or helical rotor in the water. A spiral log was towed at the end of a line behind the ship. The line, maximum length 15 fathoms, was connected to the instrument aboard and, being twisted by the revolving of the log in the water, transmitted its motion to an arbor at the instrument's central mechanism. This arbor had an endless screw, and a fly-wheel to equalise the motion. A dial plate was divided into 12 knots by divisons of a seventh of a knot. The endless screw led to a wheel, known as the first wheel, and moved the dial hand. This first wheel intersected with another endless screw, that connected with a second wheel, which turned another hand around a second dial. The second dial was divided into 12 miles by divisions of one-tenth of a mile. Yet a third dial had a pointer geared to turn once for every twenty-four revolutions of the mile dial, that is, every 288 miles. The Admiralty procured these logs both for Captain Constantine Phipps on his voyage to the Arctic and for Captain James Cook on his second voyage of exploration. Both navigators found that the log was good enough in smooth seas, but almost useless under rough conditions. (The term hydrometer is also used for an instrument that measures specific gravity and the strength of liquids. One early example was the freeboard hydrometer, basically a salinometer or salimeter, first invented in 1844 for the measuring of the salt content of water; it was a water sampler with a graduated scale, and could be used also for correcting the draught while vessels were loaded or unloaded.)

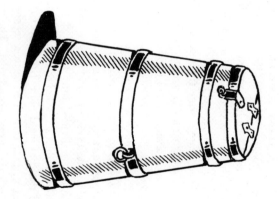

Harness cask.

I

Inclinometer. A sensitive, accurate instrument, invented in 1842, with a magnetic needle and graduated ring dial, for measuring the force of magnetic attraction exercised by the earth, also the direction of that attraction relative to the plane of the horizon. It enabled "variation" tables to be prepared on ocean surveys. The readings obtained were vital for correct navigation when a ship was being steered on a magnetic compass course; the navigator had to allow for the variation between true and magnetic north in different regions and years. This variation is shown on deep sea and ocean CHARTS BY ISOGONIC LINES.

Instruction Handkerchief. This large handkerchief had the specific purpose not of decoration or nose-wiping but of teaching the seafarer what he could not always remember of his marine craft. It was usually dyed red, and the instructional text was printed in black. Sometimes it would be used for enveloping small articles and keeping them safe in the pocket. They were not widely used, and are consequently rare.

Instrument Case. This was for geometrical, surveying, or surgeon's instruments, made of wood, and leather- or metal-lined for protection.

Isogonic Lines. These show magnetic variation as determined by an INCLINOMETER. "Isogonic" means literally the indication of equal angles (of magnetic variation). Such lines are printed on charts and on some maps.

Ivory. A hard, organic material obtained from animal tusks.

Mariners would polish and carve the material, which was more easily worked than metals. It was used on integral parts, as well as decoration, of navigational instruments such as CROSS-STAVES, SUNDIALS, GUNTER'S RULES, OCTANTS, SEXTANTS and SAND GLASSES. It was useful also for the making of SHIP MODELS, sewing boxes, needle boxes and cases, thimbles and walking-stick heads. Dieppe was the centre of the ivory trade from the 14th century onwards. An ivory-carving industry developed there, and was responsible for the famous Dieppe SHIP MODELS and ivory sundials.

Ivory Nut. The nut of a palm tree, approximately the size of a hen's egg, which was used by mariners for carving.

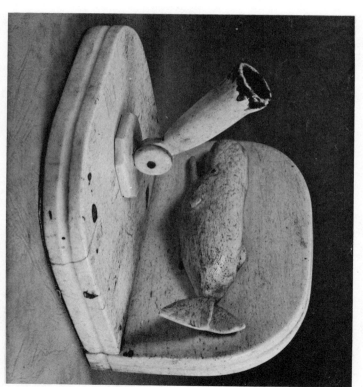

Ivory scrimshaw penholder with a whale carving in relief.

110

J

Jack. Small flag of a ship, especially the national flag which was flown at the bow on a jack-staff. The Union Jack, properly the UNION FLAG was always flown in this position. The earliest reference to the use of the word jack as a FLAG dates from 1633, when it meant a small flag on the bowsprit.

Jack Knife. A large clasp knife, supposedly named after a Belgian cutler, Jacques de Liège, about 1590. He is credited with the invention of a knife with blade or blades that folded into the handle. It was a principal tool of mariners for the making of such as SCRIMSHAW items.

Jansson, Jan (1588-1664). Dutch engraver and publisher of maps, some of which were his own, and some pirated. In 1637 he succeeded to the business of JODOCUS HONDIUS who himself took over the business and plates of GERARD MERCATOR.

Jones, William (1763?-1831). English inventor in the late 18th century of the box SEXTANT. This was an instrument to measure angles up to 150 degrees, having two coloured shades, a telescope and a lens cap. The angles were read off a graduated arc and silver vernier scale with a magnifying glass. The cover could be removed and screwed on another side for use as a handle. It was chiefly used for terrestrial observation with an ARTIFICIAL HORIZON by surveyors, but also aboard ship in the 19th century. Surviving examples chiefly date from the end of that century.

K

Kendall, Larcum (1721-1795). This watch- and clock-maker was commissioned to construct two examples of the chronometer invented by JOHN HARRISON. That of 1769 was used by Captain Cook to find his longitude during his second exploratory voyage to the Pacific in 1772-1775, and during his third voyage of 1776-1780. The second, known as the *Bounty* watch, was used by Captain Bligh during his *Bounty* voyage to the Pacific in 1772. The mutineers took it from him in 1789, and an American whaling captain acquired it when he visited Pitcairn Island in 1808. It was stolen from that owner in South America, but was subsequently purchased for 50 guineas by a Captain Thomas Herbert, R.N. He brought it back to England in 1843. Kendall also constructed two of his own, modified, chronometers, but they were inferior to Harrison's.

King, Benjamin (1740-1804). Member of an important American family of instrument-makers, of Massachusetts. This family included his father Benjamin King (1707-1786), as well as Daniel King (1704-1790), and Samuel King (1748-1819). They specialised in sextants. Benjamin King, Jr., with William Guyse Hagger (1744-1830), of Newport, Rhode Island, another instrument-maker, founded the firm of King and Hagger, whose sextants were mostly of the non-reflector type, there being a shortage of optical glass and mirrors at that time in America.

Kitchingham (or Kitchinman, or Kitchingman), John (1740/1-1781). English marine and shipping painter, whose series of pictures illustrated the whole work of shipbuilding, a craft that he studied carefully.

L

Lamb, Anthony (1703-1784). This English instrument-maker was one of the first to arrive in America. He served part of his apprenticeship with Henry Carter, the London instrument-maker, but was caught in an escapade with his dubious friend Jack Sheppard, the highwayman, in 1724. He was sentenced to hang, but this was commuted to transportation overseas. The American colonial settlement became his destination, and in 1749 he set himself up as an instrument-maker in New York. He announced in his advertisements "a newly invented quadrant for taking the latitude or other altitudes at sea".

Lamps and Lanterns. Sailing ships had a variety of lamps and lanterns, made of brass, copper and galvanised iron, perhaps painted, with clear or coloured glass windows; their purposes were various.

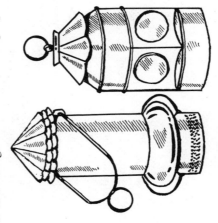

Nineteenth-century navigation lights.

There were oil lamps for the illumination of cabins, set in gimbals and with smoke shields; stern lights with clear glass showing a light to half the horizon; anchor lights with all-round illumination; storm lanterns; compass lamps; signal lamps; also red and green lights for port and starboard sides. Ships such as the *Victory* had three large lanterns above the taffrail (round the stern), and also lanterns to illuminate the light rooms, which were small chambers separated by double glass windows from the magazines.

Laurie, Robert (1750-1836). English map-publisher, who, with his partner James Whittle, issued in 1794 an edition of Robert Sayer's "The North American Pilot" in London. Laurie and Whittle had taken over Sayer's business that year.

Lea, Philip (fl. 1666-1700). English globe-maker, map-seller and geographer. His globes are mostly 26 in. in diameter.

Lead, and Lead Line and Reel. A PLUMMET or lead was used for taking soundings at sea, to discover both the depth of the water and the vessel's distance from the sea floor. A navigator would use charts that gave abbreviated depths and details of the sea floor, and compare these facts with those obtained by lowering the lead. A piece of tallow stuck in a dimple at the bottom of the lead would obtain bottom samples for comparison with the chart details. Ferdinand Magellan (1480-1521) took soundings in the Pacific during his world voyage of 1519. In the Tuamotu archipelago he used a sounding line of only 200 fathoms. It did not touch the bottom, so Magellan wrongly assumed he was over the deepest part of the Pacific. In 1620 the naval chronicler Mainwaring referred to a "lead line or sounding line" as being used in the Royal Navy, with markings almost the same as those employed today. Sir James Clark Ross (1800-1862), the polar explorer, found that his normal sounding line was not long enough during the expedition of the *Erebus* and *Terror* to the Antarctic in 1839-1843, so he had a new heavy hemp line constructed which was 3600 fathoms long, and thus made the first successful abyssal sounding. He records:

On the 3rd. January, 1840, in latitude 27 degrees 26 south,

longitude seventeen degrees 29 west, we succeeded in obtaining soundings with 2425 fathoms of line, a depression of the bed of the ocean beneath its surface very little short of the elevation of Mont Blanc above it.

As indicated, lead and line were originally thrown and hauled back by hand, although deep-sea leads and lines were in due course released and hauled back by winch, which would often take long enough. H. N. Moseley, in his "Notes by a Naturalist," made during the voyage of H.M.S. *Challenger* round the world in 1872-1876, wrote:

The vastness of the depth of the ocean [Pacific] was constantly brought home to us on board the *Challenger* by the tedious length of time required for the operation of sounding. When the heavy sounding weight is dropped overboard, with the line attached, it takes about an hour and a quarter to fall to the depth of 4500 fathoms and 35 minutes to reach the bottom in the average depth of 2500 fathoms. The winding in of the line again is a much slower process....From daybreak to night the winding-in engine was heard grinding away with a painful noise as the sounding line and thermometers were being reeled in.

Leather Hat, Straw Hat.   Mariners wore what they liked on their heads in the old days: a handkerchief knotted at the back was perhaps the most common form of headgear. Then navies gradually provided uniforms, and private owners issued clothes to seamen, when seafaring hats started to become standardised. The tarpaulin hat was introduced in the early 19th century; it was kept black and glossy with tar and oil, and had a broad black ribbon with the name of the ship embroidered thereon. The straw hat for naval persons was probably introduced in the West Indies about 1802, in response to the demands of the climate. Known as the "sennet" hat, it was abolished in the Royal Navy in 1922. Use of the tarpaulin hat had similarly been discontinued in 1890. The actual leather hat was a favourite in several navies during the second half of the 19th century; it had a ribbon round the crown, which was knotted to hang over the back of the head.

Le Roy (Leroy) Pierre (1717-1785). French watch- and clock-maker, who constructed a longitude clock given to Louis XV in 1766, and who wrote a book that, even today, contains useful principles of chronometry. He invented the word "chronometer". He was awarded a prize by the French Academy of Science for his work on time measurement at sea; his main achievement being an escapement that left the balance wheel free during the larger part of its movement. This was a key to later chronometer development; but Le Roy quarrel-led with his friend and rival, FERDINAND BERTHOUD, the result being that he disastrously decided to relinquish all further work on the chronometer.

Lemaire, Pierre (1739-1760). Pioneer French maker of OCTANTS.

Lee Metford Rifle. The first magazine rifle, with a .303 calibre and seven-groove rifling. It had a box magazine holding eight bullets. It was first issued to the Royal Navy in 1889.

Letter Seal. A form of die stamp, engraved with badge, company motif or trade mark, for pressing upon warm wax to seal a document, and used exclusively by the captain or an important officer aboard ship. Sealed orders would be given to a ship's commander in time of war, with instructions that they should be opened at a stated time or place. (See MARINE SEALS, and French PRISONER-OF-WAR WORK.).

Linstock, Lintstock. A metal rod, spiral-shaped with a length of slow-match wrapped round it, which was used for firing a CANNON through the touch-hole. The smouldering slow-match was held in a notch of a MATCH-TUB. Various types were used in different navies; the marine linstock was also different from that used on land, which was a wooden rod with an iron point or two prongs for holding the slow-match.

Liquid Compass. When the DRY COMPASS could be developed no further, and there was the problem of how to stop the wear of pin and cap, it was decided, about 1779, to experiment with liquid. The cap was enclosed in a float, and the card in a liquid, which supported the needle and, by carrying its weight, avoided wear on the pin and cap.

This device also helped to counteract violent movements of the ship. The early liquid compasses had a card that almost floated in a bowl filled with distilled water and alcohol. There was an expansion chamber to deal with expansion or contraction of the liquid, and gimbal rings so that the bowl and compass-card stayed level no matter how the ship moved. The liquid compass was in general use by the Danes in 1830 and taken up by the Royal Navy in the mid-19th century, but did not know its heyday until the early 1900s. Glycerine was used as an alternative to alcohol and distilled water; generally when the liquid used was not water the device was called a spirit compass.

Lister, Thomas (1745-1814).   Clock   and   orrery   maker,   who worked at Halifax in Yorkshire.

Locker.   A chest-like compartment in a ship's cabin, stores, or on deck, to house items ranging from clothes and personal articles to tools, nails, bolts and screws, paint and paint-brushes. Lockers used for the storing of foodstuffs came to be lined with tin or zinc.

Lodestone, Loadstone.   Magnetic oxide of iron, a black brittle mineral, which attracts metal. A piece of lodestone would be housed

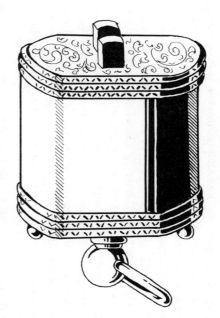

Lodestone.

aboard ship in the old days, and given a wood or metal frame, plain or decorated. The binding metal of the case would be brass. It was used to magnetise (and constantly to re-magnetise) compass needles. The lodestone was taken from its case and "stroked" on the needle or compass "wire" as it originally was. The properties of the lodestone were known to the ancient Chinese, Etruscans, Arabs, Phoenicians, and Greeks, who probably discovered that a piece of pivoted metal thus magnetised would point north and south.

Log. A device for measuring a ship's speed, the name probably being derived from the original device, which would have been a simple piece of wood - the LOG "SHIP", tied to a line and thrown into the water from a ship, the speed of which could be calculated by the time the log took to pass from stem to stern. This speed was measured in terms of the knots on the log line. An early development was the DUTCHMAN'S LOG. Later, using a GUNTER'S SCALE, a seaman could transcribe fathoms or feet, per minute or half minute, into miles per hour. The actual knotting of the LOG-LINE was in intervals thought originally to be proportionate to fractions of miles, but the modern "knot" is 6080 ft as against 5280 ft for the mile. One man or boy stood with the drum or reel for the line held over his head by the handles, while another reeled off several fathoms of the line and then heaved the attached log overboard on the lee side. As the ship sailed forward so the log stayed at a constant position in the water while the line continued to be paid out. The seaman with the reel or drum watched the line, and the other operator watched a SAND GLASS. When a piece of white BUNTING on the log line reached the rail the seaman with the drum shouted "turn", and his companion turned over the sand glass. At the end of the operation, at the final running-out of the sand, the man with the drum shouted "stop". The line was seized and prevented from paying out further, so that the ship began to tow the log, from which a wooden plug was pulled out by the sudden strain. Thus the log came to the surface and was hauled aboard. The speed of the ship was calculated from the time it took for the sand glass to run out, in terms of the knots spaced at regular intervals along the line and the "long line length", from the position of the white bunting.

Various ideas for mechanical logs were advanced in the 18th and 19th centuries, but many of these came to naught. One of the first

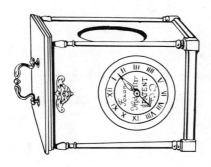

English log, 1772, by William Foxon.

reasonably successful inventions was the HYDROMETER, or English log, as developed by FOXON OF DEPTFORD. Fixed to the taffrail, it recorded the rotations of a helix towed astern of the ship, three dials indicating tens of miles, miles, and tenths of miles. But the helix made to rotate like a screw was not always accurate, so eventually the hydrometer was abandoned. About 1800 Gould, in the United States, developed his milometer that was towed astern with a submerged counter worked by a variable-pitch propeller (which could be adjusted to the average speed of the ship if known). Massey's mechanical log of 1802 swiftly superseded Gould's invention, although it was built along very similar lines. Thomas Walker, who started by manufacturing Massey's log under licence, introduced his own in 1851. It enjoyed much general use. The Walker Company patented in 1879 their "Cherub" log, which had a counter mounted on the rail, a torque-free line, a flywheel, and a propeller. One of the claimed properties of this was that it repelled the large fish which had been in the habit of swallowing earlier logs! Then in 1880 the Frenchman Fleuriais made and tested what was probably the first electric log. It had four arms or spokes with a cup at the end of each. As it rotated pulses were transmitted to a counter, and the proportion of rotations to the distance covered could be ascertained. The Walker Company developed their electric log in 1902, but it was not until as recently as

1924 that a proper electric log was produced commercially. Once again Walkers were responsible. Electric pulses were transmitted from the counter on the stern to a dial on the ship's bridge.

Log Board. Term applied to a ship's record of its voyage. Earliest due course shortened to "the log".

Log Book. Term applied to a ship's record of its voyage. Earliest known examples are from the 17th century. Afterwards two kinds developed: the official log which was confined to formal, unadorned entries; and the private log which was like a personal diary kept by the captain or other officers. Whaler captains would use a handstamp carved at one end in the shape of a whale, for ink-stamping on log pages at relevant dates to record the number of whales taken that day, and the total of barrels of whale-oil that a particular whale had supplied. The solid stamp of a whale meant a kill, an outline profile meant an escaped whale, a stamp only of a tail indicated a sighted whale, perhaps struck but lost, while the number of barrels "stowed down" was accompanied by the signs LB (larboard), SB (starboard), and WB (waist boats).

Private logs still extant can be collectors' pieces, as amusingly illustrated by the writers with drawings or even paintings of ships, harbours, whalings events, and scenes from marine life.

Whale stamp with scrimshaw work on the handle.

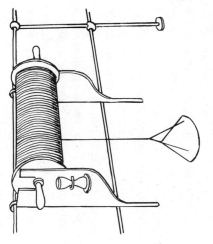

Log line and log "ship".

Log Glass.   A SAND GLASS used in conjunction with the LOG. Some of them ran for as short a time as half or even quarter of a minute.

Log Line.   A lengthy line used with the LOG REEL or drum and the LOG "SHIP" to determine the speed of a ship. After use it was placed on an oval-shaped tub, with a socket on each side to retain the reel handles in position. Thus water could drain away from the line without making a mess. Another stowing method was to hang the line and log in a housing on a rail, often the poop rail.

Log Reel or Drum.   Handles at the end of this device for holding the coiled log line were held by a man or boy during the paying-out, and could also be used for fitting into slots on the rail housing afterwards. Sometimes the line was paid out from the reel, which could revolve freely when fitted to the rail housing.

Log "Ship".   This supplanted the LOG TIMER in the 17th century. It was the actual log, a triangular piece of weighted board, or shaped like the sector of a circle, about 2 ft wide, and was attached to the line by a length threaded through a hole at one side and knotted at the back. The other end of this piece of line was attached to a wooden plug that filled a hole at the other side. The log "ship" was weighted by a

121

length of lead set into the board's edge. It was cast over the stern and the line paid out while a SAND GLASS was emptied. The line was then hauled aboard and a note was made of the length paid out. Later the line was knotted at spaced intervals so that the knots or nautical miles at which the ship was travelling could be determined. Sometimes bunting or leather was used instead of, or in addition to, the knots. During every watch the log line had to be paid out to discover the ship's varying speed during the day.

Log Timer. A Dutch invention of the 16th century to determine the time it took for a log thrown over the bows to reach and pass the stern of a ship. It was a clockwork instrument, which was started the moment the log was thrown overboard. Seconds were marked by the striking of a bell on the instrument.

Loggerheads. Heavy iron bars, heated and then used to melt pitch for caulking a ship. They were favourite weapons in private fights, hence the expression "to be at loggerheads".

Loud Hailer. A metal cone with a mouthpiece at the narrow end, held by a handle, and used to amplify the voice when hailing another ship or a person on the shore.

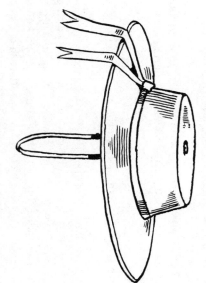

Seaman's leather hat, circa 1870.

M

Map. A plane representation of the earth's surface or part of this, with seas, oceans, coastlines, and other physical features. Early examples are inaccurate, but pretty, with drawings or paintings of seaports and other towns, including miniature items of architecture, also dolphins and other marine creatures, cherubs blowing at ships' sails, plunging and gun-firing ships, not to mention elaborate cartouches giving names and addresses of artist and printer, as well as other proper names and, in the case of sea maps, sailing instructions.

Various methods were used on old maps to indicate sea areas. German cartographers of the 16th century used simple wave patterns, but a fine, dotted stipple was increasingly favoured elsewhere. JODOCUS HONDIUS employed a moiré method of sea-shading, whose zigzag lines resembled the shimmer on shot silk. Map-makers in the 18th century used form lines drawn parallel with the shore, which increased in their distance apart as they moved away from the shore. This was the custom on early Ordnance Survey maps, which were the first purely functional kind, omitting the dolphins and other sea monsters, the ships, and the cherubs. A collection of maps or charts bound together formed an ATLAS. In the 16th and 17th centuries such a collection was called a theatre.

Most early maps were extremely inaccurate, but made up for this by their romantic interest. Non-existent places as depicted thereon, and references to deadly quicksands, dangerous sirens and mermaids, even islands occupied by gigantic cannibals, were attractions which provoked many people to go to sea and undertake fantastic voyages of exploration.

Most maps and charts were a work of cooperation between several different kinds of craftsmen, artists, engravers, printers, publishers, booksellers, and, of course, the navigator-explorers who supplied the details. The best early types are printed on hand-made paper which can be identified, even for dates, by the number of water-mark lines to the inch. Some were printed on vellum or silk. Those printed from copper plates were often hand-coloured afterwards. Some old maps have had the actual colouring done in modern times by dealers or their employees. The age of a map printed from engraved copper plates may be judged by the sharpness or otherwise of the line and other impressions. Such plates lost their sharpness with constant use. Long after the deaths of the original owners of the plates other printers would be using them - right up to yesterday in some cases. (See entries for the notable cartographers MERCATOR, JANSSON, BLAEU, SPEED, HONDIUS. Other makers were Waghenaer, Cary, Ogilby, Morden, Norden and Camden.)

Marine Seal. A seal is a device impressed in warm wax by an engraved die - used on a document or other paper or container as a proof of its authenticity. The intaglio-cut seal was usually oval or circular, and made of copper. Around the design in a border was the name of a naval or other government department, or that of a branch of the merchant service. Designs on such seals are usually nautical, such as anchors or sailing ships or naval and royal insignia. Marine seals are not to be confused with those of a nautical type used as authentication or ownership marks on ships' documents generally.

Mariner's Recording Compass. This is a curio of the 19th century. Under the compass-card was fitted a leaf of silk paper, which followed every movement of that card. The paper was pierced at regular intervals by a sharp pin as activated by a non-magnetic mechanism of bronze clockwork. The pin moved automatically outwards from the compass-card's centre, so that in 24 hours its route met the lubber-line on the rim of the compass bowl. The numerous pin-pricks could then be traced and, theoretically, the 24-hour course of a vessel could be determined.

Marlin or Marline Spike. A tool used for separating a rope's strands. It comprised an iron spike with a slight curve, and a handle like that of a bradawl or screwdriver.

124

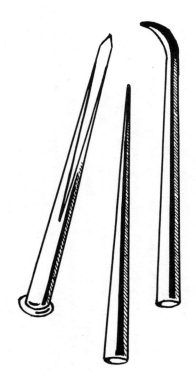

Marlin spike.

Marryat, Captain Frederick (1792-1848). English naval navigating officer and good popular novelist, who sailed as a midshipman with Lord Cochrane and was involved in much adventurous and dangerous service. He commanded a sloop off St. Helena, his duty being to prevent any attempt to rescue Napoleon. He was also involved against smugglers in the English Channel. In 1828 he was given command of the *Ariadne.* He was made a Fellow of the Royal Society in 1819, and a member of the Legion of Honour in 1833, both as recognition of his work in improving signalling methods. He devised a code of FLAG SIGNALS. He resigned from the Navy in 1830 after the success of his novel, Frank Mildmay, and thereafter became a best-seller with such adventure stories as *Peter Simple, Mr. Midshipman Easy, Masterman Ready, Settlers in Canada,* and *Children of the New Forest.*

Martin, Benjamin (1704-1782). English globe-, stick barometer-, and clock-maker, upon which topics he wrote several books.

Match Tub. A wooden tub with notches round its brim, for holding slow-matches for the firing of CANNON. The matches were fitted into the notches and kept there over water while ignited, so that there was no risk of igniting nearby gunpowder. (See LINSTOCK).

125

Maury, Matthew Fontaine, Lieutenant (1806-1873). American naval officer and oceanographer, who was promoted lieutenant in 1863, the year he published *A New Theoretical & Practical Treatise on Navigation*. In 1838 he was assigned to harbour surveying, and in 1842 was appointed Superintendent of U.S. Depots of Charts and Instruments. He then began a series of researches into winds and currents, using a strong twine sounding line to take soundings. In 1847 he issued his *Wind & Currents Chart of the North Atlantic*, following this in 1848 with explanatory sailing directions in his *Abstract Log for the Use of American Navigators*. This was universally admired and used by seamen, who cooperated by sending him information on winds and currents they had encountered. By 1853 he had devised a uniform system for recording oceanographic data. In 1854 he gathered together all the deep-sea soundings he could find (some 180), and, adding these to his experiences, in 1855 wrote *The Physical Geography of the Sea*, the first textbook on oceanography. He was consulted on the laying of the first Atlantic cable, and experimented with electric mines.

Mayer, Tobias (1723-1762). German inventor of the 1752 REFLECTING CIRCLE.

Mears, G. (fl. late 19th century). English ship portrait painter and marine artist generally, especially devoted to shipping scenes off the south coast of England. Became "Marine Painter to the London, Brighton and South Coast Railway". His ship portraits are accurate, and have appropriate seascapes. Sometimes the "G" in his signature resembles an "A" or "P", which has caused confusion in the attribution of his paintings. Noteworthy examples of his work are "H.M.S. *Devastation*", the vessel "*Woodside*", and "The Royal Yacht *Victoria and Albert* off Cowes", the last-named painting showing also the 300-ton American racing schooner *Enchantress*, famous in British events 1874-1875.

Medal. A small metal disc, resembling a coin but having no currency, with various inscriptions, struck and awarded for services in war or peace or to commemorate a special event. Attached to coloured ribbon, and represented by another small piece of backed ribbon when

Men's Quarters Equipment. The crew of merchantmen in the 18th and 19th centuries often had to take aboard their own necessities, such as drinking kegs, mess cans, wooden spoons, pottery bowls, wooden platters, a sea chest, even gear for repairing clothes and shoes. The seaman would take his own enamelled tinplate and mug. The ship provided furniture in the quarters, such as a deal or oak table bolted to the floor, benches, trays hung from the deckhead by ropes for taking cutlery, as well as paraffin lamps of copper or brass with conical black shades, not to mention hammocks and many other items which, however, varied in lavishness (if that word is permissible) according to the wealth or decency of the company involved.

Mercator, Gerard or Gerhard (1512-1594). Flemish mathematician and cartographer who first employed the method of map projection now known by his name. He was also the first cartographer to use the word "atlas" for a collection of maps. He made astronomical and mathematical instruments, and produced some large GLOBES, until in 1537 he published his first map. This was followed by a three-part atlas, published between 1585 and 1595 and entitled *Atlas Sive Cosmographical Meditationes*. Mercator's methods were followed by many cartographers after his death. Until 1606 his family continued to produce his maps, then Jodocus Hondius purchased the plates and published Mercator's maps and revised editions of the atlas until his own death in 1612.

Minute Glass. A SAND GLASS that ran for 1 minute.

Morden, Robert (died 1703). English globe- and map-maker who prepared the maps for an English translation of William Camden's *Britannia*, an historical survey of the British Isles, which was first published in Latin in 1585, and re-published in 1695.

Mortar. As opposed to a cannon, a mortar is a weapon that throws projectiles, necessarily on a high trajectory, instead of impelling them forward through a barrel. Originally - and the weapon is very old - it was exactly as its name implies: a large, open vessel or elongated pot. Naval mortars in the old days were erected on platforms, often on the "castles" of warships. Powder was put in the mortar, and then a round shot, which was hurled into the air to fall like a bomb. They were constructed of iron or bronze, and their shot would weigh up to 200 lb. The range of the weapon depended on the strength of the charge. Mortars were gradually superseded by high-angled cannon and a bastard form, the HOWITZER, but returned to usefulness in modern times, becoming smaller but infinitely more lethal.

Mother-of-Pearl. The inner shell or lining of various molluscs, notably oysters, abalone or ormer, and clams. Hard and brittle, mother-of-pearl has an iridescent sheen. It served very well as an inlay in the handwork of seamen. Large shells had their rough exterior or periostracum carefully ground away to reveal the iridescent layer beneath. A shell thus treated would be an attractive object in itself, but it would also be converted into a useful object such as a goblet. Conch shells, with the mother-of-pearl exposed, were used for the hulls of SHIP MODELS, with silver or gold thread for rigging. Mother-of-pearl plates and saucers were made. Very small shells could not easily be ground, so their exterior was removed by soaking in acetic acid.

Mudge, Thomas (1717-1794). English watch- and clock-maker who specifically invented the lever escapement (which is still used). He began in 1771 to develop a marine chronometer. The task took him three years, and the result was tested on a voyage to Newfoundland in 1774. The Board of Longitude encouraged Mudge to continue with this good work. He produced two more "marine timekeepers", but failed to win the prize offered by the Board for a completely effective instrument; this was given to JOHN ARNOLD. There were public protests, and eventually Mudge was awarded £2500 for his work; not bad considering that the pound was then worth at least twenty times its subsequent value.

Musketoon. A small MUSKET, or BLUNDERBUSS.

N

Nagasaki Prints. The subjects of these were European and American ships, seamen, and similar western maritime views, produced from the mid-17th to the late 19th centuries by Japanese artists, originally at Nagasaki, which was the first Japanese port open to foreign vessels. These prints can be finely detailed, but often the paper was poor. They were accompanied by explanatory texts.

Nantucket Lightship Baskets. These were baskets made by crew members of lightships stationed off Nantucket Island in the United States from about 1854 to about 1890, the rarest being from the South Shoal lightship. They were taken home to families, or sold ashore. They were woven from rattan, a vine of the palm family, and had wooden bases, usually oak or mahogany. They were round or oval, sometimes with handles, depending on their purpose. Nests of

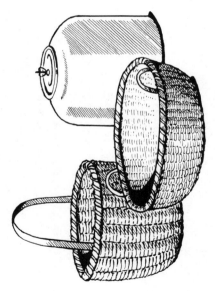

Nantucket lightship baskets.

such baskets were cunningly made, from peck size down to a "one egg" basket about 2½ in. high. Those intended for use as ladies' sewing baskets had lids, some of which were hinged. The earliest types were entirely woven, but wooden moulds came to be used, around which the basket could be shaped more accurately. The moulds were carved from a block of wood, a mast-end or driftwood, or two pieces of wood screwed together. There was an industry on Nantucket Island for the making of barrels and casks, which were supplied to the shipping and whaling fraternity. Members of the lightshipmen's families often worked in this industry, so the parts of the baskets had names derived from coopering. The circular top bindings were called "hoops", the carved handles were named "bales", and the vertical splints were "staves".

It was customary for the baskets to bear a paper label on the base stating the name and source of the maker, but most of these came off in the course of time, leaving a mark where the label was attached. A basket with authentic label still attached is especially interesting and valuable. Among the notable makers of these baskets are Captain J. Wyer, Captain Thomas James, Captain Charles Ray, Captain Andrew Sandsbury, George Swain, William Hosier, Davis Hall, David Ray, Joseph Fisher, W. D. Appleton, and William Barnard. Each craftsman had his own style, so it is possible for an expert to determine the provenance of a Nantucket basket even if the label is missing. The pattern of grooves as a design on the inside of the wooden base can often reveal the maker. When they retired and went ashore, the lightshipmen often continued to make baskets both as a pastime and source of income: such work done in retirement is perfectly genuine. The men would teach their children and grandchildren so that skills would not die out. Modern reproductions are still woven by land-based craftsmen, and these can be more elaborate than the originals, having decorative plaques of carved ivory seagulls, whales, and other nautical motifs, which are fixed to the lids.

Narrowboat Furniture, Utensils and Other Items. These were used in the 19th and early 20th centuries by the folk who worked and lived on the canal narrowboats, popularly but wrongly known as barges. Since these narrowboats were the floating homes of their occupants, who formed a distinct and peculiar community, the

Interior of a narrowboat cabin.

Measham teapot.

furniture and other articles on them were progressively made and decorated in a particular style, which became a living folk art. There were such space restrictions on the narrowboats that all articles for everyday use had to be small in size and kept in perfect condition. They represented the background of everyday life, and pride would polish them to gleaming; the copper kettles, the glass-globed brass lamps, the cooking and other domestic utensils. What was not polished was gaily painted. Wooden panels on the boats were decorated with scenes such as castles, and with the depiction of vases and bouquets of flowers, the rose being very popular (and perhaps derived from the "rose maling" of Viking ancestors). Small tables, stools, water-cans, pans, and other equipment were similarly painted, even on their undersides. China bought for use on the boats was chosen for its suitability in this bright decorative scene, particularly "Ribbon" plates with scenes painted on the centre. Such china dates from about 1880, and is identifiable by its pierced rims. Ribbon would be threaded through those rims; hence the name. The narrowboat people liked them because they could be hung by the ribbons on to cabin walls and elsewhere: thus they did not take up space and were not so easily broken. Ribbon plates were produced specially for this market both by British and foreign potteries. The British examples chiefly had complicated floral and other design centres; and the foreign ones, Austrian, German or Czech, either showed individual flower species or topographical views. Ribbon plates were also produced with scenes and legends for sale as SEASIDE SOUVENIRS from various resorts.

Another highly-prized item of decorative ware among the narrow-boat people was the Measham teapot, basically brown, but with floral, animal, and bird motifs in white and other colours. An inscribed panel on the side might convey a sentimental message, and there could be a miniature teapot on the lid. Such pots would be handed down from mother to daughter, and their life was long. Breakages aboard boats were rare.

Then there would be gilded bird-cages, and a melodeon, which was a type of accordeon much favoured by the narrowboat people for playing during the evenings or at events when many boats came together; also the wives and daughters would work in crochet or lace, the results being used decoratively in the cabins.

Meanwhile the exteriors of the boats, including the upperworks and the huge tiller, would be colourfully painted, in the lively style that also beautified showground and farm machinery and carts at that

Narrowboatwomen's bonnets.

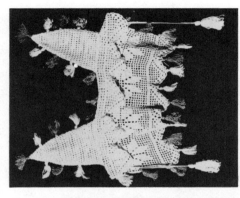

Crocheted ear protectors for the horses who drew the narrowboats.

Narrowboat water can, painted in traditional style.

time. Decorative, intricate ropework was used on fenders, and a turk's head or "horse's tail" would mark out the "ram's head" of the boat.

The narrowboat people also had their characteristic wearing apparel. The boatman's standard wear was corduroy trousers, wide leather belt or braided braces, striped shirt, a brass-buttoned waist-coat with a velvet collar and a necker-chief, then a velvet-collared jacket. The women wore bonnets with frills and layers of "curtain" at the back - on Sundays and when they were "walking out".

Many relics of these boats remain, such as the large, curved brushes used to sweep tunnel roofs clear of soot, the boards or planks emp-loyed for "legging" the boats through those tunnels, where there was no towing path, the padlocks and keys used to secure lock gates at night, the "gauging" sticks for determining the tonnage of cargo, records of which were kept in gauging chart books in the canal toll offices so that the proper tolls could be levied; and there also remain canal plans, share indentures to raise money for the building of canals, tokens issued by the canal companies when real money was short, even badges as worn by the professional "leggers" who earned their living by pulling the boats in certain cirumstances. There similarly remain painted wooden notice-boards that carried official notices and posters,

135

resolutions of the canal companies, prints and photographs, even warnings of transportation for those who damaged property or otherwise broke rules. Or one could collect the traditionally colourful harness for the horses that drew the boats, typified by the crescentmoon brasses for the heads. In summer these horses were given crocheted ear-protectors as a guard against flies. But once again it must be remembered that all such items are still being created, by craftsmen, both as reproductions and as fakes, although some of those craftsmen still work on narrowboats themselves.

Underside of a narrowboat table which folded up after use, in order to save space.

Nautical Almanacs. An almanac is a book or tables containing calendars as well as other information, astronomical and navigational in the case of nautical almanacs, which can be traced back to the astronominal tables of the Egyptians and the *fasti* of the Romans. They first appear in Europe in the 12th century, and the first printed examples are those of 15th-century France. A very early printed example in England is *The Kalendar of Shyppers*, published in 1503. Some of those subsequently used by mariners were in the form of broadsheets that were nailed to the bulkhead; others were like pocketbooks. By the 17th century these nautical almanacs were in common use. They contained much varied information, including tide tables, rules for finding high water, time by the stars, phases of the moon, and the sun's declination. The first American almanac was published by Bradford in Philadelphia, in 1687. Ephemerides are a type of almanac: a book or table of astronominal predictions calculated on a 2-year basis. The first example, entitled *La Connaissance de Temps*, was prepared by Jean Picard, a French astonomer, in 1680, for the French Bureau des Longitudes. It became the official French nautical almanac. The first British ephemeris, called the *Nautical Almanac for Lunar Distances*, was prepared under the direction of Nevil Maskelyne, the Astronomer Royal, and published 1766-1767; it contained the usual ephemerides and astronomical information, as well as tables of lunar distances showing the nearest between the moon and seven fixed stars. Ephemerides were used to arrange the current positions of the planets on an ORRERY. The 1769 edition of *The Nautical Almanac and Astronomical Ephemeris for year 1769*, published by order of the Commissioners of Longitude, London, has the calendar pages for each month printed in red and black. The first American *Ephemeris and Nautical Almanac* was published in 1852; it developed into one of the finest of all ephemerides.

Early almanacs were printed privately, but in the mid 18th century the first official *Nautical Almanac* of the Admiralty was issued. Very much later, when radio time signals could be used to check the CHRONOMETER the lunar distance method became obsolete. Lunar tables were omitted from the *Nautical Almanac* after 1906; but this official publication was always accompanied by many unofficial almanacs. One privately published example is *Brown's Nautical Almanac* which, when it was first published in Glasgow, 1877, had the notable title of *Brown's Comprehensive Nautical Almanac, Harbour and Dock Guide and Advertiser and Daily Tide Tables.*

Nautical Books. As books have been published for, and used by, seafarers through the ages, the subject is a vast one. The almanac called *The Kalendar of Shyppers* as issued in 1503 is one of the earliest printed books for seafarers. Then there was William Bourne's *A Regiment for the Sea,* England's first navigational textbook, from 1574. There succeeded *The Seaman's Kalendar* of 1602, Boteler's *Dialogues of* 1645, *The British Mariner's Guide,* 1763 (which explained how longitude could be devised with lunars), *Signals for R.N. Convoys and Sailing and Fighting Instructions,* 1746, and Cox's perennial *Companion to the Sea Medicine Chest.*

Accounts of voyages are too many to be detailed; but a collector of nautical literature would also look at RUTTERS, LOG BOOKS, diaries, and others writings of a personal nature. He would consider ship's "description" books, which are accounts or ledgers in which the purser and his clerk entered details of the ship, its complement, victuals and cargo. Another distinct subject is the "muster" books that detailed the ship's company.

Novels written about the sea are too many to be written of here, as are biographies, autobiographies, histories, and such collector's items as early bound editions of the *Navy List, Lloyd's List, Lloyd's Register* and the like.

Nautical Instrument-makers' Signs. It was customary for those who made and sold nautical instruments to have trade signs. In the 18th and 19th centuries the most common was a standing, painted, wooden figure of a mariner, holding or using a replica example of the instrument-maker's work, such as a sextant. These figures were eventually replaced by conventional signboards.

Nautical Woodcuts. Nautical subjects appear in woodcuts from the ancient beginning of that art. Their heyday was the 19th century, when they were used widely in shipping advertisements as inserted in newspapers and magazines. American examples were frequently copied from European originals. Early CHARTS were often printed from woodcuts.

Nautilus Cup. A vessel made from the shell of the nautilus, a mollusc. Early examples date from the late Middle Ages. The shell was mounted in silver. The periostracum was removed to expose the MOTHER-OF-PEARL layer in early 20th-century shades for Tiffany lamps.

Navigraph. A type of SEXTANT.

Navisphere. A navigational celestial GLOBE used in sailing schools in the late 19th and early 20th century, also sometimes employed on ships for quick identification of the stars.

Needlework Pictures. These were embroidered by sailors on light sailcloth or canvas, or "duck" (the material of which their bell-bottom trousers were made). First the picture would be drawn with chalk, pencil, or charcoal on the fabric, then the outline would be followed with needle and whatever thread came to hand; more often coloured wool or cotton but sometimes silk. The background and hulls of ships might be done in wool, and the rigging picked out in cotton or silk. Cotton-wool could be affixed to indicate clouds or waves. Subjects were usually nautical, with ships predominant, and the detail was good or bad according to the skill of the craftsman. Most date back to the first half of the 19th century, but such pictures continued to be made in steamship days. Some early examples fall into the category of PRISONER-OF-WAR WORK.

Nef. The strange name is possibly a corruption of Neptune. A nef is an elaborate model in silver or silver-gilt of a ship by one of the leading 18th- and 19th-century silversmiths. It had silver wheels significantly, and formed a receptacle to make it a very large salt cellar for pushing around on a great table. Beautiful to acquire as an investment, but extremely difficult to keep clean.

Nelson Items. No personage of maritime history has been so widely commemorated as the hero of Trafalgar and so many other decisive victories. The COMMEMORATIVE WARES that relate to Nelson range from china figures and busts to actual items of furniture, generically known as TRAFALGAR WARE. Then when the battleship

Victory underwent extensive repairs early in this century, large quantities of copper sheathing and old timber were removed and replaced. The old, worn-out material was bought by the British and Foreign Sailors' Society, and made into medallions and other souvenirs, some of these being sold; the medallions being given to schoolchildren who collected money for the Society. To this day the good work goes on of providing such mementoes for a vast number of annual visitors to the proud old ship.

Nocturnal.   A navigational instrument of metal or wood for observing certain stars relative to the pole star in Ursa Minor, and thus discovering the hour at night. Then it could be employed with an

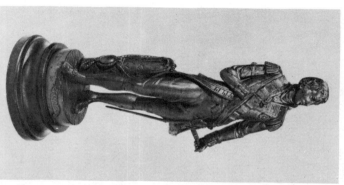

Nelson statuette, believed to be French. Possibly early-nineteenth-century.

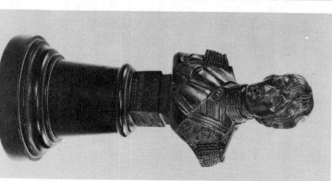

Copper bust of Nelson presented by King Edward VII to the British and Foreign Sailors' Society, probably 1905.

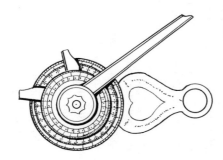

Nocturnal, 1755, signed "made by Patt. Woodside for Robert Jackson".

astrolage or CROSS-STAFF to ascertain latitude. It dates from the 15th century, and comprises two concentric discs or plates. The larger or outer disc has a handle, and is graded in twelve equal parts to represent the months from January to December in anti-clockwise order. Each of those parts is subdivided into groups of 5 days. A smaller and inner disc has its circumference divided into 24 parts for the hours, 1 to 12, and again 1 to 12 in anti-clockwise order, each again subdivided into quarters. An alidade is pivoted around the centre of the discs. The method of using this instrument is to turn a projecting tooth on the inner, toothed disc at 12 o'clock until it points to the date on the outer disc. The nocturnal is held afterwards by the handle at arm's length, and is moved until the Pole Star is seen through the central hole of the discs. The alidade attached to that centre is rotated until its bevelled edge coincides with the star line that links the stars in Ursa Major, called the fore and hind guards, when the edge will show the hour on the inner toothed disc. To obtain the latitude of the ship it is necessary to relate the position of the fore and hind guards opposite the Pole Star to the tables called "The Regiment of the Pole Star".

Some nocturnals have a tidal calculator, or a perpetual calendar and sun-dial, on their reverse. Early examples of the instrument were often quite beautifully engraved on their non-working surfaces.

North Pistol. Simeon North (1765-1852) was an American gunsmith who supplied this pistol, and other weapons, to the U.S. Navy.

Notepaper, Letterheadings. Shipping company stationery, including postcards, usually bears the company trademark or motif, whereas that used aboard naval ships in the late 19th century had the ship's badge. So many shipping lines are now defunct that a collection of their stationery can be interesting and valuable, no matter how ephemeral.

Nuremberg Diptych or Sun-dial. An instrument for determining the hour from the sun's position, being constructed on the same principles as the RING DIAL, GEMMA RING and AUGSBURG DIAL. It comprised two sides, hinged together at right-angles like a small flat box. The two sides were joined by a meridian thread. This acted as a gnomon which could be put in alignment on a north-south axis. Both interior sides had paper dials, while the horizontal side had a central compass. The hour was indicated by a shadow thrown by the thread on the vertical and horizontal interior dials. The instrument was widely used for some time, but possessed the grave disadvantage that changes of latitude had to be slight or it would not work properly. Some old examples have ornamentation or compass-cards on the exterior of the two sides.

O

Octant. An instrument for measuring angles, with a graduated arc of 45 degrees. Rather like HADLEY'S QUADRANT, it was first made in England about 1661, and afterwards in America, Ireland, and France. It was superseded in 1752 by the REFLECTING CIRCLE.

Oil Lamp. Any lamp that burned an oil to produce a light, going back to the earliest days in the Middle East when burning naphtha was first found issuing from the ground most eerily at night. Oil lamps were used on ships in various crude forms, but properly became LANTERNS in comparatively modern times when cheap glass became available. The main saloons and cabins and compartments of 19th-century steamships were illuminated by a variety of such oil lamps in the form of lanterns, until the use of electricity from the engines was learned. Lamps followed the basic style of those used on shore, with a glass funnel and dome above the oil receptacle. Some of them had a circular metal plate as part of the frame above the open funnel top, to absorb the rising heat. They would swing to the movement of the ship. The "hurricane" lamp would swing by a ring in the frame top, and was constructed to withstand both violent movements and strong winds.

Organ Pipe Glass. A type of SAND GLASS which consisted of several such glasses housed together on one mount, for the quarter, half, three-quarter and full hourly periods.

Orrery. A clockwork model of the planetary system, named after Charles Boyle, fourth Earl of Orrery. Probably the first was made by the English clock-makers George Graham (1673-1751) and his uncle by marriage Thomas Tompion (1640-1713). A John Rowley copied

143

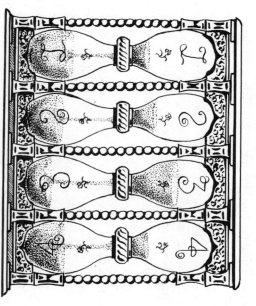

Sixteenth-century German organ pipe glass.

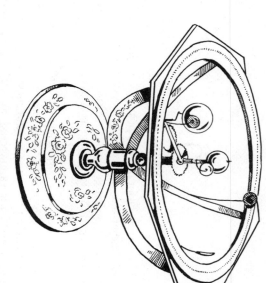

Orrery, 1750.

this about 1712 on behalf of his patron the Earl, when the instrument was given its name. The orrery has ingenious revolving spheres, which can be arranged according to the correct positions of the planets with the help of the NAUTICAL ALMANAC or EPHEMERIS, but speedily became an antique rather than an instrument thanks to the beauty of its appearance and the weirdness of its construction. A genuine example is now exceedingly rare and very valuable.

Ortelius, Abraham (1527-1598). Notable cartographer, born in Antwerp of German parents, who produced an important early ATLAS. Called the *Theatrum Orbis Terrarum*, this was published in 1570, with maps as engraved by Frans Hogenburg. Ortelius obtained much of the information for his maps from other cartographers and acknowledged this, his work being widely used until the 17th century.

Oughtred, William (1575-1660). English mathematician, author, and inventor of the EQUINOCTIAL RING. In addition he wrote a textbook on arithmetic called *Clavis Mathematica*, 1631, and was responsible for the first trigometrical abbreviations.

Overstrung Foot. The thick and heavy foot of a typical SHIP'S GLASS from about 1730 to 1775. Applied radial threads of glass, about the thickness of string, extended from the base of the stem outward and over the edges of the foot, the object being to strengthen the foot against rough treatment at sea.

Oyster Measure. A device with a central hole, made of wood or metal, and used by oyster fishermen and fishery inspectors to gauge the size of oysters as caught. If the oysters passed through the central hole then they were too small for regulations and had to be returned to their bed. Another oyster measure of a totally different kind was Whitstable baskets; these were used to assess quantities of the molluscs for sale. These baskets were based on the so-called Winchester Bushel or Tub, which equalled 21 gallons, 1 quart, and $\frac{1}{2}$ pint. Thus one Prickle Basket equalled half a Tub, one Wash Basket equalled half a Prickle, one Peck Basket equalled half a Wash Basket, and one Bucket equalled one-third of a Wash. (No wonder someone invented computers.) The total of oysters in these measures varied according to their size. A Bushel contained between 500 and 1000 oysters. Wash Baskets were similarly used at Whitstable for measuring whelks, and contained half a Prickle. (A Prickle of whelks amounted to twenty Strikes, and a Strike meant four Bushels.)

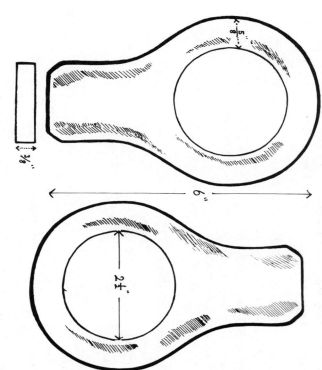

Oyster measure.

P

Paintings on Glass. Glass paintings is an ancient craft, and in its modern manifestations probably originated in the South Netherlands some 500 years ago. The craft spread from Belgium to other European countries, but may have started instead in the Balkans, where it is practised so beautifully by peasants to this day. Glass would be painted black all over, and the black paint when dry would be scraped away to make the picture, which would be appropriately coloured in the spaces of clear glass. The technique was similar to that of the etcher or engraver. Seamen were attracted to the craft as a spare-time and perhaps lucrative occupation. So much of seaboard art is the product of the infinite boredom that can otherwise mar long voyages. The maritime method would be to sketch a ship on paper with a plan of the whole picture, but in reverse. This would be used as a guide when the painted glass was scratched away on its reverse side and the gaps coloured. Then the picture appeared correct when viewed from the front. A ship picture would have the hull drawn first, then its details, and the hull's main colour added in, after which the rigging and shading of the sails would be added, followed by details of mast, flags, and other shipboard features. When the sea part was attempted the white crests of the waves would be done first; next the dark troughs; and the sky would be drawn and painted last. All kinds of paint materials would be used, from oil to watercolour, from gum arabic and varnish to bitumen.

Some old glass paintings by seafarers are signed, but most can be identified and dated only by the methods used and, most important, the name of the ship. There are sometimes handwritten labels to help. The fragility of glass makes genuine early examples very rare.

Parallel Ruler. This was used for plotting a course on a sea chart

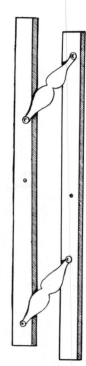

Parallel ruler.

with a compass card. It evolved from the simple ruler in the 16th century, and was used thereafter in the Royal Navy and on merchant vessels right up to modern times. It comprises two, sometimes three, rules joined by pivoted strips of metal; is usually brass, and measures from 6 in. up to 36 in.

Partisan, Partizan. A type of HALBERD. As a thrusting weapon, this long-handled pike was much used during the 16th and 17th centuries for repelling boarders.

Pebble Jewellery. Various semi-precious stones occur on British beaches in the form of pebbles. They include jasper, cairngorm, moss agate, chalcedony, cornelian, bloodstone, and serpentine. They were used from the early 19th century to incorporate in jewellery for sale as souvenirs. Some regions had famous specialities, such as the jet of Whitby and the translucent pebbles of the Harwich region; they would be mounted in rings and brooches. The Isle of Man concentrated on brooch settings in the form of anchors. Jasper and agate were used at Sidmouth in Devon. It was a favourite Victorian custom to take a pretty pebble found on a seaside holiday to a lapidary craftsman, who would polish and mount it in a piece of jewellery. The cairngorm, yellow or wine-coloured, was popularised by Queen Victoria and her guests at Balmoral. Scottish pebble brooches are large, due to the size of the cairngorm, flat cut, frequently with bevelled edges, and were set with solid backs in heavy silver mounts, furnished with a hinged pin. The fashion went out with the 19th century, but has recently been revived.

Pelorus. A compass with a lubber line, with adjustable, rotatable

148

and folding arms or rules for sighting, used for taking a bearing, and also to check the ship's compass for deviation. Mention should also be made of "Pelorus Jack", a famous dolphin which, mariners claimed, would safely lead their sailing ships through the dangerous waters in Cook Strait between the two main islands of New Zealand.

Pendant, Pennant. A long, tapering FLAG flown at the masthead of a vessel in commission; also a tapering flag used for signalling. Command pennants are flown on a naval vessel that is honoured by the presence of a high-ranking commanding officer. There are also church, cable-working, paying-off, red, blue, and white pennants, the last formerly being flown on the Navy's old Red, Blue and White Squadrons. Customs and Excise vessels had their own pennants, as did most merchant vessels. The Winner's Pennant is that flown by the Thames or Medway barge that wins the annual sailing matches.

Petarara. A breech-loading SWIVEL GUN, 3 ft long, calibre 2.5 in., weighing 125 lb. Used from the 15th century aboard ship, and suitably mounted on land, it was made by hooping together longitudinal bars of iron, together with iron rings. Loading consisted of knocking out a wedge so that the chamber came out, after which the

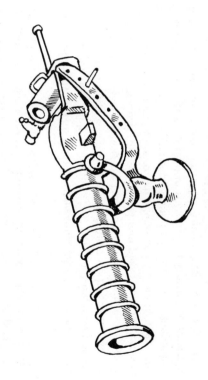

Petarara, cast circa 1545 for Henry VIII.

149

Scrimshaw pie crimper: the hand clutching a writhing serpent, which forms the handle of this item, was a popular motif for scrimshaw work.

loaded chamber was replaced and rested in the breech-piece, the wedge being driven in again and forcing the chamber hard up against the barrel. Part of its value as a weapon was its mobility, as it could be swivelled up and down or from side to side.

Pie Crimper. An implement used in a kitchen to make the design in pastry round the edge of a piece. Such would often be fabricated as part of their SCRIMSHAW work by shipboard craftsmen, using bone, ivory, or wood for the purpose. Some scrimshaw pie crimpers have a "jagging" wheel at one end to form the decorative edge on the pastry. Others have incorporated what is known as a "pie tester".

Pieces of Eight. This Spanish silver coin (dollar) was romantically the currency of Caribbean pirates, but was more important as the bullion which financed Spanish expansionism in the Americas from the 15th century on. It was the currency of the Hispano-American colonies, and remained coin of the realm in places such as Peru and Chile, Guatemala and Mexico, Honduras and Colombia long after they had wrested independence from their decaying conquerors. Pieces of eight were even used in the early settlements of Australia from 1788 onwards, and in the North American colonies, where they were current until as late as 1857. In 1792 the Americans passed legislation to introduce their own currency, which was called the dollar after the old Spanish version (derived from the Austrian thaler), but there were so many Spanish silver dollars around that they had to be used for a long time after. Other countries would use pieces of eight that had been counter-stamped with their own design. They were even used in Britain during the silver shortage of 1797; the head of George III was overstamped on these. Firms in Birmingham and elsewhere in the 19th century would sometimes overstamp old pieces of eight with their name or device and circulate them as TRADE TOKENS. A hoard of pieces of eight recovered from the wreck of the Dutch ship *Hollandia* contained some splendid coins that had been newly minted at Mexico City for the Spaniards before the ship sunk after striking the Gunner rock in the Scilly Isles in 1743. They bear on one side the Imperial Crown of Spain surmounting the Spanish Royal Family's coat of arms, surrounded by the legend "Philip V of Spain and the Indies, by the Grace of God", and with a figure eight to indicate the coin's value of eight reales. The reverse has two globes representing the Old and New Worlds, above which is the Spanish Imperial crown. On each side of the globes are pillars representing the Pillars of Hercules at the entrance to the Mediterranean, and under the globes are lines to indicate the sea that divided the Old and New Worlds with, finally, the date 1741.

On some pieces of eight the Pillars of Hercules indicated that these showed the limit of the Old World: such would have the motto "Nothing Beyond".

Such coins found in submerged wrecks are often badly worn if loose, but can be in almost mint condition when cemented in a conglomerate of sand and gravel, which can be carefully dissolved.

Pilchard Pot.   Also known as a BUSSA.

Pin-Cushion.   A small, usually hard cushion, stuffed with various materials, in which pins and needles could be stuck. Seafarers would buy these in foreign ports as LOVE TOKENS, and they were sometimes made as SCRIMSHAW work. (See SAILORS' PIN-CUSHIONS).

Pin-pricked Pictures.   These were engraved on whale teeth, chiefly by North American whalers in the 19th century. An attractive illustration would be cut from a periodical and attached to the whale's tooth so that the shipboard craftsman could use a pin to prick the outline of the ship portrait or scene through the paper to the ivory. The paper was removed and the pin pricks joined together with pencil, pen or paint. Various dyes were employed in this work, even soot, tobacco juice, ash, and tar as well as Indian ink. The same could be done not on a whale's tooth but on a plain piece of paper, a primitive but more decisive form of tracing. Several pictures cut from magazines would sometimes be incorporated into one new and pricked-out picture, as a SEAMAN'S LOVE TOKEN.

Pipe Case. One of the SCRIMSHAW carved-wood items made by seamen, usually lined or padded, to hold tobacco pipes safely without breakage when not being used (in the days when they were constructed of pipeclay, or of meerschaum).

Pipe Rack. This was another favourite item of SCRIMSHAW work, and usually consisted of a narrow and holed shelf with backing for fixing to a wall. The backboard could be decorated with nautical motifs. Occasionally a HALF-BLOCK SHIP MODEL would have a pipe rack fixed to its lower edge.

Plaited Straw Work. Straw Work that was a favoured product of prisoners-of-war during the Napoleonic wars, notably at the Norman Cross prison near Peterborough. It gave the effect of wood marquetry, so skilfully were single straw lengths plaited and pressed together.

Plans of Ships, Marine Engines, Docks, Ports. The earliest-known drawings or plans of ships are those attributed to Matthew Baker, a Tudor shipwright. They are contained in a manuscript dated 1586, which came into the possession of Samuel Pepys. He gave the manuscript the title of "Fragments of Ancient English Shipwright-ing", and left it with his library to Magdalene College, Cambridge, where it can still be seen. It comprises plans, elevations and section of Tudor ships. Since then thousands of ships' "draughts" or plans have been prepared to cover all aspects of the construction of vessels, including sail and spar plans, blueprints of engines, also plans for docks and piers and harbours.

Plates, Cockle and Eel. Small plates or saucers, 2½–3 in. wide, transfer-printed with seaside views, on which cockles and portions of jellied eel were served on street stalls or in hostelries. The majority were made either at SUNDERLAND, or at the pottery of Evans and Glasson at Swansea (a favourite view being Swansea harbour).

Plummet, Plumet. A sounding lead or weight attached to a plumb-line, also a weight attached to a fishing line to keep the float in position. Another kind was a lead weight of pear shape with a loop at the top, used by fishermen to plumb the water's depth.

Postcards. However ephemeral, these may now be classed among nautical antiques, especially those with maritime subjects such as ships, figureheads, wrecks, launchings, commemorations of naval events, and port and harbour views subsequently changed forever by development. They often provide useful information for the historian. Those which were sent home from foreign ports by seafarers give an insight into the customs and sentiments of their period, both from the subjects chosen and from the crude writing on the back.

Postcard of the royal yacht Osborne being broken up at Felixstowe, Suffolk, in 1868.

153

Another type of postcard for collecting is that issued by shipping companies for the use of their passengers and crew. These have special interest if sent from a great liner that had its own post office and post-mark. Then there are the vulgar postcards as sold with bibulous or bawdy scenes and inscriptions in resorts of the less-cultivated such as Blackpool and Brighton. One artist, McGill, erected this into almost the equivalent of a folk art, although doubtless he did not know what he was doing. A collection of his work is already valuable, and his original drawings, which he did for his printer-publisher at five shillings or 25 pence each, should eventually be invaluable and might have the same impact upon artists of the future as the Japanese wood-cutters had on the late 19th-century Impressionists.

Posters. Posters, including HANDBILLS, have been produced almost from the beginning of printing. In fact they were used more in the old days than in modern times when the media are available for disseminating shipping and other information. Those of the 17th and 18th centuries are crudely printed in heavy black and white, with sometimes an emphasised line in red. They give information about piracy, smuggling, shipwrecks, crew vacancies, cargo rates, even executions and the sale of slaves. The printing improved and became more elaborate in the 19th century: particularly interesting are those which advertised emigrant ships or voyages to the goldfields of California. As the scramble to emigrate increased, and with it the number of competing shipping companies, so the claims made by those companies increased in wildness. The destination promised was always a utopia or eldorado. Some companies would use the same woodcut or engraving of the same idealised ship for all their increasingly dubious voyages. Such emigrant posters are now being reproduced, so deceit is added to deceit, but the genuine article can usually be determined by the age of the paper.

Then the custom grew up. Towards the end of the 19th century the main shipping lines had beautifully illustrated posters produced by lithography, and this led to the modern travel poster which might eventually be regarded as one of the most important art works of our time. Some of the nicest shipping company posters were issued in the 1920s and the 1930s, when such as the Cunard, Royal Mail, P. and O., Orient and Blue Funnel lines were at their pinnacle of success (from which they were to descend so abruptly with the growth of air travel).

Yet another subject for collection is 19th- and 20th-century posters for naval recruiting, wartime maritime proclamations, naval and yachting events.

Potichomania. A variation of SAND BOTTLE work. It involved the decoration of plain glass vessels such as bottles with designs and pictures cut from magazines and brochures. These pictures were glued to the interior surface of the glass vessels by mariners who had nothing better to do. Different coloured sands were used in layers to fill the glass containers afterwards. Examples date from the mid-1850s to the early 1900s.

Powder Horn; Powder Flask. Originally an animal horn, later made in various shapes and materials to contain gunpowder for guns and to keep it dry. The priming of powder was poured from the horn into the weapon's vent. Some horns had a brass measure to regulate the amount of powder poured. The horn survives well, and old examples of the device are often found in wrecks.

Powell, C.M. (fl. 1783-1824). English seaman who became a marine artist. He was self-taught and chiefly used water-colours. He displays a delicate skill in his details of ships, particularly the rigging. Like most good artists he was a bad businessman, and could be described as a creative slave for those who employed him. Often his work, within hours of its execution, was sold by dealers for many times what they gave him. Small Powells are the best. Many are spoiled by poor varnishing. Well-known examples are "A Dutch passage boat", "Calais Pier - the Dover Packet going out", and "Harbour scene".

Presentation Firearms. As with PRESENTATION NAVAL SWORDS these were awarded to naval officers for meritorious service. They were rarely if ever fired, being ornamental and so highly valued for their associations. Pistols were usually presented in pairs, and housed in a lined case completed with accessories for cleaning and using.

Presentation Naval Swords. Given, like the firearms above, to officers as an award for a brave action or for long service. Some are outstanding examples of craftsmanship. The blade could be in gold or silver, also the hilt and scabbard, with encrustations of precious stones, while the grip could be worked ivory. Details of the deed or service, the recipient's name, and the name of the presenting notability, were usually engraved somewhere on the weapon. City companies and guilds, also commercial organisations, charitable associations, and even private philanthropists, would order and pay for the swords. The famous Lloyd's Sword originated in a Patriotic Fund at Lloyd's of London which, from 1803 until 1820, gave swords valued at £30, £50, £100, and the Trafalgar Sword. After the great naval victories in those days the Fund would appeal for donations to pay for these swords and for other commemorative items such as silver (indeed monumental) plate. The admirals and some of the captains who took part in the battle of Trafalgar each received a silver vase valued then at £300. One example of a Lloyd's Patriotic Fund Sword, of the £50 category, was that awarded to the widow of Lieutenant William Coombe, R.N., in posthumous recognition of his bravery during the capture of the French brig-corvette *Lynx* on January 21, 1807. The hilt is gilded; the backstrap and pommel are in the form of a lion's skin; the crossguard is fashioned like Roman *fasces*; the grip is chequered ivory; and the blade is etched on both sides with blue and gilt decorations and the presentation inscription. The scabbard is of black shagreen on a wooden base, with gilt-brass fittings.

Lloyd's Swords, worn with full dress uniform, are generally made with great skill and artistry. The blades are broad and curved, blued and gilt; they have ivory grips and gilt guards; and the scabbards are of gilt metal with panels of leather or embossed velvet.

Pricker. A handled and spiked implement, rather like a corkscrew, used for pushing into a cannon's vent and twisting to pierce the cartridge so that it would fire, also to remove anything that might foul the touch-hole. Also called a VENT AUGER, and similar to a PRIMING WIRE.

Priming Wire. A skewer-like implement with a thread at the pointed end, which was employed after the cartridge had been loaded,

156

to ensure that the cartridge had been properly rammed home - and to prime the cannon by piercing the cartridge.

Prismatic Compass. A compass that has a prism to view simultaneously both the card and an object at a distance.

Prisoner-of-war Work. Model ships, wooden boxes, toys, combs, and similar items, as carved or otherwise created from bone, wood, ivory, straw, by French and their Allied prisoners-of-war during the Napoleonic Wars from 1793 till 1815. The most famous camp for these prisoners was at Norman Cross near Peterborough; others were at Tonbridge, Dover, Lewes, Liverpoool, Perth, and Dartmoor. Prisoners were also confined in the hulks of old ships off Chatham, Sheerness, Plymouth, and Portsmouth. The importance of this work is its fineness derived from the French element: so many craftsmen from the Parisian region were conscripted by Napoleon and, unsuitable for war, allowed themselves to be taken prisoner the sooner. They wanted only to make beautiful articles, and, as soon as they were out of the firing line and ensconced in prison camps, turned

French prisoner-of-war wooden ship model of a 16-gun schooner, circa 1800.

to their true love again. The articles they made were sold to prison visitors, and the proceeds used for buying materials plus a few creature comforts. Perhaps the outstanding creations were SHIP MOD-ELS made of bone or boxwood and other improvised materials. Glue was obtained by boiling animal and fish bones and horn. The bone came from meat rations. At the Norman Cross prison about 14 tons of meat were used each week, so there was no lack of bone. Ivory carvers from the famous Dieppe industry set the standard for the work and doubtless taught the others, but the French included craftsmen of all kinds, even the most skilled lapidaries. Many of these remained in England afterwards and, like the Huguenots, fructified both the arts and crafts of their adopted land. It can be determined from some of the more notable ship models how several craftsmen worked on them in cooperation.

The ship models vary in size from several feet down to 2 or 3 in.; the average are between 1 and 2 ft in length; they were built as near as possible to scale, and followed a ship's construction in every possible detail, although the extent of this verisimilitude was determined by the materials and tools available. First the keel, bulkheads, deck beams, and upperworks were constructed in wood. Then clean bones were steeped in wet clay to make them easy for working; they were cut in fine lengths to make the planks that would cover that wooden frame. The natural curve of the bone was followed so that it might correspond with the curves of the ship. Such details were then added as are scarcely conceivable. For example, a skilled watchmaker would contrive spring devices, operated by cords passing through the ports, for running the miniature cannon in and out. Beautifully carved and coloured figureheads would be added, plus such deck furniture as capstans and pin-rails, side-rails, rudder hinges, anchors, anchor-chains, galleons bitts, even ship's boats. Delicate work such as the chains would be executed by jewellers and silversmiths among the prisoners. Some rails of ship models would be simply constructed, of cord or wire; others would be elaborately fashioned with cross stretch-ers or balustrades.

When the hull was completed the masts, spars, and jib-boom would be added, followed by the yards and the martingales. The standing and running rigging would be made with great accuracy, and would sometimes be as fully operable as on a real ship. Materials

French prisoner-of-war model of a 120-gun ship. The model is made of bone, and is intricately detailed.

for the rigging would include thin twine and cord, as well as human hair, or horsehair from mattresses, or very attenuated shavings of wood, as well as shredded rope and cord. It was not customary to add sails, but when these were used they were fabricated of horn. A horn would be boiled until a thin layer of laminated material could be peeled off. Then the stern and sternposts and a bone length on the keel were added; and finally the model was fitted to a wooden cradle, or by chocks to a bone and wood-marquetry base. Some of these bases had straw-plaited or even mirrored backs.

Most important models were of French ships, but sometimes the foreigners would attempt to make vessels of English design: not so happily. Unusual types were such as Maltese galleys. A deceptive practice was to attach the name of a famous ship to a vessel that did not resemble it at all, the idea being to appeal to the cash customers. Another inaccuracy was to use insufficient numbers of guns for a ship of a famous given name. Again it is not always true that fine ship

159

models were actually made by prisoners-of-war. A trade arose of having such models made by English craftsmen for passing off as prisoner-of-war models. Then models continued to be made in England by prisoners-of-war who had been released and who had decided to remain in England.

A second class of ship models made by the prisoners was of cheap boxwood, following a full-scale vessel's construction methods, but generally smaller than the bone and wood models. Often these were more accurate in details than the bone and wood types.

Another form of prisoner-of-war work are harbour models, varying in size but some 12 in. square, or less. They were made of straw and wood shavings. Lengths of straw were cut into various sizes, then split to make the hulls and sails of ships, the walls and roofs of port buildings, quays and the like. Such models are rare and valuable indeed. Other products of the captivity were the table games of bone and wood. Draughtsmen and chessmen were carved; dominoes were made from white bone with the black dots either burned in or incised and filled with soot or ink. Sets of playing cards were made from flat pieces of rectangular bone; the pictures and symbols of them were oil-painted. Such a market developed for these games that they were made in quantity. It is nice to find original examples still contained in their original bone or wooden boxes with sliding or hinged lids, boxes that are decorated with drawn designs or scenes painted in oil or watercolour.

The prisoners also made PLAITED STRAW WORK, and this is sometimes so cunningly contrived that the result resembles marquetry, consisting of straw lengths woven and pressed together. Naturalcoloured or colour-dyed pieces or slivers of straw were similarly used to form patterns and pictures when glued to a patch or trinket box, to watch stands, firescreens and many other articles. The men additionally made buttons, fans, hats, lace bobbins, seals, tobacco stoppers, miniature toys, dolls' cradles, clock cases, mirror frames, and hair jewellery. They carved figures out of wood and bone, and modelled them from clay. They wove silk and crocheted gloves, even made violins and other musical instruments. Folded paper work was a speciality, especially to make fans that had carved bone or wooden sticks. Artificial flowers were made, and dried wild flowers and grasses were used to make pictures and ornaments. Skilled artists among the prisoners produced paintings and drawings. Many of those artists remain anonymous, but we can still recognise the work of such as Jacques Gourney, M. Grieg, De la Porte, and that Louis Garneray who was a prisoner for 9 years until he was released and returned to France in 1814, eventually to become Court Marine Painter to Louis XVII.

A sinister type of prisoner-of-war model was that which showed the dread guillotine, sometimes complete with victims and with soldiers on guard. Some examples show the victim's head as already severed by the tortoiseshell blade, and ready to be tossed into a basket containing several similar heads. Surrounding blood would be realistically depicted. Happier models are those of mechanical toys, made from wood and bone and very ingenious in construction, using wheels and ratchets connected to threads and a handle for turning to operate the moving parts. Then they would make spinning wheels, with one or two women in attendance – and toy forts and castles so devised that soldiers could be encouraged to walk along the ramparts by a turn of a handle, while trumpeters would raise and lower their instruments and a drawbridge would come up and down. Some toy models were of mothers who "mechanically," nursed their babies.

There have been prisoners-of-war in all ages in every country, but no such efflorescence of art from them as from these French prisoners in England, which is doubtless an indication of relative national values. The French place artistry and craftsmanship above most other human qualities. One of the few exceptions to this is a similar outcrop of fine work in the 19th-century convict settlements of Australia. All kinds of crafts were undertaken by these unhappy men, although never so successfully as the French. The most important work was done by professional artists who had been transported "for the term of their natural life", notably the convict-artist M. Peacock. His work is primitive, but, by its rarity and exceptional historical interest, commands high prices. A very typical Peacock is his "From above Double Bay" of 1854.

Privateer Glasses. As made in Bristol from 1756 to 1770, these are engraved with the picture of a privateer ship, at a time, the Seven Years War, when English privateers and their exploits against the French were highly regarded by patriotic Britons. It is a curiosity of the genre that at least fourteen ships not known to the Navy Lists of the period are depicted on such glasses. There was usually an inscription, such as "Success to the *Eagle Frigate*", or "Success to the *Constantine brig*". Genuine privateer glasses are sufficiently rare to be nicely valuable.

Protractor. An instrument with graduated scales, for measuring angles or setting them out, and for other measurements. The chart protractor, as used aboard ship, is divided into degrees for the navigational purpose of laying off a ship's course on the chart. It is usually made of brass, and has a long jointed arm pivoting from its centre so as to transcribe the findings to paper. The semi-circular arc has a double-scale, zero to 180 degrees on some examples as read against a vernier on the movable arm. Protractors were first introduced in 1658, but an account of such an instrument was published in 1597 by Phillipe Danfrie who similarly described the first GRAPHOMETER in France.

Puget, Pierre (1620-1694). French figurehead carver who created in 1645 the famous decorative work on the French warship *Reine*. He was overseer of ship-carving work at Toulon in 1668. His figureheads and other ship carvings were large or heavy, so much so that masters sometimes ordered their carpenters to cut them off when they got well out to sea, alleging that they hampered the ship's movement; it is perhaps because of this that none of Puget's figureheads have survived. But there is in existence sufficient of his carved work to show that he was among the greatest wood sculptors of the 17th century.

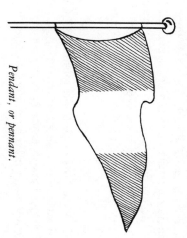

Pendant, or pennant.

162

Q

Quadrant. A navigational, astronomical, angle, and altitude-measuring or surveying instrument, used for calculating the altitude and angle of a star or the sun; probably invented by the Arabs and later used in medieval Europe. It was also used during the firing of a MORTAR. It was possible with the quadrant to estimate where the missile would fall when projected from the mortar. The actual instrument is quadrant-shaped, of wood or metal, graduated along the arc from zero to 90 degrees. Two pinnules or sights are fitted on one radial edge; from the centre of the arc a plumb-line is suspended. On sighting the horizon the plumb-line indicates zero degrees; on sighting the zenith it indicates 90 degrees. It could be used to take a sighting by a cast shadow. The user pressed the plumb-line against the arc, or took a direct sighting. The seaman's quadrant, not so heavy as the ASTROLABE, but still based on the same principles of gravity, was invented about the mid-15th century. It was superseded by the SEXTANT. Sometimes the nautical quadrant, a quarter or fourth part of a circle, is called a sextant, although by such terminology the sextant is a sixth of a circle. Old quadrants, like old astrolabes, are very rare.

Quoin, Coin. A wedge used in gun-laying, specifically for raising its level and keeping the barrel from rolling.

Quarter-hour Glass. A SAND GLASS, so constructed that the sand runs for a period of a quarter of an hour.

Quarter-minute Glass. A SAND GLASS that runs for that period.

Quintant. An instrument allied to the QUADRANT, used for measuring angles, and normally made of brass with a platinum scale. It had a

163

three-arm frame, with an index scale divided from zero to 300 degrees, read against a vernier, the radius being 9⅜ in. Rare.

Quirk, J. (fl. 1877). Possibly a Manx artist, who painted ship's portraits. His representation of the schooner *Bessy*, dated 1877, is in the Manx Museum, Douglas, Isle of Man.

Quoin. Coin. A wedge used in gun-laying, specifically for raising its level and keeping the barrel from rolling.

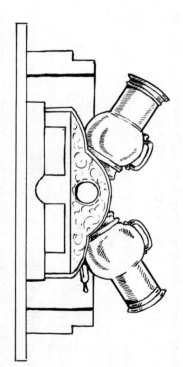

Early-eighteenth-century bronze mortar, using a quoin, or coin, for elevation.

R

Raleigh, Charles S. (1830-1925). English-born sailing ship portrait painter. He went to sea in 1840 at the age of 10; 30 years later he was forced by ill-health to become a land-lubber in New Bedford, Massachusetts. He soon established a reputation for his painting of whaling ships in that port. He produced well over a thousand paintings, of the ships and nautical events of his time. An unusual example of his work is a series of seventeen panels, 6 ft by 11 ft, altogether 197 ft long, entitled "Panorama of a Whaling Voyage in the ship *Niger*", painted between 1878 and 1880, now in the Whaling Museum, New Bedford.

Rammer. A cylindrical block of wood with a long handle, used for ramming home the powder cartridge, wads and ball in a CANNON.

Rank Badges. Badges worn on a uniform to denote the wearer's rank. Badges for petty officers were introduced into the Royal Navy in 1827, being white at first, with a single anchor and crown for a 1st-class petty officer, and a single anchor only for the 2nd-class. In 1846 a gold crown was permitted to be worn on all officers' caps above the gold lace band. Good conduct badges for periods of service from 5, 10 and 15 years were introduced in 1849, but in 1861 the periods were altered to 3, 8, and 13 years. In 1856 came the innovation of distinctive arm stripes on the full dress and undress coats of officers (but not flag officers). The black mohair band below the cap badge was introduced, replacing the gold lace band. Chief petty officers were given, in 1857, a badge on the left arm consisting of a crown and anchor encircled by laurels; the 1st-class of that ilk were given a badge with crossed anchors and a crown. These badges were white in background or blue according to the colour of the uniform (white or blue) which varied in season and place. Badges for gunnery instructors and seamen gunners were introduced in 1867; the background colour of the rating's badge was changed from blue and white to blue and red. These ratings were given gold badges in 1881; and a special badge for torpedo ratings was introduced in 1888. Chief petty officers lost their special badge in 1890, and in 1907 the rank of 2nd-class petty officer was abolished.

Reamer. A tool for enlarging the bore of a gun, or to enlarge a hole, particularly a CANNON'S VENT. It could be used to turn over the edge of a cartridge case, to open a seam for CAULKING; and "reamer" was also another name for a "WORM", which was a coil on a long handle, used to clear cartridge debris from the cannon barrel after firing.

Reflecting Circle. An instrument to measure angles up to 180 degrees in the horizontal and vertical planes. It was invented in 1752 by Tobias Mayer (1723-1762), a German astronomer-inventor. It had a circular limb graduated in 120 degrees, with a telescope. The angular distance of two observed objects was obtained by taking the mean of two readings on two opposed verniers. It would be held by its handle in the right hand, with the plane of the circular limb aligned with the two observed objects. The reflecting circle was thus employed for navigation and hydrography, to make altitude sightings and for measuring horizontal distances in longitude calculations. When made in Britain it was called the "full circle", and it was so useful that it survived until the early 20th century, being employed as a survey instrument after it had ceased to be used for navigation.

Rhumboscope. A variation of the STATION POINTER which was used to locate positions on charts. The "rhumb" was any one of the thirty-two compass points. All meridians were cut by this instrument at the same angle.

Rhysimeter. This was introduced about 1871, for measuring a ship's speed.

Ring Dial. Another name for the GEMMA'S RING, a form of sun-dial used as a sun-clock to determine the hour for any given latitude, and probably the most common and simplest form of altitude dial. It

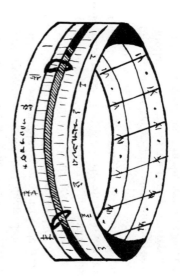

Mid-eighteenth-century English ring dial, signed "L. Proctor Sheffield".

consisted of a ring set vertically, with a small hole in the side through which a ray of sunlight could shine to show the time on an hour scale which was engraved on the ring's interior. Such a dial would be correct for just one value of the sun's declination, and there were various notions for overcoming this disability. One method was to engrave separate scales on the ring's two edges, one for winter and the other for summer; another was to have two sighting holes, one on each side of the suspension piece; but usually the hole was positioned in a sliding collar at the ring's centre, this being adjusted for declination against a calendar scale. All the same, ring dials were never very accurate, no matter what modifications were made to them and, of course, were useless when the sun went in.

Rittenhouse, David (1732-1796). American clock-maker, and astronomy professor at Pennsylvania University, who made some valuable astronomical clocks.

Rodney Decanter. A type of SHIP'S DECANTER named after Admiral Lord Rodney (1719-1792) for his naval victory at Cape St. Vincent in 1780. They are decorated with cut flutes and/or a sailor's head engraving.

Rojas Dial. Also called a GEMINUS DIAL, one more form of sun-dial, made vertically, and found sometimes on the backs of QUADRANTS,

NOCTURNALS, and ASTROLABES. It would use an orthographic projection on the plane of the meridian of the hour circles and parallels of declination. This projection would be engraved on a disc that revolved about its centre, and would be set for latitude against a scale engraved on the plate behind it. When set for latitude, the plate would be held vertically, with the sights pointed towards the sun. The intersection of the plumb-line with the appropriate declination parallel would indicate the time. When the rojas dial was engraved on a quadrant or astrolabe, the sights of the astrolabe and the plumb-line of the quadrant could be used; but if it was employed with a nocturnal a triangular arm was added to carry sights and plumb. The projection of this dial is similar to that used on a type of universal astrolabe. Probably rojas dials were in existence in the very old days, but the first description of it is found in the *Commentarii de astrolabii* of Ferdinand de Rojas, 1550.

Rolling Pin. A kitchen implement in the shape of a cylinder with a short handle at each end, normally of wood, for rolling dough. Early in the 19th century the more interesting blown-glass rolling pins began to be made at Bristol, Nailsea, Sunderland, and Stourbridge. The method might have been introduced by a French craftsman who came to Nailsea towards the end of the 18th century. They would be made in glass of several colours, sometimes flecked with enamel glass, often decorated with romantic words in gilt and with scrollwork. Such rolling pins were bought by seamen to take home as SAILORS' VALENTINES or SEAMEN'S LOVE TOKENS; apart from this sentimental purpose, it is difficult to discover their range of use. Some of them were hollow, and could be filled with various commodities, such as tea, flour, sugar, eau de Cologne, salt, or smuggled rum. When a

Glass rolling pin.

168

stopper and the contents were removed the rolling pin would be hung by a cord on the cottage wall, where the inscriptions on them would remind the wife or sweetheart of the absent donor. Such are often called ship's "rolling pins", but erroneously. They had no connection with the briny save for their being purchased by sailors for gifts. They come in all types and with many different scenes and inscriptions. The last sometimes show sailing ships, sea birds and other marine creatures, or a sailor saying goodbye to his wife or girl friend. Perhaps the most popular theme was "The Sailor's Farewell", and throughout, the emphasis, somewhat ominously, was on faithfulness: "Remember me and I will remember you". One inscription takes this a little further: "When far at sea remember me and bear me in your mind, Let all the world say what they will, Speak of me as you find." Another favourite design was of an anchor at one end and a sailing ship at the other, sandwiching the words "My Love is Thine".

The seafaring community has always been superstitious, and it was traditionally thought that if a glass rolling pin fell from the wall and was shattered, then the loved one would be lost in a shipwreck or to another woman. If the pin had originally contained salt it would be kept on the wall with the salt intact as a charm against ill fortune. Collectors' demand for these pins was so strong in the first half of our century that they were reproduced in considerable numbers.

Rolling Ruler. This brass rule, 12 in. or more long, and 3 in. wide, was introduced at the beginning of the 19th century to serve as a PARALLEL RULER. It possessed no calibration, but had two knurled wheels on its underside, and thus could be moved smoothly across a chart.

Rope Cradle. A large, circular wooden receptacle, standing on short legs, with numerous turned-wood uprights and a canework base, in which rope could be coiled to drain after use (see LOG-LINE).

Rope Mat. When rope aboard ship was wearing out, or odd lengths occurred, it was not thrown away, but often used for plaiting or interweaving into hard-wearing mats, some of which were large enough to be used as small carpets. They were useful in the ship's cabins, particularly the captain's, or taken home by seamen for presentation to their families or to make a little money. Old rope was used also for the making of bucket and sea chest handles, and in rope embroidery, such being known as "fancy work".

Round Shot. Cast-iron cannon balls, designed to do the maximum of damage to the hull of an enemy ship.

Roux, Antoine (died 1835). A French maker of nautical instruments, as well as ship portrait painter and watercolour marine artist. Like many artists he came from a family of them. His father was Matthieu Antoine Roux (1799-1872), also a nautical instrument-maker and watercolour marine artist. Other family members were Frederick Roux (1805-1870), François Jeoffroy Roux (1811-1882), and a Joseph Roux, nautical instrument-maker at Marseilles, whose shop sign consisted of two painted wooden figures of merchant marine officers, each wearing a cocked hat, under one arm a telescope and holding a quadrant. Outstanding examples of the work of the Roux family are "The privateer *L'Hirondelle*, Captain Pontus, armament two four-pounders, ready to board and take the 300-ton *Arrow*," and "The brig *Dubourdien*, Captain Mordeille, boarding the English three-master *Loyalty*".

Rush, William (1756-1833). American carver of figureheads and ornamental woodwork on ships, also sculptor and maker of sectional anatomical models. He was born in Philadelphia, the son of a shipwright, and, after apprenticeship with the English-trained carver Edward Cutbush, founded his own Philadelphia workshop in 1779 and eventually became a figurehead carver of international renown. Not only did he carve; he also prepared designs for the work of others, a notable example being the U.S.S. frigate *Constitution's* figurehead of 1797. This "Herculean figure standing on the firm rock of Independence" was carved by John Skillen to Rush's design and at his suggestion. Rush's figureheads were generally upright in posture, full-length, half-length or bust, for the frigate-type of bow which preceded the later clipper-ship bow, and they were in the French rather than the English tradition, being realistically portrayed. An example of his sculpture-like style is the bust figurehead for the U.S.S. *Franklin* of 1815, preserved at the U.S. Naval Academy,

Annapolis. Another is a fine-carved full-length female, presumably depicting the seaman's virtuous girl friend or dream wife, carved for the ship *Virtue*, and rather curiously preserved at the Masonic Temple in Philadelphia.

Rutter. A book containing information on tides, sailing directions, marine routes, entries into ports and harbours, signs and tokens of the sun, moon and stars at various times and the appearance and sound of the sea. The name is derived from the French *routier*, and the custom of keeping such books dates from the 14th century. The first rutter in English, illustrated with woodcuts of coasts, is Robert Norman's *Safegarde of Saylers or Great Rutter*, of 1590. But the text is based on a translation of two Dutch rutters, one by Cornelis Anthoniszoon.

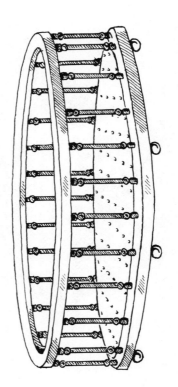

Rope cradle.

172

Sailor's pincushion.

Sailor's life preserver.

S

Sailcloth Bag.   A bag made of sailcloth, in which a seaman who assisted the sailmaker kept his sailmaking and repairing tools. Such tools would include an animal horn, sometimes engraved with a nautical motif. This horn contained the triangular needles of the craft, in several sizes. Other tools were scissors, a sailmaker's hook to pull the cloth during stitching, and two "palms", one for roping the sail and the other for wearing in sewing.

Sailing Cards.   These were actually advertisements, giving details of a passenger or cargo sailing ship and its intention of sailing, destination, time of sailing, at which pier or dock, name of the commander and ship and its size, the stowage and handling facilities, and often a glowing account of the ship's speed and safety. The card might be embellished with a nautical motif, or the details could be printed in black over a colourful nautical scene. Such cards were preceded by HANDBILLS and POSTERS but became especially popular in the 19th century as part of the emigration boom.

Sailmaker's Implements.   To make a new sail was, and is, a skilled and considerable task. The sailmaker's tools are specially adapted to it, such as "palms" for sewing and for roping the sail, triangular needles in assorted sizes for sewing (kept in a horn) and a hook to pull the cloth during sewing. The sailmaker had his own bench on which to sit; this had holes to contain the needle horns as well as several sizes of fids made of boxwood, iron, ivory or bone. Other sailmaker's tools were the scissors, prickers, mallets, iron rubbers and MARLIN SPIKES.

Sailor's Cap.   Headgear worn by sailors, with or without pom-pom according to nationality, also with a black band or ribbon bearing the ship's name or naval shore establishment in gold lettering. As originally introduced by the Royal Navy in 1857, when rules were laid down for lower-deck uniforms, it was similar to the officer's cap but without a peak (see SAILORS' HEADGEAR).

Sailor's Charm. A gift that was made or bought, such as SCRIMSHAW work or a glass ROLLING PIN, and that was intended to bring good luck both to the donor and the female recipient.

Sailor's Collar. As worn from the neck downwards at the back, this was introduced by the Royal Navy in 1857, forming part of regulations for lower-deck UNIFORMS. Three rows of white tape were designed for the blue jean collar, and it is often thought that these rows commemorated Nelson's victories. This, however, is not so, and the reason for the three rows remains obscure. The actual collar may have originated in the custom of wearing a greasy pigtail, and to protect the sailor's shirt from that grease. The pigtail developed at a time of long hair, to keep it out of the sailor's eyes in the breeze. On the other hand pigtails were never that common in the Navy, being principally worn between 1785 and 1825.

Sailor's Glass Rolling Pins (see ROLLING PINS).

Sailors' Headgear. See SAILOR'S CAP, to which may be added the following facts. A low cocked hat was worn in the Navy from about 1760 to 1780. In the last year it was authorised only for officers. By 1800 a "low tarpaulin" hat was being worn, made from tarpaulin coated with tar and grease to keep it black, glossy and waterproof. It has a broad black band or ribbon with the name of the ship. Straw hats were introduced in 1802, particularly for ships stationed in the West Indies; this "straw sennet" was abolished in 1922. COCKED HATS were worn athwarts by officers until 1795. The custom then began of turning them halfway round, and by 1825 all officers were wearing them fore and aft. Caps for officers were issued that year for wearing at sea: they had a gold lace band around them. The caps were given peaks in 1856, plain gold ones for commanders and above, and black for junior officers. The sailor's cap as such was introduced in 1857. Until 1860 senior officers had peaks with oak leaves instead of plain gold.

The tarpaulin hat was abolished in 1890. Sailors' hats have varied considerably in the different navies of the world; they have been made of hardened leather, of animal skin, and of plain or varnished straw.

Sailor's Life Preserver. Weapon in the form of a bludgeon, consisting of an oval knob of hard wood secured to a length of rope bound by cord. The oval wood was covered with cord netting, and the weapon would be secured to the wrist and hidden up the sleeve until required for use.

Sailors' Pin-cushions. (see PIN-CUSHION) Some authorities maintain that seamen never made these effeminate objects, but there are in existence many examples that have a nautical flavour with evidence of typically maritime work, such as those edged or patterned with BEADS and those decorated with Union Jacks and inscriptions like "Remember Me". It must be remembered that seafarers had to do their own sewing and mending, so would have needed pincushions themselves, but they could have been given to sailors by their sweethearts, and would have been bought by mariners in foreign ports, such as a strange one in existence that consists of two halves of a coconut stuffed with padding, fishes being carved on the hard nut.

Sailors' Valentines. Originally these were not the modern cards with which we have become familiar, but various items given by sailors to sweethearts on Valentine's Day, such as ROLLING PINS, SHELL MOSAICS, SAILORS' PIN-CUSHIONS, CRIMSHAW work, STAY BUSKS, SHELL VALENTINES and PIN-PRICKED PICTURES.

Salmon, Robert (1775-d. after 1840). English ship portrait and marine painter, who sailed from Liverpool in 1828, arrived in New York after 32 days' passage, went to Boston in 1829, and lived there until 1840, but possibly returned to England to die. Some of his earlier paintings are signed "Salomon". His work is in the Old Boston State Museum, and his "Wharves of Boston" is in the Old Boston State House. Typical Salmons are "A Sloop of War off Liverpool", and "Bidston Old Lighthouse".

Saloon Bench. A narrow bench, covered with leather or artificial leather, or with canework seating, used by the captain or other officer on duty in the chart-house for short rest periods. Similar benches were used in the captain's cabin for seating officers and other guests who ate with him. These had a pivoted wooden bar as a back-rest, this being lifted over at meal times, so the bench was made into a seat facing the food table, then turned back afterwards away from the table so the inconvenience of having to move the bench was avoided.

Sampling Bottle.   This was used on hydrographic ships to obtain water samples so that the temperature of water at depth could be measured.

Sand Bottle.   A bottle or glass vial filled with layers of different-coloured sands, usually shaped like an inverted tulip, or bell-shaped, and topped with a glass ball. Some were plain-shaped like laboratory bottles, and others in "fancy" shapes such as pillar columns, even lighthouses. The most important came from ALUM BAY in the Isle of Wight where, from the 1840s, the local coloured sand was widely advertised as a tourist attraction. Bottles were sold to visitors, who were encouraged to gather their own sand, of which there were as many as twelve different colours, for arranging in patterns in them. Horizontal stripes constituted the most common and indeed the easiest pattern. Then the sand was sold in packets for visitors to take home. The local people developed considerable skill in the artistic filling of sand bottles, and could even produce elaborate pictures, including Isle of Wight views. Seamen soon cottoned on to the idea, and would collect strange-coloured sand in exotic places and fill their own sand bottles during weary moments of the voyage. They would on occasion use earth instead of sand, especially those who touched on Chile, where nitrates produced rare colours. Chilean dock-workers sold ready-made sand bottles that they had contrived.

The later 19th century knew a variation of sand bottle making known as POTICHOMANIA. A picture cut out from a magazine was stuck inside a bottle to provide the decoration, and was backed by plain sand. This was a typical case of the progressive artistic decadence that marred the 19th century.

Genuine Alum Bay bottles, the most valuable, can have a useful old label on their base, stating "Isle of Wight curiosity arranged with

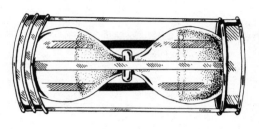

Eighteenth-century half-hour sand glass.

Early-twentieth-century souvenir sand bottle from the Isle of Wight.

•sands from the coloured cliffs of Alum Bay''. Although Alum Bay bottles were produced in thousands to meet the popular demand, they were so often broken that genuine examples are increasingly a valuable rarity (although they are still being made).

Sand Clock. Another name for the SAND GLASS, as below.

Sand Container Pictures. This is a variation of the sand bottle, as above, wherein a more or less perfect picture has been built up from vari-coloured sands inside the bottle. The outstanding master of the strange art was a deaf and dumb American ANDREW CLEMENS who lived in the 19th century near McGregor, Iowa. He was aided by the numerous coloured sands that can be found in the Mississippi valley. Clemens' early work, geometrical and floral patterns of sand in bottles, was widely purchased by tourists as souvenirs, and often brought to Europe, but in the late 1880s this extraordinary man turned to the making of actual pictures with the sand in the bottles. He gradually learned how to show a sailing ship on a storm-tossed sea, a railway engine with carriages, Mississippi river craft, birds, animals, famous people including George Washington in full uniform seated on his white horse. He would copy photographs for customers. (His secret was to make the sand completely dry by heating and rubbing on blotting paper, after which he would press it into position with a wooden spoon. He would use a home-made, curved tool delicately and patiently to put the coloured sand in exactly the position he wanted in the bottle. The pint-sized bottle pictures took him several weeks of work to complete. He used fragile bottles which, when struck heavily or broken, so disturbed the sand inside that the picture disappeared completely. Thus genuine examples of Clemens' work are very rare. There is a very valuable collection in the Iowa State Historical Museum.)

Sand Glass. This device for measuring intervals of time has two pear-shaped glass bulbs, one above the other, joined together at their pointed ends or necks by a narrow tube, through which fine sand or marble powder slowly runs down in a pre-determined space of time (that length of time being calculated by the maker after experiments with the sand or powder in varying amounts). The bulbs are protected, as well as held in position, by a stand to which they are fixed; the whole device being reversible so that it can stand on either end. Eventually they worked out how a metal disc could be inserted between the necks of the two bulbs, with a hole in it that would govern the speed of the sand. By changing this disc to one with a larger or smaller hole it was possible to vary the time. It was important that the sand or powder should not become damp in the salt air, so the places where the two bulbs and the disc joined were sealed with wax and crisscrossed with waxed thread. The stand was made strongly of brass or iron to obviate breakage or the slightest damage to the bulbs; this stand would have several upright wooden bars or spindles, turned or decorated. Sometimes the ship's name would be carved or stamped on one end of this frame. These ends might be covered with morocco leather, ornamented with gilt stampings. Others would be enclosed in a kind of tube of metal, leather, cardboard or horn. The sand glass could be "read" through the horn. Yet another container would consist of hinged doors. The mounts or stands of early models are particularly strong, and the more treasured examples have mountings with elaborate carvings that display religious or nautical motifs.

Some sand glasses were devised to run for only $\frac{1}{4}$ min; others lasted up to 4 hr. Those of short duration, called LOG GLASSES, were used for timing the log-line, and they consisted of a single bulb, pinched in the centre by the glass-blower; $\frac{1}{2}$hr glasses went out with the sailing ship in the middle of the 19th century, but the short-time versions have survived into our own period, being often retained as a standby for use with the LOG SHIP, if a mechanical log breaks down. The glass for 1 hr was frequently made in the shape of a large and pear-shaped bulb with four small bulbs below like bubbles, each of which marked $\frac{1}{4}$ hr. Sand ran into one small bubble glass, then into the others in succession. When the last bulb had been filled one hour has passed.

On the sailing ships a $\frac{1}{2}$ hr and a 4 hr glass would be sited on the poop to time the bells and the watches. That 4 hr specimen was also known as the BATTLE GLASS because it was the standby during storms or naval engagements, when other timekeeping devices might be disturbed by the movement of the ship. The term "organ pipes" was used for an arrangement of several sand glasses registering different times, in one housing. The glasses were often attached or suspended by a pair of rings against a flat surface when not in use, so that they might not be flung down and broken in rough weather.

These glasses were periodically checked against new ones to make sure they were still recording the time properly. A particular fault was the presence of grainy sand which enlarged the hole in the separating metal disc and thus caused the device to "run fast". Dampness of the sand also caused time variations.

Dating old sand glasses can be difficult, but the colour or tint of the bulbs is a help. The glass was greenish up to about 1700. During the 18th century it was darker; then in the 19th century it gradually acquired the transparency of "crystal". There were also variations in the actual sand which, prior to about 1720, was reddish or orange-red in colour. After about 1720 white or green sand was increasingly used, and sometimes this would be dyed for the purpose. Finally marble dust was employed. This came from Italy, being whitish-grey in colour. The actual marble had been crushed, boiled in wine, dried, and sifted through silk.

Sand Glass Souvenirs.   SEASIDE SOUVENIRS made of china, brass or copper, with glass bulbs in the form of a miniature SAND GLASS. They bore the coat of arms or heraldic device of the place where they were purchased, and sometimes a suitable inscription. Such souvenirs, devised as egg-timers, represented the sad but inevitable end of a considerable craft.

Sand Pictures.   These are actual pictures, in frames, made of sand in various colours that was sprinkled on a pattern or picture drawn in gum on canvas, wood, or other material. The custom of contriving such pictures dates back to about the middle of the 18th century; it became lucrative for seaside artists and bored mariners, as well as a suitable pastime for young ladies with nothing better to do. The first were probably made in the form of panels for table decoration. They were stuck on top of the table, and very few have survived, because the banging down of vessels on the table disturbed the sand. It was possibly at the end of the 18th century that someone thought of using glue as a base; maybe a certain German named Benjamin Zobel, who had trained as an artist and came to London, where he was appointed "official table decker" at Windsor Castle, and allowed to advertise himself on his trade cards as "Sand Picture Painter to George III". He married an Englishwoman, who bore him seven children, all of whom were taught their father's curious craft. These Zobel creations were sometimes signed, but most sand pictures are anonymous, and their makers can be identified only by a knowledge of styles and methods. Frederick Schwiekhardt and G.L. Haas were two other "sand" artists that we know.

The artist, maybe Zobel, who thought of the gum or glue, provided the break-through that enabled pictures of lasting value and interest to be devised. Maybe a picture would first be outlined in pencil or charcoal on card or canvas or wood. Maybe the whole area was then covered with a clear and slow-drying gum, or just part of the drawing. The artist would carefully sprinkle sands of different colours on the appropriate parts of the drawing, and excess sand was carefully removed. The method of doing the picture piece by piece became the most favoured.

Landscapes and seascapes were chosen; famous paintings were copied. During the 19th century the art, if it could be so called,

180

tended to degenerate into the usual souvenir business, becoming cruder and cruder with the passing of time. Some of the best were those made from the colourful sands of ALUM BAY in the Isle of Wight. The Victorians soon learnt how to colour sands specially for the job, and to impose them upon pictures torn from magazines. They also turned to the use of dried grass, flowers, leaves, seaweed as part of the picture. The modern "collage" thus began (see also SAND BOTTLES).

Savage, William.   A carver who was responsible for much of the fine work on the *Victory* of 1765. His work at Chatham Dockyard is referred to in ADMIRALTY DRAUGHTS.

Sawn Shot.   A solid cannon-ball would be cut into quarters, which were joined together by a rod to a central ring. This, when fired, became extended and cut usefully through sails and rigging, as CHAIN SHOT.

Sayer, Robert (died 1794).   A map publisher of London, who in 1775 issued in partnership with John Bennett (died 1787), the first edition of *The North American Pilot*. This was based on the charts of James Cook and Michael Lane. ROBERT LAURIE and JAMES WHITTLE took over the business shortly before Sayer died.

Sceptre Recorder.   An instrument for recording the water depth under a ship.

Sconce.   A metal bracket, sometimes with a reflector behind it, attached to a beam to hold a candle or lamp (a "purser's glim".) Such sconces can be seen on a deck of the *Victory*, below the waterline. The feeble light of the candles was all the surgeons had to illuminate their attentions to the wounded during and after battle.

Scott, J. (fl. 1850-1873).   This ship portrait painter specialised in merchant ships and, unlike some others, was a good painter who was not interested in ships alone. His picture of "Sailing Barques off the coast, the *Britton* and the *California*", is noted for its fine treatment of the waves. Two other examples of Scott's work are the portrait, 1873, of the British ship *Richard Rylands*, that can be seen at the Mystic Seaport in Connecticut, and the painting "S.S. *Claude Hamilton* off Dover".

Scrimshander, Skrimshander. A variation of the term SCRIMSHAW, used particularly for articles carved or otherwise created by whalemen with whalebone or teeth. There is a reference to "skrimshander" articles in Melville's *Moby Dick*. In the LOGS of early whalers we find the terms "SCRIMSHOUTING" and "SCRIMSHANTING" but it must be remembered that such men could not spell well anyway.

Scrimshanting; Scrimshouting. Versions of the term SCRIMSHAW, as particularly referred to in the early LOGS of whalers.

Scrimshaw. A nautical term for making what would today be called "fun" articles aboard ship; mainly carvings of wood and whale or other bone, also ivory from walrus tusks and teeth. (There is another school which believes the term was first applied to shell work, but the origin of the actual word is unknown: perhaps it was a sailor's name: "typical of Scrimshaw's work" might originally have been said.) Undoubtedly there is a strong whaling association, going back to the first Dutch commercial whaling from Spitzbergen in the 17th century. New England whalemen in the 19th century became quite famous for their activities as scrimshaw craftsmen. They had as long as 5 years at sea sometimes, and had to endure weeks without sighting a whale, during which they had to apply themselves to something; they used discarded whalebone, as well as walrus teeth, for making articles that could be given to wives, sweethears, and others, and even sold on return to port. Their tools were seldom more than JACK-KNIVES, sailmakers' needles, and nails fixed into wooden pegs. The teeth of the sperm whale were particularly suitable for "engraving"; the natural ridges were left on them and incorporated in the design, or scraped off with the knife and smoothed with a piece of skate or shark skin, after being severed from the whale's jaws with a chisel. Pictures would be incised of men in whaleboats after giant whales, of ships, of icebergs and islands, of maps, flags, birds, mermaids, walruses, polar bears, sailors drinking, patriotic and disastrous events and insignia, even

Scrimshaw ring box with a bone and wood lid.

religious themes, and, of course, various aspects of the feminine form. These pictures and designs would be at once more extensive and less artistic perhaps when carved on whalebone – which, however, was used not just for carving or "engraving," but also for cutting into the shapes of various useful or decorative articles, such as ornamental busks or bodice stays, pie crust crimpers, spool holders, clothes pegs, yarn winders, lace bobbins, napkin rings, rolling pins, small eating utensils, pen holders, shoehorns, clothes pins, work boxes, thimbles, needle cases, tobacco jars, door handles, hooks, baskets, bird cages, paper-knives, yard sticks, rulers, compasses, seals and counters, cane heads and tool handles, children's toys.

Some scrimshaw items are worked very finely and display considerable artistic skill. The rarest are those made from BALEEN. Men of all nations took part in the good work: a nice eye is required to differentiate between them, but national motifs help, such as flags and coastal scenes. It is helpful when names of a ship and its home port are included. The types of ship are useful; it is a good point that English seafarers tended to incise the whalebone and walrus teeth rather deeper than the Americans. The last-named were also inclined to be more realistic in their work, whereas the English were more fanciful.

Scrimshaw work in other materials than whalebone was generally done by mariners who voyaged outside the whaling grounds. They used driftwood, or ends of timber obtained from the ship's carpenter, as well as meat bones from the galley (usually from salted pork). American seamen would carve their items in wood and sometimes have them cast in metal on their return to port.

Another type of scrimshaw consists of carved wall plaques depicting whales, pen and ink stands, coat racks, tool handles, belaying pins, rigging blocks, fids for line splicing, many with seafaring motifs.

The modern interest in scrimshaw has naturally led to a considerable industry among reproducers or forgers. When sold as reproductions these items are honest; when sold as originals they are not so good. The forgers use dentistry equipment, engraving quickly with the drill; they "age" the bone and tooth ivory by various chemical means. It is possible to detect such deceptions after becoming closely acquainted in museums with truly original scrimshaw work.

Scroll Work. A form of SCRIMSHAW in which sailors curved paperd into scrolls either as a decorative object in itself or attached to an object for the purpose of adorning it. PRISONERS-OF-WAR used tightly-curled paper with gilt edges, which they glued to boxes.

Seaman's Chest. This can be an important, if off-reproduced, antique, but was originally just a wooden chest or box with a hinged and curved or flat lid, in which seafarers kept their spare clothing and other personal possessions. Then some craftsmen started the practice of carving and painting such chests artistically, and even of affixing paintings to the inside as decoration. The chests were generally about 3 ft by 18 in., and another 18 in. deep in the old days, making them portable, and they had either short wooden legs or wooden strips underneath to raise them from the deck. They formerly had rope handles at either end. These early chests usually possessed lids of a flanged type that overlapped the sides, and there were either iron key-locks, or a clasp on the lid and ring on the front side which could take a padlock.

Then the seaman's chest gradually grew up. It developed drawers, and became beautified by brass "furniture", particularly escutcheons and protective corner-pieces. Senior officers required fine chests to be made for their cabins by skilled cabinet-makers in the ports. Good aristocratic chests were "discovered" by collectors soon after the World War II, and some obtained enormous bargains as a result of their prescience. But this item of antique furniture is basically so simple to contrive that it exists today in thousands of reproduced examples, which, if they ever went to sea, might become exceedingly sick.

(The largest seaman's chests are those made for deep-sea fishermen, who used them as tables; there is also the SHIP'S MONEY CHEST.)

Seaman's Pay Book; Seaman's Discharge Book. These were carried by seamen in the merchant navy. They contained records of the ships in which the man served, together with dates, details of duty, and wages received. Sometimes such books cover the entire seafaring career of a man and, as such, are valuable historical documents as well as human-interest stories and valuable items for collecting.

Seamen's or Sailors' Love Tokens. Items purchased, or hand-made by the seafarer, to present as a token of affection to loved ones at home: items such as glass ROLLING PINS, SHIPS IN BOTTLES, STAY BUSKS, knitting needles, apple corers, wooden spoons, PIN-CUSHIONS, shell-work plaques, WALL PLAQUES, PIN-PRICKED PICTURES and SCRIMSHAW generally.

Sea Sack. A receptacle in which a man kept his spare or dirty clothing, sometimes ornamented with EMBROIDERY.

Sea Service Pistol. A flintlock or percussion weapon, brass-mounted and with a belt hook, used aboard ship or by coastguards. In particular, two models of a British flint-lock sea service pistol of .56 calibre were produced, the short pattern, 15 in. overall with a 9 in. barrel, and the long pattern, 18 in. overall with a 12 in. barrel. The percussion sea service pistol was 11½ in. overall with a 6 in. barrel, of 567 calibre, a swivel ramrod, and a lanyard ring on the butt.

Seaside Souvenirs. Objects, useful or ornamental, purchased during a visit to the seaside as a souvenir, and introduced at the end of the 18th century when the Prince Regent and his friend Mrs. Fitzherbert had suddenly popularised coastal holidays and in particular transformed Brighthelmstone into Brighton. At first the souvenirs were made locally, and early examples have a sufficiently salty flavour, but soon their fabrication became an industry for such places as Birmingham. The local souvenirs of real interest are those based on the geology of the region. They were contrived from interesting stones, even fossils. Then SHELLS were engraved for use as dishes and other small receptacles, or incorporated into nautical pictures, shell-sided purses, and glued to items such as trinket and pin boxes. Local shells were similarly used to make shell pin-cushions, of which there are two main types, as made from bivalve or univalve shells. The bivalves, from mussels or scallops, had the stuffed padding for the cushion held in position between the two hinged valves by thread through bored holes. The univalve was simpler to make into a pincushion: it was just a matter of glueing the actual cushion into the single shell of such as a large whelk, and then sometimes fixing that shell to another to make a base. Some such inscription as "A Present from Worthing" would be painted on the device.

The most important type of seaside souvenir, however, became the pottery item. These were "toys" or miniature objects made of white or cream-glazed pottery or bone china and decorated with local coats of arms and/or inscriptions in colour. Nearly everything was reproduced, from busts of famous men to chamberpots, but the most popular items were tea cups, jugs, vases, shaving mugs, egg cups, and the inscriptions were standardised in the familiar wording: "A Souvenir from Hastings"; "A Memento from Margate". From the beginning of the 19th century Staffordshire potteries enterprisingly produced these wares in vast numbers: one day their shards may be all that will remain of that civilisation. The collector has a very wide range of choice. He could specialise in the blue and white transfer-printed items with topographical views that have, alas, become

186

increasingly difficult to find. He could acquire pieces for each seaside town, or those that commemorated notable events. He could look for the "pink" ware that came for a long time from Germany, or concentrate on one of the aristocrats of the genre, which was SUNDERLAND PINK LUSTRE. Another aristocrat is Goss-ware. W. H. Goss, a master potter and designer of Stoke-on-Trent, was the small genius that every craft produces sooner or later. He made thousands of the usual items but always of a fine body and sometimes with exquisite attention to detail. His busts in particular have great value already. It was possible 20 years ago to buy his tiny cauldrons and jugs, and reproductions of local antiquities, for a few pence each; now they are worth many, many pounds - when they can be found. He had many imitators, but none could produce his fine, almost eggshell and nearly translucent porcelain: they couldn't afford to produce it. He was the usual artist who possessed no commercial sense, hence a producer of lasting interest and beauty. His mark, without which none of the work claimed for him is genuine, is a punning rebus - a gos(s) hawk ducally gorged. Jones and Son, Stoke-on-Trent, with their Grafton china, and Arkinstall and Sons (A. &S.) of Stoke-on-Trent with their Arcadia, were the nearest rivals of this foolish-fond little genius of the promenade shop.

The collector could also turn to such small objects that have a specific nautical flavour, reproductions in china or other substance of ships, lighthouses, lifeboats, or fish. Or he could concentrate on such things as glassware, particularly seaside paperweights with hand-coloured views (photographs after 1890). Or pot lids (beautifully transfer-printed in the rarer specimens). Indeed the entire gamut of miniature creative activity is covered by the seaside souvenir, including a great number of the items mentioned elsewhere in this dictionary.

To be ranked among seaside souvenirs are also POSTCARDS, as well as old illustrated guides and albums of views.

Seaweed Album. One more favourite occupation of the Victorians, especially the ladies, was the collection of seaweeds and their insertion in a suitable album for study and remembrance. Possibly the Queen was the initiating culprit again, from the days when she first went to the Isle of Wight for holidays with her mother, the Duchess of Kent, in the first quarter of the 19th century. We know that she presented such an album of seaweeds to the young Maria da Gloria, Queen of Portugal, in 1833. There were two kinds of album: one was of the common scrapbook type; the cover was plain board or cloth-covered board, and contained thick paper pages upon which the seaweeds were mounted and classified. The other type was provided more or less ready-made, or ready-collected for a purchaser, and this was more elaborate, often with a shell-encrusted or pictorially-decorated cover. A group of ladies at Jersey in the Channel Islands developed quite an industry of producing such ready-made seaweed albums for sale on behalf of a local school, St. Aubin's. Their albums contained as many as 200 specimens, and the enterprise was so successful that it covered the school's expenses for 14 years.

A sideline of this sport was the sale, in seaside shops, of cards upon which a seaweed specimen was mounted, together with educational details. Holidaymakers would buy these cards for slotting into albums. A complete collection of such could still be made.

Yet another item for collectors is the shell container of seaweed specimens. Two large and fairly flat shells were chosen, such as those of scallops. Holes were drilled in them, through which ribbon was threaded. Between the shells were placed leaves of papers with sea-weed attached to them, and the ribbons were tied to hold the shells together. *The Lady's Newspaper* of 1852 describes these in the follow-ing words: "A fanciful and very elaborate book, the binding of which is composed of two large fan-formed shells, enclosing leaves whereon seaweed is secured". A pioneer of this curious craft was Mrs. Margaret Gatry (1809–1873), a popular author who became such an expert on the subject that she produced the definitive work *British Seaweeds* in 1872. This contains a chapter "Rules for the Preserving and Laying-out of Seaweeds". Mrs. Gatry herself devised a considerable number of seaweed albums, which she sold in aid of various charities; one of them to Queen Victoria herself.

Seaweed Picture. The custom of making such pictures arose towards the end of the 18th century, when the Prince Regent and his lady friends first made holidays by the briny a social event. The problem was to find rewarding occupations during those holidays. The collecting of seaweed was suggested, and some of the more artistic ladies started to make pictures with these specimens. They dried them, and stuck them on to a drawing in pencil, ink or watercolour, usually to represent the flowers and foliage thereon. It was a primitive form of collage. A typical specimen is "The Avenue", constructed (if that is the word) by a Miss Jane Parminter of Exmouth in the late 18th century. It shows a distant house, with an avenue of trees on the right and a single tree on the left-hand side; the sky is watercolour blue; the grass, ground and drive are sand, stuck and coloured on the paper; but the tree trunks are made of pressed seaweed in various colours, also the tree foliage and the bushes, giving a strangely natural impression.

The art came of age in the 19th century with often remarkable manifestations. One was the seaweed basket, a picture on hand-made paper in a wooden and glazed frame, sometimes gilt and oval-shaped, which consisted of the depiction of a small wicker basket from which protruded a mass of dried and unpressed seaweeds. The Coralline type was used as stems, and the foliage of other kelps could be diversified with attached seashells. First-class examples of this genre can look very natural when hanging on the wall, much depending upon the degree of preservation of the seaweeds, which in turn depended originally upon how they were treated before attachment. Properly handled seaweeds would retain their colour and not fade to a dirty brown. A good specimen can have remarkable arrangements of shells among the kelp, or as intricately designed borders to the picture. The "floor" of the picture might be devised of sea mat and sea urchin skeletons as well as small shells. The top corners might have dangling swirls of seaweed in the form of many-petalled "flowers" and frail-looking "foliage".

There came a more commercial development in the mid-1860s. Uncoloured prints were sold in seaside resorts; these prints which would later be coloured by purchasers and decorated additionally with pieces of seaweed; or seaweed was wreathed around the coloured picture. If the purchaser did not want to have the trouble of collecting his own seaweed, then he could buy it, ready-dried, from the same shop. This amusement, originally for adults, degenerated into a children's pastime later, as do so many human activities.

The Victorians might have been childish, but at least paid lip-service to the liberal arts. Thus the seaweed picture was often accompanied by suitably composed verses. Some specimens of this literary efflorescence remain for our delectation, such as:

Ah! Call us not weeds, but Flowers of the Sea,
For lovely and gay and bright tinted are we.
Our blush is as bright as the Rose of thy Bowers.
So call us not weeds, but the Ocean's gay Flowers.

Not nursed like the plants of a Summer Parterre
Where winds are but Sighs of an Evening Air,
Our exquisite fragile and delicate forms
Are reared by the Ocean and rocked by the Storms!

Whoever composed this had a kind of immorality for his pains. The verses became so popular that they were continually used and often varied in their wording, even to a third stanza that ran:

And thus 'tis in life, like weeds thrown away,
As many who bask not in fortune's bright ray,
Whose sunshine of life would shed lustre around,
And in weal, or woe, brightly tinted be found.

It became almost a little seaweed mania for a time, and was accompanied by many instructional books (that are still sold and collected today), such as Gifford's *The Marine Botanist* of 1848, the Rev. Mr. Lansborough's *A Popular History of British Seaweeds*, 1849, Clarke's *Common Seaweeds of the British Coast*, 1865, the Rev. J.G. Wood's *The Common Objects of the Sea Shore*, 1864, Professor W.H. Harvey's *Phycologia Brittanica*, 1846-51, and Johnson and Croall's *Nature Printed British Seaweeds*, 1859-60 (not forgetting Mrs. Gatry).

Sector. Known in France as the *compas de proportion*, this mathematical measuring instrument has two limbs or arms, and is essentially a brass-jointed ruler, the arms of which are engraved with various sets of graduated lines of scales, or tables, sines, tangents, and the like. These sines, tangents, secants, chards, and polygons were standardised on English sectors during the early 18th century. The sector

Sector, circa 1760.

would be unfolded or opened so that the ends of the two arms were as far apart as the length of the line to be divided, then verticals were dropped from the scale to the line. By using the sector with a pair of DIVIDERS it was possible to solve any problem that involved right-angled triangles or ratios. As long ago as the 1590s a form of sector was made by a Thomas Hood of that period; this was adapted in 1606 by EDMUND GUNTER for use in navigation. Instructions were in Latin, but a considerable number were made for the use of navigators. Gunter published English instructions in 1623, then introduced (1624) his GUNTER SCALE. The first sectors were intended for the use of surveyors, but were employed aboard ship, both for navigation and gunnery.

Seller, John (fl. 1669-1691). Chart printer and map seller of Wapping in London. His *The English Pilot* of 1671 used copper plates from Holland, and was continually reprinted for the next 150 years.

Serres, Dominic (1722-1793). Ship portrait painter from Gascony in France, who specialised in historical incidents. His water-colours were first drawn in thick ink, then tinted in his favourite blues and greys. He ran away to sea as a boy, and rose to become master of a Spanish trading vessel, which was captured by a British frigate in 1758. Serres, a prisoner, was taken to England, where he was be-friended by, and became a pupil of, Charles Brooking. Eventually he was appointed marine painter to George III, became a founder member of the Royal Academy, and was made librarian of that institution in 1792. Two of his sons, Dominic and JOHN THOMAS became marine artists. A good example of the father's work is "A squadron of Dutch me o'war in a fresh sea".

Serres, John Thomas (1759-1825). Eldest son and pupil of the above Dominic Serres, who became drawing master at the Naval School in Chelsea, then was appointed marine painter to the King and the Duke of Clarence in succession to his father. He was "Marine Draughtsman" to the Admiralty in 1793. His watercolour style is very similar to that of his father, with the same pen-drawings tinted in greys and blues, but with some touches of rather brighter colours such as greens and yellows. He published in 1801 *The little Sea Torch for Coasting Ships*, and, in 1825, a handbook for marine painters entitled *Liber Nauticus*. In spite of all this he died penniless and ensconced in the Kings Bench Prison (this state of affairs was blamed on the extravagances of an eccentric wife). Good examples of his work are: "Fishing boats with an American and British ship off Liverpool"; "A brig in a fresh gale, with a view of Dover"; and "The *Royal George* becalmed at Spithead".

Settle, William Frederick (1821-1897). As a specialist in watercolours and crayons, he was appointed marine artist to the Royal Scottish Yacht Club. Queen Victoria commissioned him to execute marine pictures for some of her famous Christmas cards.

Sextant. An instrument used by navigators for discovering latitude and longitude. There are two types, the nautical and the box, the last being a small portable version of the nautical sextant, housed in a box which was held one-handed by a projecting handle. The more familiar brass nautical sextant has an arc of 60 degrees. The outer surface is calibrated, which calibrations are crossed by the lower part of a movable alidade, that has a sighting telescope, and the other has another, fixed, mirror. It was originally to be an improvement on HADLEY'S OCTANT, whose wooden frame tended to become distorted during humid weather conditions. The sextant was basically the same as that octant, but more practical because of its wider arc. The octant, with its smaller arc, was unsuitable for observations of the moon. A Captain Campbell of the Royal Navy was responsible in 1757 for making suggestions that led to the creation of the nautical sextant. He suggested specifically that the arc of the octant should be enlarged to 60 degrees, so that angles up to 120 degrees could be measured. It was necessary to measure lunar distances that exceeded 90 degrees.

Basically the sextant was used to measure the height of a star. First a note would be taken of the alidade's position when the star's image was reflected from the pivot to the fixed mirror and into the telescope, being coincidental with the horizon when viewed through the unsilvered part of the fixed mirror. Being suitable both for vertical and horizontal work, it was preferred by mariners to the octant, and, being portable, it could be carried about on deck easily, and even taken up to the crow's nest or up mast rigging to get a better vantage point for observations. Edward Troughton, a founder member of the Royal Astronomical Society, patented a brass sextant in 1788. Strips of metal plate in duplicate were used on this to make the limb; brass pillars effected a jointure. The use of this Troughton or double-frame sextant continued well into the 19th century. Another maker, Jesse Ramsden (1734-1800), used thicker-gauge metals in experiments, and tried other methods of manufacture to obtain rigidity in the instrument. He created the "bridge-type" sextant. A 1794 specimen of Ramsden's making has a radius of $8^5/8$ in., a brass double frame and wooden handle and a platinum scale, together with three coloured glass shades for the index glass and three for the horizon glass. There are three sighting telescopes, the scale being divided from zero to 130 degrees; there is a vernier with tangent screw plus a spiral screw adjustment. Later Ramsden produced sextants with a radius of $9^1/8$ in., of brass, double frame, bridge type. These had handles of lignum vitae, platinum scales, four shades for the index and horizon glasses, two sighting telescopes, and the scale was divided from zero to 130 degrees; the vernier had a tangent and clamping screws, plus a reading microscope. Another maker, Fraser, produced a similar bridge-type sextant. Troughton's remained the most successful, but the problem of how to overcome strain on the sextant was not resolved satisfactorily until new metal alloys were discovered. During the 19th century it was common practice to use bell metal alloy with 7 per cent tin, which made the weight of a sextant ideal for nautical use, at about 4 lbs. Another problem to be overcome was the avoiding of distortion caused by the improper grinding of glass for the plane mirrors. The two faces had to be ground parallel and silvered with mercury and tinfoil. If the grinding of the glass did not produce an absolutely flat surface the instrument was inaccurate. It was similarly important that the telescope used with the sextant should be made perfectly; the eye-pieces were either of the Ramsden or the Huygens type, and the last-named obtained the best results.

The sextant proved of immense value during the great exploratory years of the 18th and 19th centuries, and the instrument survived in useful service until the end of the 19th century. Captain Cook used it when exploring the coastline of New Zealand from 1769 to 1770, and around some 2400 miles of Pacific island coast. There was also a brass pocket sextant, employed for obtaining quick meridian bearings. This was not so accurate as the nautical sextant. Its radius was $2\frac{1}{2}$ in.; it had a silver scale divided from zero to 130 degrees; the index arm was adjustable by a tangent screw on the outer, toothed edge of the scale's arc; and the vernier had a lens mounted in a hinged arm for reading the scale and with two shades for the horizon glass. (A stellar sextant is an astronomical sextant with telescope and mirror.)

Shadow-box Model. The American term for a HALF-BLOCK MODEL—half a ship model with rigging and masts fixed to a background, the hull on a painted base to simulate the sea, and all enclosed in a glass case or frame.

Shark Walking-sticks. These were made from the spines of sharks. The ribs were cut off, and then a metal rod was inserted in the spine to strengthen it. A handle was affixed, sometimes the beak of an ALBATROSS.

Shells. These were probably the first natural objects to be collected. They were used by the pre-Dynastic Egyptians as ladles, dishes, containers, as musical instruments, and for religious purposes. The voyages of exploration and the opening up of trade routes brought home many exotic varieties. These were sold, exchanged, and collected; there was a steady import trade, from which shrewd

194

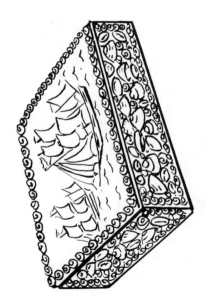

Eighteenth-century shell trinket box.

seamen profited. Thousands of guineas were sometimes paid for a rare shell in the 18th century, but not afterwards: there has been a steady decline in the value of these objects since that century (during which nobleman and their ladies on the Grand Tour collected shells as moderns acquire gold bars and Swiss francs). During the Victorian period shells were displayed in cabinets by wealthy enthusiasts. They were used in vast quantities to make SHELLWORK JEWELLERY such as SHELL CAMEOS. A particularly fantastic use was to cover the clothes of a doll entirely with them; one hand of the doll would hold a basket encrusted with tiny shells, and the other hand a bouquet of miniature roses made in the same way; there would also be shells above and below the brim of the doll's bonnet. The finished doll was housed in a glass dome on a wooden stand, for display as one more Victorian ornament. Such dolls date back to the 1830s. Sometimes shells, like the pearly nautilus, had their outer surface or periostracum ground away to reveal the layer of MOTHER-OF-PEARL and were thus made into plates and saucers. A real decorative shell craze in the 19th century followed the 18th-century shell-investment craze, and all kinds of objects were made from them: trinket and money boxes, vases, mirror frames, wall plaques, framed nautical prints, paper-weights, plant containers, pincushions. They were used together with dried flowers, leaves, fern, cones and SEAWEED to create wreaths around various objects and pictures. They were used to adorn furniture, even entire chimney pieces. We know already about their part in the industry of SEASIDE SOUVENIRS.

That is going so far, but our ancestors were capable of anything, and went even farther. They widely used shells for the embellishment of outside buildings and monuments, such as pavilions, grottoes and follies. A fashionable pavilion adorned in this way would have inner, and even outer walls, sometimes ceilings, entirely encrusted with these back-ends of molluscs. Some grottoes were veritable artifical caves made of shells, crystals, and rocks. The Duchess of Richmond and her two daughters spent most of the years 1739 to 1746 at creating their own shell pavilion in the grounds of Goodwood House. But years before this, the owners of Woburn Abbey made their 1640 Grotto Hall, wherein figures riding dolphins stood out in relief against a shell background; the ceiling was given a classical design in shells. Other famous examples were at Mereworth Castle in Kent, where Lady Fane designed a grotto with floral and geometrical designs in shells, and "A La Ronde" near Exmouth, a "cottage orné" or small house in the folly style. Here the sisters Jane Parminter (who made the SEAWEED PICTURES) and her sister Mary lived in the late 18th century after completing their inevitable travels in Italy. They used shells to decorate the octagon or hall of the building in imitation of the church of San Vitale at Ravenna.

Shell Bouquet. A cluster of "flowers" and "foliage", made of shells and sometimes standing in a similarly shell-encrusted container. Small lengths of coral were often involved. Such items were probably made in the 18th century, a shell-dominated era, but most of the surviving bouquets date from 1840 to 1870. Some of the "flowers" were based on a circle of card, to which the shell "petals" were glued, particularly fine examples being of the compound flowers such as chrysanthemums, globe flowers, and dahlias. Buds and delicate sprays were made by threading small shells on copper wire. Holes in the shells were made by egg-blowing drills. The wire was covered with silk. Leaves could be made from small oval and oblong shells appropriately slanted when fixed to the wire; in lowly examples of this art the leaves would be made from green paper or green wax on wire. Plain white shells would be painted to make them resemble petal tips and leaves with veins. Such bouquets were housed under the favoured glass "bells" of the period to keep dust and prying fingers at bay. The most valuable shell bouquets today are those made in pairs. A variation was the early flower bouquet made of shells, standing in a basket or urn, all being created against a flat base board, which was itself surrounded by a gilt frame, sufficiently rococo with more shells. Then some are depicted under a canopy made with shells, and occasionally there are Chinese or Turkish-type figures as an integral part of the construction. It is believed that the first shell bouquets were made in the Mediterranean region.

Shell Cameo. A cameo created from the carved white under-layers of suitable shells, such as the conch and helmet. It could be cut in an oval or rounded shape to fit a mount suspended from a chain as a necklace, or cut so that the white engraving stood out in relief against the colours of the shell's exterior. The engraving could also be done in such a way that the design or scene was created by the exterior colour remaining of the periostracum, which would stand out in relief against the background of the exposed white under-surface. Jewellery cameos usually depicted the head and shoulders of a woman in side view, but larger shell engravings on helmet and conch shells were more catholic in scope. All kinds of scenes were shown, together with messages of a sentimental nature, such as "I'll love you always", "To dear Mother", or just "A Souvenir from . . .". The craft originated in southern Italy, and is still carried on there. If, by the way, a cameo has a pinchbeck mount, it is usually old.

Shell Mosaic. This is what the words imply, a design or picture made from various coloured shells stuck mosaic-wise in glue or cement. The various "pockets" of the mosaic were separated by thin strips of card or wood. The mosaic was made in a wooden frame, often cedar and six- or eight-sided, with glass on top of the picture. Two such shell mosaics could be hinged together to form a wall plaque. Large examples were used as table-tops. The craft was not entirely for young ladies, and became a cottage industry in many parts by the sea. The best work was done in the first half of the 19th century, but the craft has not entirely died out to this day. A special kind was made in the West Indies, where they were purchased in the 19th century by sailors and brought home as SAILOR'S VALENTINES. Examples from the

Barbados of that time have since been taken apart for cleaning or renovation, and it has been found that the bases were lined with cuttings from strange local newspapers of the distant period. Occasionally the mosaic actually states "A Present from Barbados", picked out in dark shells to form the letters against a white background, or the original firm's or maker's label survives to prove their origin. It has been incorrectly stated that sailors themselves made these mosaics aboard ship, with shells obtained in their travels. They may have used shells in their SCRIMSHAW generally, but so far as is known, not shell mosaic pictures. A variation of the craft was the box divided into partitions, each containing shells but not with a glass covering, which were prepared in India in the early 20th century for sale to mariners.

Shell Roundels. A frame; round, usually wooden, covered by various shells, the centre of the roundel usually having a drawing, painting, or printed picture. Motifs can be nautical: a ship, a jetty, a lighthouse; and roundels were used as wall ornaments. Not only shells but also coral and dried seaweed could be incorporated. There could be a small looking-glass in the centre. The custom of making these objects dates from the second half of the 19th century.

Shell Valentine. A type of SHELL MOSAIC which has a mosaic-like design made in the form of compartments, or which is a picture made of shell flowers. It was also known as a SAILOR'S VALENTINE, because so many were brought home from the West Indies especially by seafarers as love tokens (with the usual messages, "Truly Thine", "Forget Me Not", and the like).

Shellwork Jewellery. This is jewellery made from shells, or from the iridescent nacre or MOTHER-OF-PEARL obtained by stripping shells. The practice is probably very old, but naturally flourished in the Victorian period of beach-combing and home handicrafts. The favourite production was necklaces, made from shells cut to a suitable shape to fit a mount and attached to chains or, in the case of small cowries and cones, drilled and threaded on wire. Varnishing made them bright at first but eventually yellowish. They were manufactured wholesale for the souvenir industry, but were also constructed after seaside holidays by the Victorians and Edwardians, who found it a sentimental pastime during dull suburban evenings.

Ship and Sailing Craft Blocks. A block is a pulley used in the rigging of ships to lead the ropes in several directions. A large number of different blocks were necessary for the standing and running rigging of a sailing ship such as a windjammer. Consider for example the swivel block, the gin block, and the snatch, fiddle, flag halfyard, iron sheet, purchase, iron lift, mast, yard, reef tackle, quarter leech-line, headsail, staysail, brace, brace leading, halliard, triple, leading, guy purchase, double sheet, double vang and even the single vang blocks.

As such, the block comprises a case or shell of wood or iron, also a sheave and a pin. The shell can be of many shapes and sizes. The sheave is made of lignum vitae or iron, and is circular or flat. It has a groove around its circumference, and a hole through the centre which takes the pin, the hole being bushed with brass to avoid wear if it is a wooden sheave. The iron or steel pin has one end squared to prevent its turning. An ordinary block shell has two cheeks of wood, usually elm or ash for strength and water resistance. These cheeks are oval, and held apart at their top and bottom by two small distance-pieces, fractionally thicker than the sheave, to form a gap or slot between the two inner faces of the cheeks called the swallow. Each cheek also has a

Ship glass, circa 1760, with radial trails of glass on the overstrung foot.

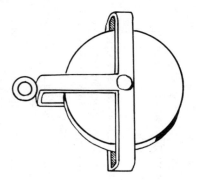

Ship blocks: gin block.

199

hole, one of which is squared to take the squared end of the pin; these holes are bushed, known as bouching, to avoid wear. When the sheave and pin are in position a square of metal can be tacked over the end of the pin so that it will not come out. Then the cheek's outer face was curved and a scorchline made in it for a hemp or wire rope strop-made by splicing a short rope length to create a ring. Blocks without such a strop had a hook or eye at the upper end, also an iron strap that lies in a groove made in the inner faces of the cheeks; this hook or eye was welded on while the pin passed through holes bored on each side. The wooden cheeks of this type of block are not intended to streng-then the block but to guide the rope and sheave.

In the type called the iron-bound block the iron strap is affixed to the outside rather than the inside faces of the cheeks.

Some blocks are made entirely of iron or other metals, and some of the hooks may be made to swivel. The eye, if used instead of a hook, is either facing the same direction as the swallow slot, or is placed at right-angles to that swallow. Blocks also may be made single or double, and some have an eye, the becket, at their lower end; this is for shackling. The type known as a gin block has a metal shell so cut that it forms a horizontal member to support the pin, and a vertical member to which a swivelling hook is fitted.

Ship Glasses. These date from about 1730 to 1775 in their original crude form, which was very similar to that of the firing glass. The last were so-called because drinkers liked to rap them sharply on the table, hence it was necessary that their feet should be unusually strong, up to ½ in. thick. Ship glasses were similar to those firing glasses, but not the same. Their thick feet were designed to keep them upright on tossing and lurching surfaces. Mid-18th-century ship glasses have what is known as OVERSTRUNG FEET. Their stems could be plain, opaque twist, air twist, or cut; and their bowls were far more variable in shape than those of true firing glasses.

Ship Letters. Letters marked with a handstamp indicating they were landed from or accepted for transport by a ship. A kind of official post office was in existence as long ago as 1688; it accepted and sent mail to and from Falmouth/Spain, and employed sailing vessels for the purpose, known at first as post barques, then as sailing packets; it

Top: reverse of a letter sent to Bordeaux in 1814 which bears two superb strikes, one with inverted date. This item is believed to be unique. Below: A letter carried on the ship Pigon from Pennsylvania to Poole, Dorset in 1788. It bears an example of the very rare LIMINGTON SHIP LRE marking.

was originally a minuscule service between Falmouth and Spain and then between a few other ports, at bi-monthly or monthly intervals. Most overseas mail in those days went by ordinary merchants without any intervention of a post office as such. Merchants and governments confided the letters to the masters of such ships, paying a small fee. This system continued for about 200 years. Letters coming from abroad were handed by the ship's master to a branch of the post office in the port, who conveyed them to anywhere in the British Isles, and collected a fee from the recipient on delivery. Parliament enacted in 1710 that the post office could pay a penny fee to a ship's master for each letter he handed to them, which penny was charged to the recipient plus what that delivery had cost the post office, according to distance and the weight of the package. Each letter was hand-stamped by the post office at the port; early examples have the name of the port and the words "ship letter", with a hand-written legend showing the fee charged. Some of these hand-stamps, for the main ports, are common enough, but there are exotic examples of those used in remote or difficult places. An interesting example is that used on letters brought ashore by pilots from vessels lying offshore, as in the roads of Deal off the Goodwin Sands. Rare hand-stamps are those showing the original spelling of ports, such as "Limington" for Lymington, and "Brighthelmstone" for Brighton. Island hand-stamps are interesting, notably those used in the Channel Islands. The first example of these dates back to 1802 and has a crown in an oval frame with the words "Jersey Ship Letter". The oval became a box in 1834 and was stamped in black until 1843, although a red-framed type with the words "Ship Letter Jersey" was occasionally used. From 1843 to 1853 the stamp was unframed and in black ink, although blue was used in 1851, and mustard brown in 1852.

Collectors like to find ship letters that had the name of the carrying ship hand-written on them at the time of their going aboard, but the custom of the ship letter as such went out with the modern development of the international postal system, and should not be confused with modern letters and POSTCARDS posted in the post offices of great ships and given their mark.

Ship Models. Not to be confused with votive ship models or EGYPTIAN RITUAL SHIP MODELS. The ordinary type is that made by seamen from available materials during long voyages. Some of the makers were highly skilled at wood carving and produced models of considerable intricacy and beauty. These were rarely longer than 3 ft, due to the difficulty of finding storage space for them. Models in the round were made of pine, deal, or mahogany. The rigging, handrails, anchors, blocks, and chains were devised from materials to hand; thus sails could be made from paper that was originally an old parchment chart. Many models were cooperative ventures: a carver would cut out the hull with a clasp-knife, a sailmaker would undertake the rigging and sails; a metal-worker would contrive the anchors and chains and the miniature cannon. Primarily such models were made for the sheer love of it, but inevitably some would be sold for useful cash to other

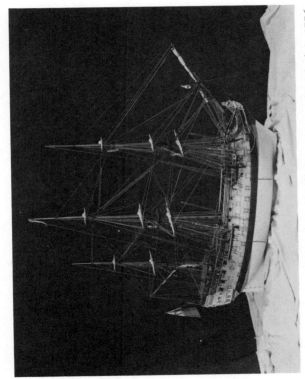

Shipyard model of the Duke, a British second rate 98-gun ship rebuilt in 1776.

crew members or ashore to dealers, and a certain number would be proudly brought home for presentation to mother or sweetheart or even to wife. Seamen often found that what they learnt while making models aboard ship was useful to them when eventually they were cast ashore and could sail no more. They created the models in their forced retirement, and sometimes made some money from them, although more often than not the profit was the dealers'. When a ship model is larger than 3 ft long it is usually the product of such work in retirement, as the shore base has the single advantage of offering more space.

The reader should also consult entries for HALF-BLOCK MODELS, SHIPS IN BOTTLES, and PRISONER-OF-WAR WORK.

The most attractive models have ever been those of sailing ships, but the age of steam brought its own practitioners, notably professionals who constructed very fine replicas in miniature of famous vessels for display in the showrooms of shipping companies and travel agents. Then there is the naval DOCKYARD AND SHIPYARD MODEL, constructed to help naval architects in their work and to "sell" proposed ships to Admiralty officials and civil buyers. The HALF-BLOCK MODEL came out of this. It was eventually the custom to make quite large models to scale for tank tests at dockyards. They were sometimes made large enough to carry one or two men on a suitable sheet of water. William Froude (1810–1879) was the first to use model ships in such tests to discover the behaviour of new hull designs. An English engineer and mathematician, he was assistant to Isambard Kingdon Brunel from 1837 to 1846, but retired after this to devote himself to experiment and investigation in hydrodynamics and naval construction. He did much to improve knowledge of the rolling and stability of ships. What he discovered in tank tests was utilised in improved shipbuilding. His first complete testing tank was built by the Admiralty for Froude in 1870. Some of his subsequent models ranged in size from several feet to as much as 25 ft. They were often a shell made of wax about an inch thick, cast in a mould, then reduced to accurate hull dimensions with the use of a profiling machine. Few of these models have survived, because the wax was melted down to make another hull afterwards.

Ship portrait of the schooner Alabama, built in 1873, painted by Renault, Leghorn, Italy.

204

Ship Pictures. The term is applied to original portraits of ships as painted or drawn by professional and amateur oil painters and water-colour artists, but it is also used specifically for ship portraits pro-duced by hack artists in Naples towards the end of the 19th and at the beginning of the 20th centuries. These would cover canvases with stock backgrounds showing the Bay of Naples and Mount Vesuvius. When a ship arrived at Naples the artist would ask the captain or passengers if they would like to have a painting of Naples with their ship in it. A fee would be arranged and the job was quickly done; rather too quickly for real art: but surviving examples of this genre are now sufficiently rare to have considerable value.

Ship Portraits. This is the proper term for a painting or drawing of a ship, usually broadside on, to show all its main details with the same function as a photograph, for the use of architect and owner, and as a remembrance for mariners. Ships have been thus depicted by artists throughout history, but surviving examples date mainly from the 18th century, when artists first tended to specialise in ships and marine subjects. Prior to that there were no specialists in ship portraits as such. Such painters would reside in ports and obtain commissions from ship owners or from captains who wanted a perma-nent record of a proud command. Early examples are too often unsigned or undated and thus difficult to assign, although the style of the work and backgrounds and ships' names can be helpful.

Another type of ship portrait is that executed by crew members themselves, on sailcloth or canvas. These were painted to show the folk at home what the mariner's ship looked like, or to sell ashore or to the captain. They were fixed sometimes to other articles, such as the inside of DITTY BOXES and SEAMAN'S CHESTS. They are easily distingu-ishable from the products of shore-based artists by their crude materi-als and generally naive appearance. Brush-strokes were inevitably wide; colours were limited; and rigging was often drawn in pencil with a ruler, then traced over by a nail dipped in black paint. Their nautical details can be superior to those of landlubbers at the art, but not their workmanship. They can still be wonderfully found, espe-cially inside chest lids (see also PAINTINGS ON GLASS).

Shipboard Journals and Publications. As produced for the purpose of informing and entertaining crew and passengers these date back to at least the 18th century, when they were written and illustrated by hand. The contents included articles, home news, foreign news, advertisements, letters to the editor, even poems. They varied in size from single sheets to several pages. The historian can learn much from them, as the brighter examples mentioned unusual shipboard events, the health of crew and passengers, the ship's speed, accidents, landfalls, and included religious sentiments. On the whole they published information that it would be difficult to disseminate in any other way. They were chiefly produced on merchant ships; the Royal Navy did not encourage them generally, although troopships on long voyages often had a newspaper. When the luxury liners arrived so did really lavish newspapers for the entertainment of passengers. At the same time the development of radio telegraphy enabled up-to-date world news to be printed each day.

An early shipboard publication of considerable interest is *The North Georgia Gazette and Winter Chronicle*, produced for the crew during the expedition of H.M.S. *Hecla* and *Griper* to find the North-West Passage in 1819. Another is the *Great Eastern Telegraph*, issued on the ship of that name during the laying of the Atlantic cable between Britain and the United States in 1866. A *Champion of the Seas Times* was published aboard a famous clipper ship of that name while voyaging between England and Australia in the 1860s. *The Birds of Passage* was a troopship magazine as published on H.M.S. *Malabar* between Britain and India.

By the end of the 19th century regular printing presses were being carried on the larger naval and merchant ships, and a crew member with literary skill and mechanical dexterity combined usually had the working of them, but the luxury liners eventually signed on professional printers for the job. An important professional example was *The Superb Gazette*, produced on the passenger liner Superb, that travelled to Australia. The 20th century saw newspapers and journals on all the main lines, and a few survive to this time of writing when so many of the great ships have reached their final port.

Shipping Company Ware. This was made for shipping companies to their prescription: plates, cups, saucers, jugs, dishes, teapots, and bowls, made of pottery, porcelain, Britannia metal, or silver. It had the owners' trademark, or the name of the ship with that trademark, which was transfer-printed or hand-painted on the china and stamped or engraved on metalware. There was a time when to collect such ware was neither interesting nor profitable, so much of it being in existence, but the sudden and otherwise unhappy disappearance of the great ships gave rise to many auction sales at which these articles were disposed of to far-sighted dealers. Today a piece of china from an Atlantic liner of the 1920s is already rare enough to be extremely valuable. (It is also intrinsically valuable, because it was made to last at a time when planned obsolescence were dirty words.) (See TABLE-WARE.)

Ships in Bottles. A type of seaman's SHIP MODEL that is self-explanatory, but one of the most attractive items to proceed from the long hours of idleness that characterised shipboard life on long voyages. It is not known when the custom began; but it was a custom that appealed particularly to the great Victorians, being both romantic and useless, besides incorporating a gimmick that amused children and people at evening parties.

First a small ship model was made, complete with masts, spars, sails, and rigging, but these were hinged or otherwise devised so that they could be folded down to the deck. The height of the ship model hull plus the folded-down rigging was rather less than the diameter of the chosen bottle's orifice. Material to represent the "sea" was painstakingly inserted into the bottle with a long, thin tool, painted, then smeared with glue. Cottons were attached to the rigging of the ship

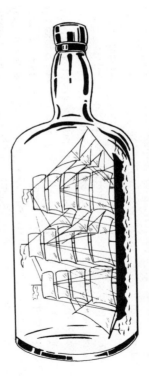

Nineteenth-century ship in bottle.

model in such a way that, when the ship was inserted into the bottle and the glue had adhered to its hull and dried firmly, those threads could be pulled and the masts would come upright. The cottons were carefully burned off, and finally the bottle had its lasting cork.

Various materials were used for the base or "scene" in the bottle, ranging from layers of painted, scuffed putty, to a mixture of cork, sand, and glue; even plaster. The laying of this base was regarded as the most important part of the work. Pint-sized bottles were the most popular with the shipboard makers, but quite large ships have been inserted in gallon bottles, and very small ones in miniature vials. Flat-sided bottles required no outside stand; round bottles were usually given a wooden cradle, sometimes edged with rope and adorned with nautical motifs. A crude method with round bottles was to apply sealing wax to one side, under the "sea" and ship, and smooth this out flat while it was still soft. Then the bottle would "stand" on that side. A rarer type is the bottled ship mounted on a backboard for use as a wall decoration.

Inevitably some ships in bottles were beautifully contrived and can be regarded as small works of art, but most tended to be crude and relied for their effect upon the simple mystery of how the full-rigged ship got into the bottle. A virtuoso would insert two ships into a bottle, together with other miniature objects for flabbergasting beholders, such as a background of "land" with a church whose spire (cottoned up) could "never" have got through that narrow bottle's neck.

Ships in bottles are still made, in some cases by souvenir manufacturers with the juvenile and seaside market in mind. It is often difficult to tell what is "genuine" and old, but one of the best indications is the bottle itself. Old glass is crude and greenish; then all materials fade or otherwise deteriorate with age, and it is possible for the expert to assess how long it took for that paintwork to fade, that woodwork to crack, and those sails to turn yellow. Moreover the makers would sometimes decorate their ships with flags and names of their own particular period, although these makers could of course themselves be fakers. One of the best evidences of identification and dating is the actual ship. There is no reason why a modern faker should choose an 18th century merchantman with the odd name of *Prospect of Hades* for his forgery. The historian can refer to his books, however, and find that such a ship was regularly on the Lisbon run in the 1760s, and, since the bottle is 18th-century and the paintwork on the ship badly faded, it could all well be genuine. Early steamship models in bottles also have a good chance of being old. There is one bottle in existence which contains a miniature seaman holding a minuscule bottle which itself contains a ship.

Ship's Articles or Papers. These are documents carried during a voyage, giving detailed descriptions of the ship and crew. The details about the crew are the most historically interesting. We learn their names, ages, ranks, terms of service, and discover how and when they were taken on, also details of their behaviour and how they had enjoyed leave or deserted, lost overboard or died during the voyage (also their adventures with pirates). The ship's articles as such were stamped by consuls at ports where the vessel called; they, and the ship's papers generally, were kept by the captain, in the old days, but by appointed officials on the great warships and liners. They were housed in the SHIP'S PAPERS BOX, and included the registry and clearance certificates, the LOG BOOK, the charter party contracts for cargo loading, and the BILL OF LADING.

Ship's Badges. These are badges bearing the ship's name and perhaps a motif appropriate to it. When FIGUREHEADS were abolished they were replaced as decoration by ornate scroll-work on the bows. This sometimes involved a coat of arms or other heraldic device, until, as warships became more practical in design, even this was abolished. It was during the transition period, between about 1860 and 1914, that naval vessels began to have unofficial badges as a matter of pride and identification. These were fixed to the foreside of the bridge, although the ship's name could still be carved in raised letters on the stern, to be replaced eventually by a nameplate mounted on the after-super-structure. The unofficial badges gradually became accepted as an integral part of the ship, and were even used on the ship's stationery and letterheads. Such a badge was also placed on the gun tampion (disc or plug for the mouth of the barrel). Badge-making flourished during World War I, with the great expansion of the Navy but as the designs were not always completely decorous, a Ship's Badge Committee was set up by the Board of Admiralty in 1918, and from then on such badges became official. They were thereafter designed to include the ship's name, a reference to its history, and a suitable motif. Each class of naval vessel had its own shape of badge: circular for battleships; pentagons for cruisers; shields for destroyers; and diamonds for aircraft carriers, submarines and auxiliary craft. The basic design involved a gilt surround of endless rope, surmounted by the naval crown, with the name of the ship immediately below it, and below this the motif and maybe a motto in Latin or English. Such mottoes could refer to old British families, like that of the *Revenge*, which recalled the Grenvilles. It showed an avenging sea dragon.

The first ship's badges were carved in pine and then cast in brass. Modern examples are of epoxy resin and fibre glass. Needless to say old badges are of importance to keen collectors' items.

Ship's Bell. The ship's bell on Royal Navy vessels is traditionally positioned or hung on the quarter-deck. In the old days it was used in conjunction with a HALF-HOUR GLASS. The bell was struck each time that glass was turned, a practice that survived in the Royal Navy until 1857. "Bells" was the term used for the half-hours of the watch as struck on that ship's bell. Eight bells were struck at the end of each watch of 4 hr, at 4, 8 and 12 o'clock.

Some ship's bells weighed as much as 50 lb, and eventually had the ship's name engraved on them, plus the port of registration of a merchant ship and even the date of the vessel's construction. Possibly the bell custom originated among the ancient Chinese, who are known to have used gongs for signifying the passing of time aboard a ship. When the Normans brought their invading army to Britain they heralded their arrival by striking bells on their ships. But the custom dates back to about the 13th century in British records. On early sailing ships the bell mount was constructed in the form of a small church belfry, with roof shaped like that of a pagoda, and with carved sides; the bell depended from a beam. During the ornate 19th century the frame of this belfry could be ornamented with dolphins, and made of brass, gun-metal or cast iron. Aboard sailing ships the bell could hang from a curved iron stirrup, usually mounted in an ornamental frame of metal, the decorative motif being appropriate to the ship's name. It could be highly polished, or painted in green and gold or black and gold. On ships such as the *Cutty Sark* the ship's bell was hung within easy reach of the helmsman, maybe on the after-edge of the monkey poop in front of the wheel.

There was another bell, at the fore part of the ship within reach of the lookout on the forecastle. On the *Victory* the belfry housing the ship's bell is amidships, abaft the galley funnel; before that the *Victory's* original bell, together with the first steering wheel, was shot away during the Battle of Trafalgar. The present bell, dated 1795, came from H.M.S. *Africa*, which was also at Trafalgar. Maybe the *Victory* had yet another bell, because some years ago a paper was discovered in Bradford Church, Devon, that stated: "There existed a bell on the roof of the rectory, which is reputed to have been taken from H.M.S. *Victory* by Captain Hardy and given to the rectory." But the whereabouts of that rectory bell are now unknown. (Ship's bells from wrecks were often used by churches; there are many legends connected with the ship's bell as such. Crews in the old days regarded the bell as the spirit of the ship. They claimed it always rang when the ship sank, and, if it rang when all otherwise seemed well, then it was a presage of disaster.)

Ship's Candlestick. This is made of metal, and usually has an expanded, heavy, circular base for reasons of balance, and at the same time this catches the waste spilled from the candle as it gutters. The upright part of the holder is mounted in gimbals which are screwed to the cabin wall so that as the ship moves the stick can swing and remain reasonably upright. Glass covers are fixed on projections from near the top of the candlesticks to protect the flame from draught.

Ship's Clock. A simple, lever-escapement timepiece, fitted usually in a round brass case with a flange for screwing to a bulkhead or panel in a cabin. The term "marine clock" is sometimes used for it; and there is also the ship's bell clock, similar in appearance but, as first introduced in 1850, striking an interior bell at every $\frac{1}{2}$ hr to mark the watches.

Ship's Decanter. A type of stoppered glass decanter, dating from the late 18th century, made from crystalline flint glass, that had a wide, heavy base, sometimes over $11\frac{1}{2}$ in. in diameter, and sloping

211

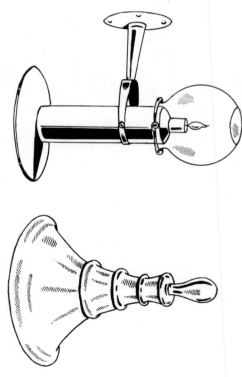

Ship's candlestick.

Eighteenth-century ship's decanter.

sides, with a triangular profile, which tapered to the base of the neck. The neck as such would either be cut plain or have three or four applied neck-rings. They can, of course, be identified by their special design. The wide heavy bases were designed to keep the decanters upright under rough conditions. Until such were devised it was necessary to use heavy or wide-based bottles aboard ship. One of the first ship decanters as such was that made after 1780 to celebrate Rodney's Battle of Cape St. Vincent. They came to be known as RODNEYS. Ship decanters thereafter tended to be plain in appearance. The chief decoration was an occasional fluting on the upper part of the body and the neck. Some "Rodneys" had a sailor's head engraved on them. Of course decanters became more decorative after 1830. Queen Victoria brought fussiness, and in the 19th century there were many kinds of "amusing" decanters, such as those made in the shape of a broad-mouthed bell. The 20th century has been largely concerned will collecting these - and reproducing them.

Ship's Name Panel. The name of a merchant ship was sometimes carved on a wooden panel of long, oval shape, and decorated with scrollwork. One would be fitted on each side of the steering gear box.

Ship's Papers Box. This came into being for the purpose of housing the ever-increasing amount of documentation that merchant ships had to carry in the 19th century in order to satisfy their legislators. It would be not too large, thank to the confined space of shipboard, and would be oblong in shape, and made of wood with a hinged lid and lock and key. The ship's name, class, and tonnage could be indited in gilt lettering surrounded by a wreath of foliage, this inscription being below the lock, but also sometimes on the lid. A small painting of the ship with its name and tonnage could take the place of that inscription. A duplicate of this box, containing copies of the ship's papers and other documents, was often to be found in the offices of the owners.

Ship's Wheel. This comprised several parts: the rim, the spokes (with projecting ends), the hub, and the brass boss. The names of the ship and her port of registration were inscribed on a brass ring at the centre of the wooden wheel. In sailing ships one of the wheel's spokes was differentiated from the others, either by projecting farther outwards, or by being capped with bronze or brass. When this spoke was at the top of the wheel it was known to the helmsman that the rudder was in its central position: the helm was "centred". By the middle of the 19th century the average ship's wheel had become a modest wooden circle of spokes, 3 ft in diameter, but sometimes larger to give it weight, aiding the steering.

Shipyard Plate. This is not a utensil, but a bronze or brass plate inscribed with the name of a shipyard where a vessel was built, together with date of launching and net and gross tonnage. Such plates were often fixed to the poop bulkhead on sailing ships, varying in size from 12 to 18 in. A typical example bears the following inscription: "Lower mast of H.M.S. *Hercules*. Battleship, built at Chatham Dockyard. Commenced 1st February, 1866. Completed 21st November, 1868."

Signal Flags. FLAGS used to convey messages between ships when they passed at sea, according to a recognised code so that two ships of different nationalities, speaking different languages, could still communicate with each other. The flags are hoisted on halyards rove through BLOCKS, and flown high so as to be clearly visible. Such flags are housed in a box, together with fore and aft signal halyard ropes and the International Code Book. Mariners must have employed some form of visual signalling from the earliest days of seafaring; it would have been necessary from the beginning. But our modern system did not begin until the 18th century. The ships of the Royal Navy, by 1780, were using fifty different flags for their signals. By 1799 it was necessary for the Admiralty to issue a standard flag signal code book. The novelist CAPTAIN MARRYAT was a navigation officer in the Royal Navy, and devised a flag signal code for merchant ships (1817). This later became the basis of the modern International Code of Signals, which makes use of twenty-six alphabetical flags, ten numeral pennants, three substitute or repeater pennants, and an answering pennant. Each flag or pennant is of distinctive colour and design so that it can be immediately recognisable at the limit of vision.

Signal Slate. An oblong length of wood-framed slate on which were written the messages from flag signals, superseded in the Royal Navy by signal pads of paper. The nautical term "wash out" comes from the cleaning of the message from the slate.

Small Sword. This is a type of hunting sword, much worn by naval officers in the 18th century. A variety that has the guard decorated by five balls is known as the five-ball small sword.

Smith, Captain John (1580-1631). Sailed from England in 1605 to establish the first official English settlement in what is now the United States of America (Virginia, 1607). He produced in 1612 a map of Virginia that was revised many times and used by other cartographers. Then he wrote A Description of New England, 1616, and a History of Virginia, 1624. He was romantically saved from death by the Indian girl Pocahontas, the "princess" daughter of a chieftain who had taken Smith prisoner, but it is thought that the Captain invented this story. It is known that Pocahontas married an Englishman and died in Gravesend.

Smuggler's Keg. A small cask, holding 3½ pints; 10 in. high; of oak, brass-rimmed. The smallest container used by the distillery trade. Probably it was devised in the first place to be easy to stow in the false bottom of a lugger. As many as forty would be carried; twenty on each side. They could also be easily transported on horses at night through the lanes of the Isle of Thanet. Such casks were made on both sides of the Channel; they, as well as the specially designed luggers, cutters, and ketches, were designed for the particular revenue-defying purposes of a brave, earlier age. The same shipyards, however, built the revenue cutters that pursued the smugglers.

The chief item smuggled was spirits, often contained in larger casks, even in hollow oars. If it was too risky on occasion to land the cargo, then the casks would be roped together and secured with two anchors on the sea bed, or tied by fishing line to a bladder and an anchoring bag of shingle on that bottom. Later a grapnel was used to fish the casks out.

Indeed a collection could be made of smuggler's items; it probably has been made. It would include especially a flasher, which was an ordinary FLINT-LOCK PISTOL that carried a hammer and flint with an enlarged pin for the powder, but no primer. The weapon would cast no ball but gave a brilliant and comparatively noiseless flash. The smugglers called this signal "flashing off". Specimens of crow lamps could be collected: they were first devised by smugglers who used Crow Gap, near Beachy Head, Sussex. The lamp was an ordinary LANTERN whose tapering funnel or tube, about 15 in. long, ensured that the light was cast only in one required direction.

Soil Bottle. A variation of the SAND BOTTLE, made by mariners from soils collected at their ports of call, or obtained by the trading of European goods for bottles already filled by Chilean dockers with the curious soils of their country.

Speed, John (1552-1629). English cartographer, who produced his *The Theatre of the Empire of Great Britain*, 1611-1612; from map plates engraved by JODOCUS HONDIUS in Amsterdam. He similarly produced *Prospect of the most Famous Parts of the World*, 1627. It was not until 1676 that his famous four maps of North America were published (One shows New England and New York, and another depicts California as an island.)

Spencer, R. B. (fl. 1840-1870). English ship portrait painter, most of whose work was undertaken on private commission. His ship portraits are very accurate; his backgrounds not so perfect. Examples of his work are: "The *Earl of Balcarres* and other vessels off Dover"; "Portrait of the clipper ship *Columbia*"; "Clipper ship off Dover"; and "The Battle of the Nile".

Spermaceti Candle. Candle made from spermaceti, a white, fatty material contained in solution in the heads of sperm whales.

Sphere. A globe representing the earth or the apparent surface of the heavens. There are two main types, of which the first is the planetary sphere. This mechanically represents the relative movements of the planets. The other type is the celestial sphere which shows the fixed stars, but also the equator, being provided with equatorial and meridian rings in which the vault of the heavens can rotate. It is possible with the celestial sphere to study astronomical problems involved in the rising and setting of various stars and their moving through the meridian, and to solve those problems visually and without abstruse calculations. Both spheres are normally made of wood or brass. Small examples were made for use aboard ship; large ones for landlubbing astronomers or for teaching in maritime schools. The ARMILLARY SPHERE is a navigational instrument, much used at sea in the 16th and 17th centuries.

Sponge, Sponger. An implement, made of boarskin or sheepskin on the end of a long pole, used for cleaning the bore of a CANNON, by pushing up and down before or after firing.

Spontoon. A small, short-handled pike or HALBERD, as used particularly in the 18th century.

Spun Glass Ship Models. These are sailing-ship models, not usually of any particular vessel, as spun by glassblowers. Most are small, up to 6 in., with rigging but not with sails, all made from finely drawn twists of glass; clear glass save where the coloured variety was used for features such as flags and bulwarks. There are also large examples, based on a glass "sea" (that might have a lighthouse in opaque glass) and notable for the extremely fine work in their rigging, which consists of numerous thin threads of glass. These were usually housed for protection in a glass dome on a wooden base, and superb examples have survived rather well, partly because of those domes and partly because they are so large and beautiful. Such models could be produced as "friggers" by glassblowers in their own time after a day's work. Then, in the 18th and 19th centuries, there were itinerant glassblowers who travelled from fair to fair. They would blow and spin and deftly construct the little models while the gapers watched. Such glassblowers also proceeded to seaside resorts and rented shops or stands there, where they would produce not only glass ship models but also such as fish, birds, animals, walking sticks, and long-stem pipes.

The main glass centres, Nailsea, Newcastle, Sunderland, and Stourbridge produced such glass models wholesale for the attraction of sailors in ports, who bought them to take home as gifts. Some manufactories are still engaged in this trade. The making method was fundamentally to heat glass rods or canes over an intense tallow flame in a small furnace, until the end of the rod became a paste that could be drawn out and manipulated to any thickness.

Square. An instrument used similarly to GUNTER'S SCALES for working on a sea chart.

Station Pointer. A three-armed protractor, for determining a point on a chart, but mainly used in hydrographic surveys. When only three points were visible the station pointer was helpful to locate the position of the instrument station on the plan or chart. Murdoch Mackenzie, a Scottish hydrographer, first devised the station pointer in the 1780s. It consists of a brass circle and scale, from the centre of which three arms are projected, two being adjustable and one fixed. The adjustable arms are moved to known bearings on a chart, and sooner or later the ship's position is determined. An English station pointer of 1830 has an 8 in. diameter brass circle with wooden arms or pointers. The scale is silvered, and divided to readings by a vernier (small movable scale). At the centre there is a mounted reading telescope.

Stay Busks. Without the unfortunate whale there would have been

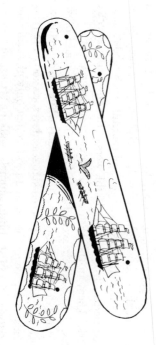

Stay busks of baleen engraved with a needle.

no hour-glass figures for females in the 19th century. Strips of highly pliable and almost indestructible whalebone were used by seamen in hours of moonlighting to make busks for the stiffening of stays and corsets. These busks were, somewhat strangely, regarded as LOVE TOKENS when brought home to roost. Sometimes they were ornamented; at other times they were made of alternative materials such as animal bone, wood, and ivory. Genuine examples as made by actual seafarers may be identified by the names, initials, verses, and crude scenes scratched on them, and stained in ink, lamp black, or red dye.

Steamer Chair. A kind of DECK CHAIR with a long, low seat and reclining back, usually of slotted wood and collapsible, that was used on the decks of passenger ships from the mid-19th century on.

Stern Board. A richly painted and/or carved board with the name of a sailing ship. FIGUREHEAD carvers usually supplied most of the carved stern boards at the same time that they made the figureheads. They used a variety of nautical motifs for decoration.

Stern Lantern. A large lantern with panels of convex or bull's eye glass, used in the 18th century at the stern of a ship. It contained an oil lamp, the light of which was magnified by the glass.

Stern Light. A lantern with clear glass, showing a light to half the horizon.

218

Stores. Many items of ship's stores have already been described in this dictionary, but it was necessary in the old days of very long voyages for an extremely wide range of articles to be carried out. Many of these can be usefully collected if found and properly identified. Apart from the usual crockery and cutlery, there were for example fire-irons, muskets, bayonets, pistols, ball cartridges, handcuffs, lamp scissors, flour scales and weights, coffee mills, steel yards, flour scoops and dredgers, candle boxes, corkscrews, dustpans and brushes, and cabin stoves with copper funnels. Those were included in what was known as the cabin stores. But there was also the ship's chandler's store, that would comprehend such things as brass speaking-trumpets, hides of pump leather, deck-scrubbing brushes, paint brushes, mops, cabin-sweeping brushes, oil tanks, shark hooks, fishing lines, portable water filters, lead lines and reels. Then there was the cooper's store, specialising in casks, buckets, tubs, water-cans and funnels, bread boxes, and mess kits. The carpenter's and boats-wain's stores held pump spares, sail booms and yards with blocks, rigging screws, tarpaulins, handspikes, capstan bars, pitch pots and ladles, chain hooks, oars, tar brushes, grindstones and troughs, anchor fish-hooks, boathooks, ballast shovels, hen coops, cork fenders, boat chocks, pig houses, crow bars, chains, purchase gaffs, iron

French stern lantern.

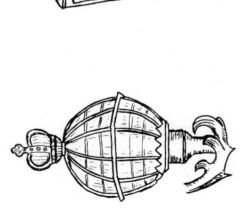

English stern lantern.

slices, files, hooks, thimbles, buoys and ropes, flare guns, cork life-buoys, anchor shackles, fore locks, washers, fids, nails, screws, pumps, even a fire engine with leather hoses.

Straw Boxes. These were plain wooden boxes decorated all round and on the top with pictures made from straw. They comprised one more 19th-century phenomenon of folk art. First the design or picture was drawn on the wood, then pieces of various-coloured straws of different lengths were glued on to create a raised picture. The theme was usually maritime, and, as always, the majority of straw boxes were crude while a few could be remarkable and even beautiful. As the "art" progressed so did the actual seamen cease to make such boxes that were latterly the produce of souvenir firms ashore. They had briefly known a height of accomplishment as PRISONER-OF-WAR WORK at Peterborough and other prisons during the Napoleonic Wars. Straw boxes were varnished on completion to keep out dust and damp. When such a box has been damaged by damp it can scarcely ever be repaired satisfactorily.

Straw Marquetry. The decoration of the surface of an object using small pieces or slivers of split straw. These pieces were either natural colour or dyed. PRISONER-OF-WAR WORK is the most interesting and valuable, and bright-surviving colours give additional value. Often hastily contrived dyes would fade fatally away. The French prisoners-of-war used a tool contrived by themselves, called a splitter. It was a small wheel in a wooden frame, having sharp divisions like spokes in its centre. A spike protruded from the axle, and on this a piece of straw was placed and pushed through. The cutters and spokes of the instrument divided that straw into the required kind of slivers. The "rice straw", or inner side of the slivers, was used for the marquetry work. It was chiefly "Dunstable" straw that they employed for the purpose; unsplit.

Items decorated in this way included sewing, patch, and "book" boxes, also tea caddies, needle-holders, firescreens, watch-stands, picture frames, and, rarest to survive, pieces of small furniture. Different effects were achieved by various methods. The straw slivers could be glued at angles to each other in order to create a design. Cameo and intaglio impressions could be given. Pictures of scenes and people, and of flowers and fruit were cunningly devised with coloured straws. When prisoners of war undertook such work it might be complete from start to finish, or just straw applied to objects supplied by customers. Those at the Peterborough prison had the additional advantage of a straw industry in the neighbourhood, where English straw plaiters made hats. These workers often turned in their spare time to straw marquetry, but never achieved the fine results of the imprisoned Frenchmen. There came a point when the local workers complained of competition, so the prisoners were told they must make no more. They got over this by doing their straw marquetry work in secret and smuggling it out. There are records of court cases brought against those who assisted this smuggling from outside. The craft of straw marquetry thereafter spread to other countries, notably Austria, where it degenerated into an industry of tourist souvenirs.

Straw Pictures. As above, but in the form of framed and glazed pictures. A favourite theme was "The Sailor's Farewell", but it was not in those days what a sailor's farewell would be now. Made aboard ship, ashore by commercial firms, and again by prisoners of war.

Sully, Henry (1680-1728). English clockmaker, who did considerable work on marine timekeeping instruments.

Sunderland Pink Lustre Ware. Staffordshire potters in the early 19th century developed the art of so glazing their wares that the finish was smeared and metallic in appearance, as if the colour had dripped round the article with iridescent effect. Pink "lustre" was actually gold of that ilk applied to pottery with a white body or white glaze. It was done in such a way that the gold solution resulted in various shades from pale pink to deep purple, this depending on the quality of the ingredients used and its thickness when applied. "Speckled pink" was the most usual kind, especially as done in the Sunderland area, where several potteries used the brown clay of the region. A favourite subject was a transfer-printed view of Sunderland Bridge. This was the Wearmouth Bridge over the river Wear, opened in 1796 as "the longest single-span cast-iron bridge in the world". It was 236 ft long, and 100 ft high at low-water mark. It had the national fame at the time of an Eiffel Tower or New York skyscraper subsequently.

Pictures of this bridge were continually printed on jugs, vases, plates, bowls, dishes, and mugs, and pink resist was the favourite finish. Some thirty-three different transfer-printed views of Wearmouth Bridge were used on the BRIDGE JUGS. The pictures were mostly printed in black, but sometimes in blue and green. Others were hand-coloured. The transfers were supplied from a common source to several unrelated potteries. The common type of Sunderland pink lustre ware falls into eight categories, mostly of jugs which, for some reason or other, have survived better or have become the most popular. There are other categories, but these are exceedingly rare and correspondingly valuable. Sunderland jugs can be big, holding as much as 2½ gallons in some cases. Complete sets from small to large are now very difficult to assemble. Far too many copies have been made, and are being made to this day. These betray themselves by an unnatural whiteness of background which turns brownish quite quickly with exposure to light. Put your purchase in a window and you will soon find if it is genuine. "Crackle" is another indicator of age. A genuine old jug should have a certain amount of this, but not too much. Fakers creake an over-bold, mechanical kind of crackle.

In addition to their resist jugs and other household articles, the Sunderland potteries also produced nautical WALL PLAQUES. These were made in the form of a frame, either pink-lustred or painted yellow to resemble gilt, and this frame surrounded a transfer-printed design with various seafaring motifs, sailing ships, shore or coast scenes, often with patriotic or sentimental verses appended. Famous naval events were commemorated by such Sunderland plaques, particularly those dealing with Nelson's victories. Sunderland's seafaring traditions also evoked souvenirs, and such verses as the following about a Jack Crawford who climbed the mast of his ship to nail a Union Jack there at the Battle of Camperdown in 1797:

At Camperdown we fought
And when at the worst of the fray
Our mizzen near the top, boys,
Was fairly shot away.
The foe thought we had struck
But Jack cried out "Avast"
And the colours of Old England
He nailed up to the mast.

Other items from the Sunderland potteries included much "gift china," or "SEASIDE SOUVENIRS". Then their characteristic pink lustre was increasingly copied by other potteries in coastal places, at Liverpool, Bristol, Swansea, and Newcastle. The last two tended to specialise in the production of such ware for sale to seamen as gifts. They often used the same verses, notably the famous "From rocks and sands and barren lands, Kind fortune keep me free, And from great guns and women's tongues Good Lord deliver me."

Sun-dial. This was devised to show the time, according to the sun, by the shadow cast on gradations from a central pointer. It goes back to prehistoric times, when a stone column was set in an open space, wherefrom the shadow described an ellipse. Various types were developed for use at sea. One was the equinoctial or equatorial sun-dial, which had an hour scale set parallel to the plane of the equator. The large dial was revolved until the sunlight on it shone through a vent in a sight - but the device was of limited use because it could be used only for a fixed latitude. One of the best makers of equinoctial dials was George Adams (1704-1773), instrument-maker to George III. His were precision-made dials, and some of them had mechanical working parts. Other forms of sun-dial were the NUREMBERG DIAL or diptych, the RING DIAL or GEMMA'S RING, and the AUGSBURG DIAL.

Swift. Another name for the YARN-WINDING REEL, made by seamen from bone and ivory.

Swivel Gun. A lightweight weapon, made of bronze, with a cannon-type barrel. The trunnions fitted on to a pivot called the pedestal, which was fixed to the bulwarks, so that the weapon could be easily turned from side to side to give raking fire. The term was also used for a heavy musket with a spike attached at the point of balance in the middle. This spike fitted into a sock on a stand, so that the musket could be swivelled around.

Swords and Scabbards. These came in several shapes for naval use, one- or two-edged, straight or curved, triangular in section and hollow-ground if single-edged, but lozenge-shaped if double-edged.

223

The back, opposite the cutting edge of a single-edged blade, could be flat or rounded. The thickest part of the blade near the hilt was called the shoulder, and this could have the maker's name and date of manufacture. A normal hilt had one or two quillons and two shell guards. These guards were usually engraved with an anchor on naval swords. The grip, made of metal, wood or ivory, was riveted to the tang, a long metal sliver extending upwards from the blade. Wooden grips were covered with leather or shagreen, and might have grooves in which metal wire was wound. Above the grip was the pommel or knob; the end of the tang was riveted into this. The place of riveting is indicated by the tang-button at the end of the pommel. A sword-knot could depend from the hilt; it was formerly used for attaching the sword to the wearer's wrist, but is now chiefly seen on officers' ceremonial swords; the kind that are never used. This knot could be decorated by a tassel of varying design.

Sword scabbards for seafaring use were made of brass, iron, or leather, and were sometimes lined with wood. The point of the scabbard, known as the chape, was reinforced with metal. The scabbard had at its other, open, end a locket and catch, or a ring, for attaching to the wearer's sling or belt. This locket was actually the top mount of the scabbard, and sometimes had the maker's name inscribed on it. Scabbards of PRESENTATION NAVAL SWORDS could be little works of art.

By the 18th century naval officers were chiefly using two types of sword: the HANGER and the SMALL-SWORD, but in 1800 the Admiralty ordained that these should be abandoned and two more types should be standardised: an ornamental sword for the ceremonial purposes of officers, and a plain sword for the dirty work. These last were straight, and had langets engraved with an anchor, lion's head pommels, gilded brass hilts and grips covered with fish-skin. They remained so for approximately 100 years.

A typical British naval officer's sword of the late 1800s has a 37-in., single-edged, deeply-fullered blade; the hilt pattern includes a lion-headed backstrap and pommel with knuckle guard that has a rope and fouled-anchor motif; the fittings are brass, while the wooden grip is covered with sharkskin and has a brass wire wrap. The scabbard is of black leather with brass fittings.

Consider, however, a naval sword of 1817 (but 1805 pattern), as intended for the use of commanders and upwards. It has a 28½-in. double-edged, centrally pointed blade; the hilt has a lion-head back-strap and pommel with P-shaped knuckle-bow; the crossguard langet has the motif of a crown, rope, and fouled anchor; the grip is ivory; the blade is blued, and etched with Britannia, foliage and arms in gilt; the scabbard is black leather, with mounts and hilt fittings of silver-gilt, nicely hall-marked.

There was a period about 1856 when naval officers preferred a highly-curved blade (as made by the famous Wilkinson firm), after which we frequently find claymore-type blades, straight with two grooves, white fish-skin grips, and half-basket guards ornamented with a crown and anchor badge. There was a temporary fashion for "pipe-back" blades, of which the blades' back edge had a rounded, pipelike "spine".

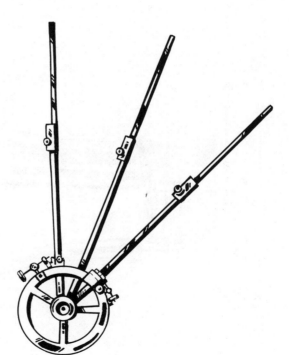

Nineteenth-century station pointer.

225

Nineteenth-century telescope with twin eyepieces.

T

Tableware. It is known from discoveries in submerged wrecks that ships of former days carried a remarkable quantity of tableware, plates, dishes, bowls, tureens, mugs, glasses, and tumblers. This ware was of pewter and coarse pottery, but also of gold and silver as well as fine porcelain. Devices on the articles would range from simple makers' and ships' names to elaborate and artistic heraldic, royal, and nautical emblems. The extent and variety of this ware is explained by the fact that voyages were so long: mariners regarded their ships as their permanent homes. The value to collectors of such pieces proceeds from their beauty and general good craftsmanship. Prior to the machine-age articles, hand-made ones were not necessarily better; they were always nicer to handle and regard.

With the coming of that machine age, and especially of the steamship and its ultimate product, the ocean liner, marine ware became standardised, but often has interest for various reasons: the name of the ship, or owner, or company, and its sheer luxuriousness in the case of some passenger lines. We have seen in our time the auction sales of such wares that have thrown on to the market a great quantity which will progressively become rare and valuable (see SHIPPING COMPANY WARE).

Warships had their own tableware and cutlery, adorned with the anchor and other motifs, or the ship's badge. Quantities of this have since been sold off to the public as navies have declined. We have reached the stage now when tableware of the thinnest plastic or even cardboard suffices for aircraft and car-ferry voyages of short duration. What remains of sturdy value on cruise ships will be among the true nautical antiques of the future.

Taximeter. An early 20th-century navigational instrument for taking bearings.

Telescope.   In its simplest form this is an arrangement of lenses in a tube, for bringing distant objects into closer view. Generally speaking there were two types of telescope in the old days: the refractor, which just used that combination of lenses; and the reflector, which used mirrors. It is believed that the refracting telescope was invented in 1608 by a Netherlander named Lippershey. He made optical spectacles, and noticed that children playing with them, two or three at a time on their noses, were able to make a distant church spire look closer. Lippershey mounted lenses in a cardboard tube, obtained remarkable results, and approached his government, who thereafter supported his work because they thought it might enable them to obtain a closer view of a military enemy. Galileo in Italy improved on Lippershey's invention; his Galilean telescope of 1610 had a lens sited at the far end of a tube; at the other end was a plano-convex eyepiece, the whole giving a magnification of thirty times, and the name being a perspicillum. It is understood that at the same time Thomas Harriot, Sir Walter Raleigh's mathematical tutor, was working in England on his "perspective glass", a very similar instrument to Galileo's. Very soon the word telescope was being used, and Isaac Newton was working with mirrors to overcome the aberration in lenses. The resulting telescope of the reflecting type had to overcome several difficulties, notably tarnishing of the mirrors by bell metal containing copper, which was used to construct the early instruments. Among those who made reflector telescopes were James Gregory and JOHN HADLEY. Hadley closely followed Newton's principles, and in 1726 he developed Gregory's device with moderate success. James Short (1710-1768) overcame one of the major difficulties by making his mirrors of glass backed by quicksilver. Dolland's achromatic lens of short focal length enabled the device to become more practical, but still difficulties remained, in particular the narrowness of the field, which was a great disability on a rolling ship. Makers of the 19th century tried to overcome this by using only a single extrusion tube on their marine telescopes. Characteristic versions were made lightly of brass measured about 19 in. long when closed, and had a diameter of about 3 in. The outer tube was covered with leather or leather braidwork, and frequently bore signal tables. Lens attachments included a hood against the sun and rain, and a lens cover for general protection. The eyepiece was covered when not in use by a pivoting disc. It is interesting to find a number of rings scratched with a sharp tool on the ocular tube of old ship's telescopes. These provided a kind of distance scale, which facilitated focussing prior to observation. Another curiosity was the Y-shaped telescope, made with one lens and two eyepieces as far back as 1677 and used well into the 19th century. It was to take advantage of the considerable demand during the Napoleonic Wars for hand telescopes from both Navy and Army that Peter Dolland (1730-1820) built up his renowned business.

As short-focus lenses suffer from aberration, long-focus types had to be used until the end of the 18th century. Then again it was necessary in those days to limit magnification to three or four times in order to get a field large enough to absorb the ship's movements (the field gets smaller as magnification increases). To obtain better results the tubes had to be extended; some early telescopes have eight to ten tubes extending to over 4½ ft. Those early makers also had the problems of chromatic aberration and spherical aberration, which they tried to overcome by using types of glass of different refractive indices; crown glass and flint glass would be coupled in a single lens system. A concave lens of flint glass was first combined with one of crown glass by Chester Moor Hall in 1729. The achromatic lens of a kind was thus created. A precursor of this method had been Christian Huygens. John Dolland (1706-1761) developed his true achromatic lens in 1758 after obtaining details from George Bass, who had been a lens-grinder to Chester Hall.

Old marine telescopes are good to collect because the fakers have not yet really got on to them, but they are increasingly rare to find.

Theodolite. An instrument which, superseding the CIRCUMFERENTOR and GRAPHOMETER, is used for general surveying purposes and by naval hydrographers. It is capable of a high degree of accuracy.

Thermometer. This measurer of temperature is another shipboard instrument of vital importance. Probably Galileo (1564-1642) made one of the first modern examples, his thermascope. That was 1592; and some 50 years later the work was continued in Italy by instrument-makers of Florence, who used a straight or spiral glass tube that contained alcohol or water, with a bulb at the bottom, and sealed at the top, plus calibrations in the form of coloured glass globules on the exterior of that tube.

The first reliable marine thermometers were introduced in the 18th century. They used mercury and the fahrenheit scale from 1717, then the reaumur scale with spirits of wine in 1730, and the celsius or centigrade scale in 1742. But 18th-century thermometers were varied in type and sufficiently curious at times. There was no agreement about the scales, that followed several patterns, with temperatures for freezing at one end and for boiling water at the other. The 19th century progressively standardised methods. There was even a fluorescent thermometer, used for readings in the dark; it contained alcohol, and was taken on several polar expeditions, including that of Scott. Then came the invention of the self-registering thermometer, upon which readings could be retained for later study: like the "memory" of a calculator. The depth or deep-sea thermometer was invented about 1878 not only for discovering how cold it was at great depths, but also for retaining that knowledge until the instrument was drawn up. A ship's deck thermometer of the 19th century, housed in a mahogany case, is very similar in design and gradation to a modern thermometer. It was, of course, frequently incorporated with a BAROMETER. (See DEPTH THERMOMETER.)

Thomson, Sir William, 1st. Baron Kelvin (1824-1907). This Scottish physicist, mathematician, and engineer was knighted in 1866 for the researches into the transmission of electric currents in submarine cables that led to the success of the great Atlantic cable; he was created a peer in 1892 for that and much other important work, including what he did for the MARINER'S COMPASS. He invented sounding apparatus and a tide-predicting machine as a result of his remarkable research work in hydrodynamics, particularly wave motion; not only his home town Glasgow but also the entire world owe a great deal to him.

Tide Calculator. An 18th-century circular card device, about 12 in. in diameter, pivoting on a central button, that has around its fixed outer edge a scale graduated clockwise from 1 to 12; concentric with that is a graduated, 30-day circle. An inner pivoted card is graded from 1 to 48 anti-clockwise, and against each number is a comment for each place, such as "T.F. in all Harbours and Ports between Sheerness and Dover". "T.F." meant "tides flowing by the shore or on the ground". A fleur de lys or index pointer is opposite one of the numbers, while the circles are flanked on either side by two columns of place names, from A to Z in alphabetical order. The most common examples of tide calculators cover places on the coasts of Britain and north-west Europe.

If the index pointer is set to the day of the moon's age on the day circle, and opposite to the arrow at the end of the numbered radius, this gives the time of the "tides flowing" in the desired locality. One old calculator of this kind has a cartouche with the proud pronouncement that it is "a new and correct tide table for the British Channel, German Sea, Bay of Biscay, etc., showing the time flowing of the tide by the shore and its time run in the offing for every day of the moon's age on the coasts of England, Ireland, Scotland and Holland, Flanders and France." A well-known 18th-century purveyor of such cards was ROBERT SAYER.

Tiller. The bar or lever fixed to the head of the rudder, worked by hand in small vessels. It was sometimes of considerable length to give leverage, and often carved by the crew with various motifs or with simple barley-sugar spirals. Tillers of NARROWBOATS were painted gaily in the traditional "showground" style of those craft.

Toilet Cabinet. This was developed first in the rich cabins of high-ranking officers, then in passenger vessels, and became in the 19th century a kind of fixture, up to 6 ft high, made of mahogany with brass hinges and other fittings, together with a hinged, three-sided tray that pulled down and revealed a washbowl. Above were shelves for articles of toilet, then a cupboard with mirrored door. In the early days that cupboard housed a copper tank, that was periodically filled with water, and sent that liquid by narrow pipe to the basin. Below the basin was a cupboard to house, in the early days, a chamber pot. Before great liners and warships had proper plumbing the dirty water from the bowl would be run off, when the bowl was tipped up, into a drain or tank for later emptying. Not many items of furniture were developed only for ships, and this was one (but also used on passenger trains).

231

Törnström, Johann (1743-1828). Swedish maker of ship's FIGUREHEADS, who began as a furniture carver in Stockholm, but from 1782 to 1818 held the position of official carver at the Karlskrona naval dockyard. A considerable number of his figureheads survive. They are chiefly full length, and show delicate figures with separate fingers, hair curls, drapery folds, and detailed weapons, some up to 12 ft high.

Trade Token. This is a small piece of metal with the appearance of a coin, issued by tradesmen to provide their customers with small change at times when the national currency was in short supply. Canal and shipping companies often issued these, and many had nautical motifs. Lead tokens were issued as long ago as 1404; there were many in the 16th and 17th centuries, but most of those still in existence date from the 18th and 19th centuries. Not all were circular: some are square or diamond or octagonal. A 17th-century octagonal penny-value token issued by John Mitchell of Little Somers Quay, near Billingsgate, London, has a tilt-boat on one side, being rowed with passengers; such tilt-boats were ferries with protective tilts or canvas covers. John Mitchell was doubtless a fishmonger. Indeed there are numerous tokens with pictures of ships on them. One example is that issued by a Gosport draper, John Jordan, in 1794. This is of a halfpenny's denomination and, because Gosport was then an iron-founding centre, especially for the making of chains and anchors, it shows a collier on the reverse. Another, from a Deptford ironmonger,

Trade token.

Thomas Haycraft, in 1795, is similarly for a halfpenny, and gives a stern view of the *Royal George*, with the wording "Prosperity to the wooden walls of Old England". Then there are many tokens that commemorate famous naval men such as Jervis and Nelson. Canal company tokens include that issued in 1795 by the Thames and Severn Canal Company, value a halfpenny, which shows on one side a Severn trow, or sailing barge of 40-80 tons: the reverse has a view of the entrance to the Sapperton Tunnel. Or there is the shilling token of the Basingstoke Canal Company, issued for payment to their navvies. The front shows a Thames sailing barge with the words "Basingstoke Canal", and the other side has a wheelbarrow, pickaxe and spade, with the words "John Pinkerton, value one shilling". (Pinkerton was Secretary to the Company). Other canal tokens depict coats of arms, incline engines, bridge views, horse-drawn and sailing barges.

Trafalgar Chair. Following the Battle of Trafalgar in 1805 many items of TRAFALGAR FURNITURE were produced in commemoration; one of these was the Trafalgar chair. It is elegant and lightly made Regency, with caned seat and back, sabre legs, and carved mouldings to represent rope. That is the true Trafalgar chair. Another example goes back to Sheraton for inspiration, and is adorned with several nautical motifs, rope, anchors, dolphins (see below).

Trafalgar Furniture. In addition to the chairs (see above) there were other items of furniture for selling to people who had been encouraged by the famous victory to loosen their purse-strings. A lot of this was made by Morgan and Sanders, a London firm of cabinet-makers, who, between 1801 and 1822, not only supplied sea-going furniture and pieces for travellers generally, but also used the brand name of "Trafalgar". Nelson was himself a customer of Morgan and Sanders, who made a cellarette for him that is now in the National Maritime Museum, Greenwich. Such cellarettes, the precursors of the cocktail cabinets taken in Rolls-Royces to the races, often accom-panied long-distance travellers in coaches. Then there was the Edin-burgh maker of Trafalgar furniture, C. Munro. He made, for exam-ple, a fine couch in mahogany, 78 in. long, the head shaped like a large scallop shell and the feet like dolphins; small panels on the sides have nautical motifs carved in the hard wood.

Trafalgar Sword. Valued originally at 100 guineas, this was presented by the City of London, together with the Freedom of that metropolis, to Captain Thomas Masterman Hardy in 1806, as recognition of his gallant behaviour on the *Victory*. Two other true Trafalgar swords were subsequently given by the City to Vice-Admiral Lord Collingwood and Rear-Admiral The Earl of Northesk, but the term has also been applied to PRESENTATION SWORDS as given to Nelsonian and subsequent worthies by Lloyds of London.

Trafalgar Table. An extending table made by Morgan and Sanders of London as part of the TRAFALGAR FURNITURE in which they specialised.

Trafalgar Vase. This was designed by John Flaxman (1755-1826) when he was designer and sculptor for Rundell, Bridge and Rundell, London silversmiths and jewellers. It was a pastiche of an ancient Greek vase, and was presented to sixty-six senior naval officers who took part in the Battle of Trafalgar.

Trafalgar Ware. A vast amount of china was made to commemorate Trafalgar, including figures of the Admiral himself that often bore little resemblance to the poor man. All kinds of pots and mugs and plates and cups and saucers were offered, usually with transfer-printed views of Nelson and/or his ships and battle, but the most popular were Trafalgar jugs that showed a plan of the naval engagement.

Trail Board. This means the woodwork on either side below the bow of a sailing ship, and particularly the carving thereon, of foliages, scrolls, stars and the like. They lead aft from the figurehead, often with a finial scroll at their juncture. The original trail boards of the *Cutty Sark* showed naked witches in hot pursuit of Nannie, the beautiful seductress in Burns's "Tam o'Shanter". This was typical of the marine carved work that so increasingly shocked the Victorians, and led to a virtual 19th-century ban of the depiction of the female figure on a ship. Instead the mariners had to make do with the dullness of foliation.

234

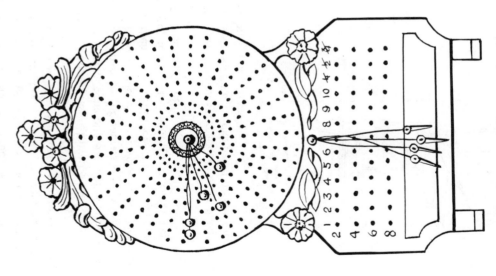

Eighteenth-century wooden traverse board.

Traverse Board. A device for keeping a record of the course steered and distance covered by a ship; from the 18th century, and basically a compass-card with eight small holes drilled along each of the thirty-two rhumb-lines at 11-25 degree intervals around its circumference

235

to form eight concentric circles, each acting as a 30 min period of time. A small peg was inserted at the line of the ship's course, and this was read (the course) from a compass each half-hour by the officer of the watch. An oblong board beneath the compass card had a variable number of rows of holes in horizontal columns of four, into one of which a peg was put each hour by that officer. This indicated the ship's speed in knots measured by the LOG. The matter might be difficult to believe, but the officer could eventually plot the ship's position on the chart by the courses steered and the nautical miles covered in his duty time. Some traverse boards were made by ship's carpenters; then they could be crude in appearance, with the compass-card in black and white, and sometimes embellishments according to nautical motifs.

Turnspike. An implement made of iron or wood tipped with iron, used with the HANDSPIKE for manhandling the carriage wheels and raising the breech of a CANNON.

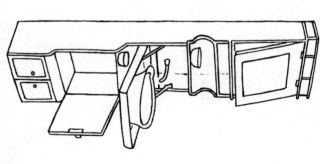

Mid-nineteenth-century toilet cabinet with folding washstand.

U

Uniforms, Naval. The first uniform officially required by the Admiralty was that of 1748 for admirals, captains, commanders, lieutenants, and midshipmen. It consisted largely of an embroidered blue coat with white facing, which was worn unbuttoned, ranks being indicated by the cut and shape of the lapels and cuffs. Until that moment it seems that officers and men wore what they liked. Their garb was often strangely feminine in appearance. Drag might have begun there (an essentially nautical term). By 1760 sailors chiefly wore a pea-jacket and petticoat trousers; the last resembling a skirt. A COCKED HAT with low brim was often worn up to 1780, and buckled shoes were favoured. The second half of the 18th century was the age of buckles (which make a good item for collecting). By 1800 the general wear had changed to a blue jacket, a checked shirt, and white trousers, the last being either bell-bottomed, or worn short (rather coyly to reveal coloured stockings). The black tarpaulin hat surmounted this rig-out, and a black silk handerchief around the neck could serve as a sweat rag. A rumour arose that this was worn as a mark of respect to Lord Nelson after his death, but it was worn before that, black being chosen to save washing. Even so there were still no regulations in force to govern sailors' uniforms, and the men continued to be individualistic in their choice of clothes, as did the captains who sometimes chose those garments for them. Thus the captain of the *Harlequin* in 1853 had his men dressed like harlequins, but was not so bad as the captain of the *Vernon*, who in 1840 had ordered his crew to wear quite-feminine frocks of red serge.

A kind of uniform for warrant officers had been introduced in 1787, and 1795 had seen the coming into being of EPAULETTES for officers. Gold lace on officers' sleeves was their reward that same year for the Glorious First of June. Admirals were given three rows, vice-admirals two, and rear-admirals one. In 1825 civilian grade officers were given badges of their branch on their collars: three anchors for masters, a snake twisted round an anchor for physicians, and two anchors with cables crossed for pursers. In 1837 engineer officers were given a uniform similar to warrant officers. In 1843 executive officers were ordered to wear coats with double breasts, while civilian branch officers remained single-breasted; the various branches were distinguished by the spacing of their buttons. (This was a time of peace when the Admiralty had little better to think of.)

Distinctive arm stripes were introduced in 1856, three rows for captains, two for commanders, one for lieutenants. Then in 1857 the lower deck at last got its official uniform, which at first comprised a blue cloth jacket, a cap similar to those of officers but without a peak, and a collar of blue jean with three rows of white towards the end of the cloth. Monkey jackets for use aboard ship were introduced in 1879. White uniforms for officers on foreign stations were ordered in 1885, the distinction of rank being in the form of white silk lace on the sleeves. The blue jacket and tarpaulin hat for the lower deck were abolished in 1890, and, in the following year civilian branches were given double-breasted coats. This famous year shoulder straps were introduced with white uniforms, as well as ball dress and mess dress. The ratings lost their cloth trousers and even their frocks in 1906 - save on the royal yachts of Edward VII.

Union Jack; Union Flag. The union flag as designed by order of James I in 1606 had only the crosses of St. George and St. Andrew; that of St. Patrick was added in 1801. The name British or Britain flag was used for the concoction between 1606 and 1625, when the name union flag was first employed. The bunting was flown both by naval and merchant vessels, but an order was issued in 1634 commanding that the union flag should be worn only by naval vessels for identification purposes, so that British merchant ships could give the customary "Salute in the Narrow Seas" to men-of-war; but the merchantmen continued to wear very similar flags in order to frighten and to obtain courtesy privileges from foreign warships. Then a stricter order was issued in 1674 that British merchant ships should carry only a RED ENSIGN with a white jack (cross of St. George) in the corner.

The word JACK as such was first used about 1633, being referred to then as a small flag for wearing on the bowsprit. At first such jacks were flown both at sea and in harbour, but the introduction of fore and aft headsails and the disappearance of the sprit topmast caused fouling at the flag-staff, so the jack came to be flown only in port. To use the term union jack for all union flags is incorrect; strictly a union jack is a small union flag to be flown only in one place; at the bows of a naval vessel. Jack really means miniature.

V

Varley, Cornelius (1781-1873). Not only a marine and landscape watercolour artist, but also an inventor of several optical instruments, including the graphic telescope. He was trained by his uncle Samuel Varley, the watch and scientific instrument-maker, but decided in 1800 to become an artist. He executed etchings, and was a pioneer of the then-new art of lithography. Examples of both are contained in his *Etchings of Shipping*, issued from 1809 to 1811, three of his lithographs being in this volume. He patented his graphic telescope in 1811, and was awarded a gold medal when it was shown at the Great Exhibition of 1851. A good example of his work is "Fishing boats and craft on the river Thames".

Velde, Willem van de, the Elder (1610 or 1611-1693). One of the best Dutch marine artists, perhaps because he was the son of a Flemish sea captain, and spent his own early years as a sailor before settling down in Amsterdam as an artist (prior to 1636). But in his teens he was already an acclaimed artist in a country that knows how to appreciate them. His early work was marine subjects in black and white. He was commissioned to produce paintings for the Dutch Navy after 1634. A small vessel was made available to him by the States of Holland so that he could witness naval actions; and he was thus a pioneer war artist, being present at numerous sea fights during the Anglo-Dutch wars. He came to England in 1672 at the invitation of Charles II, and, with his son Willem van de Velde the Younger, was appointed painter to that monarch, having the Queen's House at Greenwich as his studio. He concentrated on the "taking and making of draughts of sea fights", while his son's work consisted of "putting the said draughts into colours". When van de Veldes are not so precisely drawn then they were probably wholly executed by the son.

240

The father used ship models to achieve wonderful accuracy in details of masts, sails and rigging. Outstanding pictures are "Men o'War" and "Dutch East Indiamen near the shore".

Velde, Willem van de, the Younger (1633-1707). Known to have started work in England in 1672, when he arrived there from Holland with his father, because a painting of his carries that date and is inscribed "In London". Appointed jointly with his father as painter to Charles II in 1674, for which they received £100 each yearly. Usually the father drew the pictures and the son painted them. Young van de Velde did mostly marine work at first, but chose more general subjects in his later years. His early work is the best; doubtless because it was based on his father's superb draughtsmanship. His larger paintings of naval actions, originally conceived when both father and son worked in Holland, are of more than artistic value, being helpful to naval historians. Young van de Velde wrote over the ships their name and that of their commander. Under his own vessel he inscribed "V. Velde's Gallijodt", or "Mijn Gallijodt". He was an extremely prolific painter, and it is difficult to separate his work from his father's. A van de Velde is best regarded as a composite production. When it is inferior in draughtsmanship and shows a ship or scene rather obviously after 1693 in date, then it is the entire work of the Younger. A painting of the van de Veldes (H.M.S. *Resolution*, 1669) shows the first UNION FLAG on the mainmast, also the elaborate carved and "gingerbread" work which decorated the sterns of warships at that time. Other van de Veldes of note: "The Royal Yacht *Mary* (built 1677) racing another yacht, the *Charlotte*"; "A Dutch packet in stormy weather"; "Dutch ships of war saluting"; and "Sea Piece with Men of War saluting".

Vent Auger. An implement for piercing the cartridge of a CANNON; also called a PRICKER.

Vent Bit. This was used for cleaning the vent of a CANNON.

Vent Cover. This was made of lead, and used to cover the vent of a CANNON during preparations so that the weapon would not fire prematurely.

Vent Scourer.   An implement for cleaning the bore of a CANNON.

Volley Gun.   The name for an unusual carbine of the naval 18th century, fired from the rigging fighting tops, for the same purpose as a DUCK'S FOOT GUN. The best were made by Henry Nock to the design of James Wilson, and had no fewer than seven barrels, each 20 in. long and of .46-in. calibre smooth bore. Six of the barrels were fitted in a circle around the seventh. The weapon was, however, made lightly, only 12 lb, so that it could be taken up the rigging. We know that the Royal Navy was employing some 600 of these ancestors of the machine gun at one time in the 18th century. When H.M.S. *Pandora* went to Tahiti in 1791 to search for the *Bounty* mutineers, her crew used volley guns very successfully to drive off attacking, but suitably surprised natives.

Votive Ship Models.   Votive meaning religious thanks, such models were given to coastal churches by seafarers as thanks for escaping the perils of the deep. Melville's greatest of nautical novels, *Moby Dick*, describes a church which is filled with such offerings. The practice was more common in European countries than in Britain. Some churches in Dutch ports still contain considerable numbers of models, hanging from, or placed on, beams. When Spaniards and Portuguese returned, rich with plunder, from the unfortunate New World, they would be so grateful to their deity for allowing them to get away with it that they would order magnificent ship models of gold and silver to be made, even to be encrusted with jewels. Such are still preserved in some exotic churches, high out of reach in glass cases, or in museums. Cromwell's Puritans did not allow many such to remain in English churches.

It is a strange fact, however, that votive ship models are rarely so accurate in their details as normal SHIP MODELS, and they are not so often representations of any particular ship as of a generalised vessel. Those remaining in English churches are, indeed, not the finest examples of shipboard craftsmanship. More interesting to the antiquary are votive ship models unearthed by archaeologists in places such as Crete, Cyprus, and Carthage. Probably the best examples which remain *in situ* in England are those at the Shrine of Our Lady at Walsingham in Norfolk.

242

W

Wall Plaques of Sunderland Lustre. These were produced at Sunderland potteries from about 1805 (date of Trafalgar) partly for domestic consumption but also for sale to seafarers for taking home as gifts. The SUNDERLAND PINK LUSTRE WARE has a pink border surrounding scenes of ships, sailors, and the famous Wearmouth Bridge, also verses that could convert the plaques into SEAMEN'S LOVE TOKENS. A typical literary effusion is headed "The Token of Jack's safe return to his true love", and reads: "If you loves I, as I loves you, No pair so happy as we two". And another: "My ship is moored, my wages paid, So let me haste unto my maid".

Wall, William Guy (1792-1862). Irish watercolour artist who worked in America from 1818 to 1836. Engravings from his watercolours were published in *The Hudson River Portfolio* (Megarey, New York, 1823). Many of his drawings of American scenes were used to decorate blue and white transfer-printed ware of popular provenance.

Walter, Joseph (1783-1856). English ship portrait and marine painter, who also painted harbour and river scenes. Examples of his work: "*Great Western*"; "The *Ajax* in the Bristol Channel"; *Great Britain* struck by a sea".

Walters, Miles (1774-1849). This English ship portrait painter was usefully trained at first as a shipwright, then became a sailor himself. Father of SAMUEL WALTERS who collaborated with him. Their pictures were signed "Walters and Son". Examples: "The *Jamaica* of Liverpool"; "The *Princess Charlotte* of Holyhead".

Walters, Samuel (1811-1882). Son of the above: a self-taught marine oil painter, who in his later period treated chiefly of coastal subjects and seascapes. He was actually born at sea, and later assisted his father in his ship portraits, from which experience he was able to launch himself into a successful career of painting portraits of their new ships for Liverpool and American owners. His son George Stanfield Walters (1838-1924) himself became a landscape and marine painter. Examples of Samuel's work: "The steamship *President* leaving her berth"; "The New York packet ship *Waterloo* off Holyhead"; "*The Ocean Monarch* on fire;" "Prussian brig in a light breeze"; "The Port of Liverpool".

Ward, John (1798-1849). English ship portrait painter and specialist in Humber shipping scenes, who was the son of a master mariner Abraham Ward (that father may be responsible for a picture of the whaler *Swan*, dated 1784, which is in Trinity House, Hull). John Ward served an apprenticeship as a house and ship decorator, but produced some paintings in his spare time that were seen by the Scottish marine artist William Anderson (1757-1837), who encouraged and influenced the young man. Ward developed considerable skill in drawing ships. He produced several books with plates of naval and mercantile vessels. He visited the Arctic, and painted whalers. His work is sometimes signed "J. W.", or "J. Ward." Typical examples of his work: "H.M.S. *Pique, Nautilus* and *Greyhound*"; "H.M.S. *Britannia* and other units at Spithead"; "Northern whale fishery; portrait of the *Swan* and *Isabella*"; "Dover Pier"; "From the quay at Antwerp".

Ward, William (1761-1802). This English marine watercolour artist himself owned a fleet of whaling ships.

Wax Maquette. A model of a proposed ship's figurehead made of wax, in miniature or full-size, for approval before permission was granted for the wooden figurehead to be carved. The soft and pliable nature of the wax saved time in the making of a sample model, but that nature of the material prevented the survival of many specimens. A very few remain, mostly from the 18th century, and of Dutch and Danish origin.

Webber, John (maybe 1752-1793). This landscape, topographical and marine watercolour artist, also etcher, specialised in South

Seas subjects, and was the son of a Swiss sculptor named Weber. He studied in Berne and Paris, and was chosen in 1776 to accompany Captain Cook on his third and fatal voyage around the world in the *Resolution*. When he returned to England in 1780, he was employed by the Admiralty in making complete drawings from the sketches done on the voyage; these were published, 1784, in the official account of the expedition. One of his most famous drawings is that of the death of Cook, which he had witnessed. He published a set of views of the places he had visited, etched, printed, and aquatinted by himself. Examples: "A party from His Majesty's ship *Resolution*, on Captain Cook's last voyage, shooting sea horses in the year 1778"; "View at Cracatoa, an island in the China Seas".

Wellings, William (fl. 1778-1790s). English silhouette maker, both bust and full-length. His work has interest because he used light shades to show details of the clothing of the time, including naval uniforms. Examples of the last include a silhouette of Captain Sir William Burnaby leaning on an anchor, and a Captain Macdougal standing on shore with his cutter in the background.

Westall, William (1781-1850). Marine artist and book illustrator who was chosen by the Admiralty to accompany Captain Flinders and make drawings on his voyage to Australia in 1801-1803. He was shipwrecked on a coral reef, taken to China, and later visited India, Madeira, and the West Indies. Examples: "Cape Wilberforce, looking into the Gulf of Carpentaria, from the Indian Ocean, Australia, discovered by the late Captain Flinders in H.M. ship *Investigator*"; "View of the Bay of Pines, New South Wales, etc."; "Wreck Reef Bank, Australia".

Whalebone. Bone from whales, particularly the jaws and ribs. Note that BALEEN is not whalebone. Whalebone had a variety of uses but was especially employed for the making of supple stiffeners for the female corset; it then became a favoured raw material for sailors' SCRIMSHAW. To this day can be seen, in and near ports once frequented by whalers, whole whalebones erected as arches (from Whitby, Yorkshire, to Lyttelton, New Zealand, and even in the grounds of Buscot Park, Oxfordshire as erected once by the original owner, a whaling master).

Whale Tooth.   The sperm whale has over thirty teeth on each side of the lower jaw; such were much used by mariners in their SCRIMSHAW work.

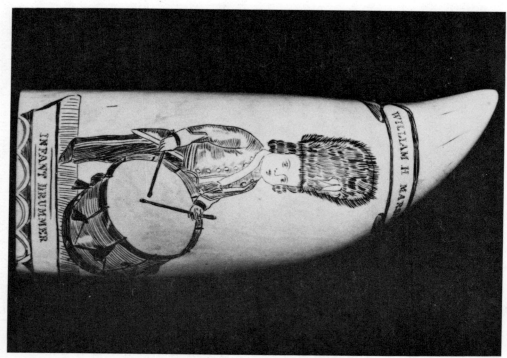

Scrimshawed whale's tooth, etched with the figure of a young boy in full military uniform, complete with shako and drum.

Whaling Tools. Thousands of these were required, and some remain for collecting. There are, for example, the long-handled knives and cutting shovels for dissecting the great animal and cutting its blubber into small portions. Then there are the BLUBBER POTS, that were used for reducing and refining that blubber into oil that could be stored in casks. These cauldrons were of cast-iron and had massive lugs. When whaling developed into a mass-production and modern trade the ancient pots were abandoned, and will still be found on remote shores, such as those of Greenland. Others serve various decorative and semi-commercial purposes in and near whaling ports of the past.

Willard, Simon (1753-1848). A member of a famous family of Massachusetts clockmakers, that also included Aaron, Benjamin and Ephraim Willard. His personal immortality is a lighthouse clock, which stands on a cylindrical wood base to represent the tower of a lighthouse, the entire instrument being enclosed usually in a bell-shaped glass cover.

Williams, H. (fl. 1779-1792). This functionary of the Navy Office had the hobby of painting ships, and views of salty places such as Greenwich. Examples: "The head view of His Majesty's cutter, the *Rattle Snake*, 10 guns and 180 tons"; "Greenwich Hospital".

Williamson Rice (c. 1740). London maker of stick BAROMETERS.

Willoughby, Robert (1768-1843). English painter of ship portraits.

Wilson, Samuel Henry (fl. 1850-1870). English ship portrait painter of such as: "H.M.S. *Monarch* and the U.S. *Plymouth* conveying the remains of the late Mr. George Peabody to America, leaving the Channel, 1870"; "Opening of the Albert Dock, 1869".

Windlass. An apparatus for hoisting or hauling by means of a rope or wire wound on to a horizontal drum or barrel. It was operated by two long levers with cross-bars at each end. These were pumped up and down by members of the crew; the levers and bars were above deck and the gear wheels and winch barrels were below. The levers and bars were removed and stored away when the windlass was not being used. Principally found towards the end on sailing vessels such as barges and lighters.

Witham, J. (fl. late 18th century). English ship portrait painter; example: "The ships *Henry Fernie* and *William McGilvery*", Mystic Seaport, Connecticut, has a Witham painting of the American ship *M.P. Grace*, 1880.

Wood, B. English marine barometer maker, who worked in Liverpool, *c.* 1800.

Wood, Thomas (1800-1878). English self-taught marine watercolour artist, whose paintings are historically accurate, and executed with meticulous detail as regards the particular ship's construction and rigging. Examples: "H.M.S. *Queen* in Portsmouth Harbour", 1853; "Near Alum Bay, Isle of Wight"; "Mont Orgueil castle, Jersey"

Woodcock, Robert (1691-1728). English marine oil painter, who abandoned a government job to become an artist. He had a useful working knowledge of ship design, and often made models of fully rigged ships with precise accuracy before starting a painting. He was one of the first British marine painters to carry on the tradition of the VAN DER VELDES.

Worm. A coil on the end of a long pole, used to clear the wads from the bore of a CANNON if it misfired, or to remove any smouldering remains of a cartridge after the firing. Also sometimes called a REAMER.

Wright, Richard (1735-1774). A marine painter, popularly known as "Wright of the Isle of Man", whose name was contemporaneously made by a picture "The Fishery" of 1764. A "water wagon" had been developed, to transport fish freshly from landing port to customer. Fifty guineas had been offered for a painting on the subject. Wright received first prize for his attempt, awarded by the

Society for the Encouragement of Arts. Another example of his work: "A view of the storm when the queen was on her passage to England, painted from a sketch drawn on board the *Fubbes* yacht".

Worm.

Y

Yarn Winding Reel. One of the items of SCRIMSHAW popularly made by American whalers in off-duty hours to take home as a gift to a loved one, chiefly in the second half of the 19th century. Bone or ivory was used for the stand and numerous arms of this complicated device. Also known as a SWIFT.

Yates, Lieut. Thomas, R.N. (1760-1796). Amateur marine water-colour artist and engraver, who joined the Royal Navy in 1782. A series of his drawings of "Celebrated Naval Actions" were engraved by him and published. His ships are well-drawn, but his backgrounds are not so good. His short life was terminated by a family quarrel, during which he was shot dead. Examples: "A squadron of men of war lying off Gibraltar Bay, taken from the King's bastion"; "A ship of the line towing into Portsmouth".

Yorke, William Hoard (fl. 1858-1903). Little is known about this marine artist, save that he specialised in ship portraits, particularly in the Mersey and off Liverpool. It appears he worked only for local patrons, and did not exhibit his pictures. The Mystic Seaport, Connecticut, has Yorke's portrait of the American ship *Benares*. Dated 1858, this is his earliest known painting. His latest known is of the ship *Cumberland*, signed and dated 1892. Other examples: the ship *Reliance*, signed and dated 1885; the schooner *Snaefell* of 1870; and a "General Trading Barque off the South Stack lighthouse, Anglesey", inscribed "Liverpool, 1879".

Z

Zobel, Benjamin (fl. late 18th to early 19th centuries). German maker of SAND PICTURES, who, after arrival in London, was appointed "official table decker" at Windsor Castle, and allowed to advertise himself on his trade cards as "Sand Picture Painter to George III". His seven children helped him in this work as they grew up. Sometimes Zobel signed his productions.

Bibliography

The History of Cartography, by Leo Bagrow (C. A. Watts & Co. Ltd.).

How to Identify Old Maps & Globes, by Raymond Lister (G. Bell & Sons).

Investing in Maps, by Roger Baynton-Williams (Barrie & Rockcliff).

Discovering Antique Maps, by A.G. Hodgkiss (Shire Publications).

A History of Nautical Astronomy, by Charles H. Cotter (Hollis & Carter).

Collecting and Restoring Scientific Instruments, by Ronald Pearsall (David & Charles). Has lists of British and American 18th century instrument makers.

The Guardian Book of Antiques 1700-1830, by Donald Wintersgill.

Scientific Instruments, by Harriet Wynter and Anthony Turner (Studio Vista).

The Antique Collectors' Illustrated Dictionary, compiled by David Mountfield (Hamlyn).

The Antique Buyers' Dictionary of Names, by A. W. Coysh (David & Charles).

The Collectors' Glossary of Antiques and Fine Arts, by J. R. Bernasconi (Estates Gazette Ltd.).

A Dictionary of British Marine Painters, by Arnold Wilson (F. Lewis Pubs. Ltd., Leigh on Sea).

Nautical Antiques for the Collector, by Jean Randier (Barrie & Jenkins).

Old Ship Figureheads and Sterns, by L. G. Carr Laughton (Halton & Truscott Smith Ltd.).

Ships' Figureheads, by Peter Norton (David & Charles).

Discovering Ship Models, by Norman Boyd (Shire Publications).

Ships in Bottles, by Donald Hubbard (David & Charles).

Royal Navy Ships' Badges, by Peter C. Smith (Balfour).

Guns, by Dudley Pope (Spring Books).

254

Antique Weapons A-Z, by Douglas J. Fryer (G. Bell & Sons).

Edged Weapons - A Collectors' Guide, by Frederick J. Stephens (Spurbooks).

Shell Crafts, by Elizabeth D. Logan (Hale, London; Scribners, New York).

A Present from . . .Holiday Souvenirs of the British Isles, by Larch S. Garrad (David & Charles).

Victoriana, by Violet Wood (G. Bell & Sons).

Victoriana, by Jean Latham (F. Muller).

Travelling By Sea in the 19th century-Interior Design in Victorian Passenger Ships, by Basil Greenhill and Ann Giffard (A. & C. Black).

The Cutty Sark, by C. Nepean Longridge (Model & Allied Publications/Argus Books Ltd.).

Coins, Ancient, Medieval and Modern, by R. A. G. Carson (Hutchinson).

Trade Tokens, by J. R. S. Whiting (David & Charles).

Still Looking for Junk, by John Bedford (Macdonald).

The Origins of Some Naval Terms and Customs, by Lt. Cmdr. R. G. Lowry, RN (Sampson Low, Marston & Co.).

The Romance of Sail, by Michael Leitch (Hamlyn).

Smugglers' Broadstairs, by William H. Lapthorne (Thanet Antiquarian Book Club).

Nantucket Lightship Baskets, by Bethany Strong (*The Antiques Journal*, U.S.A., October 1976).